TWO CODES FOR MURDER
A True Crime Story

By

Dorothea Fuller Smith

It happened in beautiful San Diego where the Jacaranda grows

Ode to a Conmaniac

She knows where you are, in your tiny cell
    You'll stay there without a sky,
Your plans to kill *her* did not go well,
    The price you are paying is high.

Was it worth the trade, *her* love you lost,
    Would you like to turn back time?
No regrets can speak the words that it cost
    For the pain caused by this crime.

Yours to wonder for the rest of your life
    Where and with whom *she* has gone
You were *her* husband and *she* your wife
    Until you began the con.

To *her* you are little more than a ghost,
    Predestined alone to die,
What's left to ponder, to hope for the most?
    The burning question of Why?

TWO CODES FOR MURDER

By

Dorothea Fuller Smith

A DiefFesco Book
www.DiefFesco.com

First edition
Second printing, 2002

ISBN 0-9700726-0-0

Library of Congress Control Number 00-091443

Published by DiefFesco Publishing Co., Inc.
P. O. Box 140098
Saint Louis, Missouri 63114
www.TwoCodesForMurder.com

Graphics Credits:
Cover Design: CFM Graphics, Catherine Westrich
Photos: Courtroom scenes:
Courtesy of KGTV Channel 10, San Diego CA.
Illustrations: Phyllis Hornung, New York, NY
                    Jacarandá tree; Dancers

The events depicted in this story are true. However, for dramatic and other reasons, some partly fictional characters, scenes, dialog, and locations are used. Partly fictional characters are indicated by an asterisk (*) used on the first reference of the character. —The Author.

In memory of

Nicole Brown Simpson, young and beautiful mother brutally murdered after many instances of spousal abuse, and Ron Goldman whose future was denied him by a bloodthirsty killer.

Dedication

To all those women who have suffered unspeakable abuse at the hands of men who believe they have an inbred right to do so. God knows you are far above them. If all your stories were told to the world, they would be felt by everyone.

A Special Note

Two wonderful girls suffered quietly and valiantly with a tear or two through what must be called a severe crisis in their lives. They did not know what to think or say, but stood by their mother, ready to share her pain. Thank God the bad times are over and you can go back to the normal life you so richly deserve. We love and appreciate you more than words can say.

Acknowledgements

I wish to thank and give credit to my daughter and my husband who did a great deal of work, even though troubled and distressed by the events of this story, and without whose input this book could not have been created.

Many law enforcement people in San Diego, particularly Al Rushing and Ron Johnson, assisted me in the early stages of this book's development. A private investigator in San Diego, Patrick Delucia, also aided me tremendously. As for the long list of attorneys recommended by the Bar Association and consulted in San Diego, they for the most part thwarted me in going forward with the justice process and cared mainly about what money they would earn. Exceptions were 1) Herbert Bowman, deputy district attorney, who prosecuted the trial—one of the central issues in this book, 2) a divorce attorney, Stephen Dimeff who earned no fee but supported me when I was most disturbed over the crime, 3) a personal injury attorney, Catherine Richardson, who recognized the enormous injustices that had come to my daughter and tried to counteract them, and 4) Constance Klein who fought for us.

PART ONE

HOW TO BELIEVE IN A LIE

Humility is only doubt
And does the sun and moon blot out
Rooting over with thorns and stems
The buried soul and all its gems
This life's dim windows of the soul
Distorts the heavens from pole to pole
And leads you to believe a lie
When you see with not through the eye.

-William Blake
1757-1827

Charlene Mitleider's story of self-deception, disenchantment and hard-learned lessons is told with dignity and conviction. *How to Believe in a Lie* is followed by a brush with reality which forces her to face life after the lie is exposed and the problem of *How to Live* supercedes all. It begins here in an ordinary courtroom, but *ordinary* does not describe the tale.

Prologue

San Diego, California
Superior Court
August 2, 1996

The TV camera was set up on a sturdy tripod behind the railing of the bar, an eager cameraman testing the lighting. Attorneys and court personnel were inside the bull pen, some seated at tables, others milling around. Judge Kennedy was at the bench looking at a batch of papers, oblivious to the commotion. For Charlene some of the attorneys and Herb Bowman, Deputy District Attorney, were traces from the past. They had all been here in May for the trial today being concluded. The court reporter, her stenorecorder set up before her was ready to begin preserving the words of this day in Department 28. The words would be lengthy, even boring, and would decide the fate of four defendants. And what happened to them would determine what would happen to Charlene.

Somehow the atmosphere was too relaxed. It was indeed informal for a court. But this made her rigid tension all the more brutal. It was not the place nor the moment to be unguarded or frivolous.

There was no jury. Their job was over. In their place the four defendants, dressed in street clothes, sat with their wrists flattened to the arms of their chairs, chained securely. Charlene scanned their faces quickly forcing her to focus on one of the defendants. In a flash her eyes met Floyd's for no more than a blink. It was enough to make her remember the first time she had seen them and the beginning of a hellish nightmare.

1

Getting to Know You

"Charlene, I never dreamed that I would meet a girl like you through Heart-to-Heart," continued the voice of this man who called himself Floyd.

Charlene tried desperately to put a face to the sound. He said he was tall and muscular and had black slightly curly hair. He liked to keep in shape. He said he was a businessman. He was a bicycle enthusiast and worked out at the gym regularly. He was not a smoker or drinker. He drank orange juice and Gatorade. This pleased Charlene who could not breathe around cigarette smoke and who did not ever want to date a "drinking man."

"But how do you know what I'm like, just talking to me on the phone for the past half hour? The fact we attended Brittany Junior High at the same time doesn't tell you that much. That was a few years ago."

"I can tell. I can always size up a person. You're just not like other girls. You are genuine, honest, truthful," Floyd asserted. "I wish I had known you back then."

Charlene agreed to go out on Saturday. Until she knew him better, she would not let him know where she lived. They would meet at her parents' house in University City, a place they both knew well.

"It'll be all right, Mom, you'll see," Charlene implored. "I know how you feel about dating services, but Susie* met Will* that way."

"If you ask me, she took an awful chance," continued this over-protective mother. "A man who has to get dates through a dating service must have a problem or two. I don't care how much he impresses you, the fact is he must have something wrong with him or he wouldn't go through Heart-to-Heart, he'd have other ways to get women to go out with."

Her mother's words stuck in her mind only briefly. She would not let them spoil her dream.

"We made a date for Saturday, Suze," Charlene reported. "I think I am going to like this guy."

"Didn't I tell you? You needed a little extra zing in your life. You've got to get back into the swing of things. Being the great Mom you are to Jericha* and Tracie* should only be a part of your life; not your whole life."

"I know that," Charlene acknowledged, watching her two eager "cooks," their arms wrapped in oven mitts taking a cookie sheet of burnt sugar cookies out of the oven. "I am a better mother and make them happy when I am happy myself.'

"Here, Mom, try one," said Jericha extending a warm black-edged cookie to Charlene. "They're a little too baked," she admitted.

"Thanks, sweetheart," Charlene said, munching on the offered morsel. Returning to her phone conversation, she continued, "Suze, don't think I'm ungrateful. Thanks for making me take the dare. It was just a little hard to accept that I had to resort to a dating service. I used to think that was only for losers."

"You sound just like my mother," Susie remarked. "And mine, too," Charlene laughed.

Come Saturday, Charlene packed up the girls' things for an overnight stay with her parents in University City, an affluent suburb of St. Louis, in a ranch-style brick home more than thirty miles from where she lived in St. Charles.

She was sure Floyd would be impressed by her old home. There were years of charm and elegance there that her own place lacked, the difference between a thirty year residence on the one hand and a twelve and a half year marriage to Bart. Once inside the old homestead people were always taken by the décor with a flare for the international.

Evidence was everywhere of the travels to faraway places in which the family had been involved. The parents, Charlene's brother Steve and Charlene had all participated in travels abroad and meeting people very different from themselves. This family liked to keep the world at their fingertips with mementos from everywhere, oftentimes gifts from esteemed foreign friends.

Susie and Will were seated on the long armless blue velvet couch under the huge wall-mounted ceramic Santa María and Spanish Coat of Arms. The children were playing in the family room deeper into the interior of the house. Floyd arrived promptly at 8:00 and introduced himself when Charlene opened the door. She could see he had left out a few details in his self-description. He was only mildly muscular, had a medium build but had a forceful carriage reminiscent of a bigger man. He had a "little boy" element that seemed to seep through his personality. His hair was unkempt and frizzy and was thinning on top. But he had a captivating smile and deep blue eyes that became bolder as he spoke. After Floyd had been presented to the crowd, he took Charlene's arm and guided her to the door. They stepped out the door into the chill of the November evening. Charlene felt his touch but thought it was nothing special, nothing warm.

2

Getting to Know All About You

"You know, Jewish men treat their women right," Susie had admitted. "I don't know why I didn't realize that long ago, before my first marriage and a series of mistakes."

Charlene had not wanted to be blunt, but Jewish was not what a Gentile girl like her was looking for, exactly. But she wouldn't shut him out because he was. She had always been open and tolerant; she didn't know any other way of living her life. "We are all God's creatures," was a theme taught to her by her parents. By the time the first date with Floyd came around, she was used to the idea that this would be a different experience for her.

◆◆◆

It was winter and everyone said 1991 had been one of the coldest in St. Louis history. But it seemed to Charlene that very few in her thirty-four years had been mild. She soon appreciated the good manners of her date; he opened the car door for her and hopped around to the driver's side in a choreographed manner. He let her out in front of the restaurant and told her to wait in the foyer inside while he parked. It was a fine restaurant where Charlene had never been before. "No need for both of us to get cold," he said politely. "They should have valet parking in this place."

The evening went well. Charlene found Floyd gawking at her several times while they ordered and ate dinner. "I can't get over it. I have been dating women for fifteen years and I have never seen one as good-looking as you. You're the right height and weight, you have beautiful skin and light-brown hair, my favorite color and I like the shoulder length."

"Wait a minute," Charlene protested. "Aren't men supposed to favor blondes?"

"You're close enough. It's your figure that's model perfect. And you've had two kids? Incredible. Do you work out?"

"I work at a job and basically take care of my daughters. I don't work out at a gym. I was sick with pneumonia recently and lost a lot of weight. I decided not to put it back on, so, in a way, I am dieting, or at least you could say I am eating less. I used to be very athletic and P.E. was my favorite class at school."

"I just knew you liked sports. That's important to me."

"I didn't say I liked sports. I think quite a few professional football, basketball and baseball players are disgusting, and those unsportsmanlike hockey players give the sport a bad name," Charlene declared, but not wanting to offend, added, "Collegiate sports are okay. I watch them sometimes. And I do like being active."

"You have the wrong idea. Sports are for the enjoyment of the spectators. The personal lives of the players or a little hanky-panky just make watching the games more fascinating. Those guys know how to get away with almost anything. They make the money. And then there's the gambling."

Floyd did not like it when Charlene declared, "To each his own." He changed the subject. In fact during their conversations at times Charlene felt like he was cutting her off and not letting her fully express her opinion.

"Enough!" he declared whenever he wanted to change the course of their conversation. Charlene thought it was rude. It was as though he was the referee and the blown whistle put an end to one phase so the next could start.

He left a big tip for the waiter and told Charlene he was sympathetic to service people, that he himself had worked as a waiter during college days and did not appreciate all the cheapskates who came into restaurants.

Charlene and her newfound friend continued to go out on the week-ends. As time went on, she found there was a consistent difference between what Floyd said and what Floyd did.

Charlene felt she must report to Susie at first. "He's like a good book I can't put down. I can't skip even a single page. I feel compelled to get to know all about him."

"How does he relate to the kids?" Susie wanted to know.

"I'm not really sure, but I don't think he knows how to relate to kids. He never had any in his first marriage."

"He can't help but like your kids, Charlene. They are about the sweetest kids I've ever known."

Charlene's reports to Susie became less frequent. She began to feel guilty enjoying herself so much.

It was just before Christmas when Floyd took her to Cheshire Inn for a late night dinner. Their waiter was a very short olive-skinned man who spoke with an accent. Charlene thought she recognized the manner of speaking as Indian or Pakistani, trying to make the distinction from what she knew out of her experience with foreign students at the college where her parents taught.

"This is not what I ordered at all," Floyd burst out. "I ordered trout. T- r- o- u- t. Does this look like trout to you?"

The young waiter bowed as he spoke. "I am very sorry, sir. Please forgive me. I will be back soon with your order."

Charlene didn't know whether to begin eating her prime rib or not, so she picked at it with her fork and delayed. She reached for a roll in the napkin-covered bread basket. Floyd noticed and began yelling.

"Troll, troll. Come here."

Charlene at first did not realize he was calling for the waiter.

"There is no bread in this basket. Get her some."

"Yes, sir. Right away."

Floyd became impatient again when his fish was not brought out very quickly. He called for the waiter twice before the meal was served, each time using his term *Troll* to get his attention. Charlene was embarrassed, trying not to show it, and wondered where Floyd's sympathy for waiters had gone.

Their relationship moved along smoothly and it became automatic for Charlene to overlook some of his temperamental outbursts. She reasoned that she had some faults of her own. But she did feel like a student in a small classroom where she was getting lessons she did not want.

Floyd always had plenty of money. This made Charlene feel secure. Financial problems had plagued her through a marriage and divorce and the subsequent era of being a single mother.

"I own two paper routes for the *Post-Dispatch*," Floyd told Charlene. "Technically you can only buy one, but I found a way to get two. Both of them are very lucrative," he confided. "The LaDue route is a real money-maker."

He said he hired others to do most of the delivering, paying only moderate wages. He said it was good business practice. He was fortunate to find reliable workers to whom he could pay little. "I know what I'm doing," he boasted.

"Why do you like this kind of work? Didn't you say you had a good job with Maybelline before this?"

"I wanted to be self-employed. I don't have some Dork for a boss; I'm my own boss. And there are income tax benefits when you work for yourself."

For the holidays Floyd did not participate in their Christmas activities but brought Charlene a gift. He said he wanted their relationship to go on and on.

As the weeks and months passed, Charlene realized that Floyd's athletic prowess was prominent to his persona. He made several trips to the gym each week and went on cycling tours with fellow enthusiasts. One in particular, Tim*, was eager to please Floyd and did all the mechanical work on Floyd's mountain and racing bikes. "The only thing I don't like is the bicycle maintenance," Floyd confessed. "Tim loves to change tires, adjust the gears, lubricate the axles. It's a good thing. He's got nothing else going for him, and he's a pest."

"I thought Tim went with you on rides. When he was out here last week, he seemed like an okay sort of kid."

"Kid is right. Brainless, shallow. But he'll do a good day's work on my bikes for a meal at Rich and Charlie's."

Tim was not home and Floyd needed him to fix up his favorite bike for the next day's ride. Floyd left him a message on his answering machine: "Listen, Phlegm, I need you. Be over at my place tomorrow by 8:00 in the morning, or forget our plans for later."

"Who are you talking to?" Charlene asked, hearing Floyd's harsh words.

When he told her, she imagined Tim really was brainless, to be ordered around, permitting Floyd to call him names. She told Floyd he treated his friends in a very shabby manner. Floyd shrugged his shoulders.

3

A Man's Best Friend

Floyd could not be concerned with Charlene's evaluation of Tim. She tended to be a nuisance in a way, but he was attracted to her and had learned to ignore the remarks she made which offended him. He knew he was superior. He knew she was inclined to believe in him. *Let her rant and rave*, he thought. *What she doesn't know now she'll never know.* He was glad to be in his own place where he could have things the way he wanted them. He had set up an appointment with a favorite call girl.

"No, your regular girl can't make it tomorrow," Lily had told him when he called. "But Reva can. Who knows? She may become your new favorite."

"Tell her my name is Chuck," Floyd instructed.

"It matters not to these girls," arranger Lily went on.

"I know," Floyd acknowledged, secretly thinking his regular girl *would* care. He knew she had a thing for him, and he was flattered. But no woman would ever get to him again. Pat* had been one sweet girl when he married her, and it was so nice to have it whenever he wanted it. But she became as routine as all the others after a while and she actually wanted to become pregnant. He vowed from that time on to be like one of his best friends, Frankie*.

"Women only get in the way," Frankie often said. "You'll sure never see me marrying one of them. The merchandise they have to offer can be bought one piece at a time." They both shook with laughter, a custom of theirs when either of them struck a note of gratifying humor.

When she arrived, Reva caressed Floyd while he removed her clothes. He gave her momentary approval for Body; now to find out how the Sex would be. He was impatient to get started and told her to shut up when she began some inane conversation.

"I'm not paying you for small talk," he told her as he roughly hiked up her legs and kissed her open lips. There was little foreplay. His tongue went to the depths of her mouth and then he aroused her quickly sucking on her large breasts.

His panting and throbbing lasted to the climax which he tried to prolong. She pretended to urge him to stay inside her and try to come again but he was through and soon pushed off to regain his normal composure.

She's not bad, Floyd thought. Not as good as Delores, but pretty damned good.

He couldn't help it. The round fullness of her buns was right there, at his eye level, and within a split second, his chance would be over. It was too much of a temptation, so he reached out and smacked her hard, leaving a pink spot on her pale skin.

She spun around and grinned at him. "You devil, Chuck," she cooed.

"You know you love it," Floyd continued. "You loved what we did in bed, too. I got my money's worth. Did you?"

The girl reached for her clothes where Floyd had flung them and was mentally composing an answer to his unexpected question.

Floyd grabbed her viciously. "I asked you a question. Was it good for you?"

"You know it," she said, picking up the cash on the bedside table. "Got to go now, Chuck."

Floyd lay down again after her departure, sorry to see her go.

"I was just getting started," he laughed to himself.

He picked up the phone and speed-dialed Frankie's private number in Atlanta. He needed to hear from the only other superior being he knew.

He could hear a barking dog in the fenced-in yard of the house adjacent to his building. "Put a muzzle on him!" he commanded, thinking of his own dog Load, left at the family home in the care of his parents. A man's best friend might be an alley dog, he mused, but would never mean as much as a real best friend. His pact with Frankie was held secure in the definitive sphere of his brain and his being. Frankie outranked his loyal dog and everything else in his life. His other good friend who often advised him in business deals was another plus in his life. They both outranked any woman, even Charlene, he sighed, even Charlene.

"Hello, my friend," he began. "Got time to talk? I want to fill you in on some more details . . . yes, about what we were saying yesterday," he hesitated. "Yeh, Charlene is fine, maybe too fine. I don't think I can go along with your drop-trailer idea. I think I love her too much."

4

Ménage à Trois

Charlene wondered if Floyd had any real feelings for friends until he told her about Frank, a buddy of long standing whom Floyd seemed to worship. Another close friend was mentioned less frequently, but there were ties.

"You're going to love Frankie," Floyd promised. "He'll love you too. You're our kind of woman." Once mentioned, Frank became a permanent part of their conversations. He was always there with them, sitting across the table or plopping on the couch between them while they watched TV. They were a *ménage à trois* except that one-third was a silent partner.

Charlene had no idea of how verbal this third was; he liked to dictate to Floyd on a day-to-day basis about everything that affected their lives, even Charlene's.

"What's his wife like?" Charlene wondered.

"Frankie's? Oh, no, he's single."

"You've told me how smart and good-looking he is. How has he escaped matrimony? Have you guys been so busy that in these thirty-some years you haven't been to the altar?"

"I was married. Ended in divorce. Not Frankie. He just doesn't make mistakes. He'll never marry."

Charlene winced at Floyd's references to marriage as a mistake. But he was describing Frankie, not himself.

"Frank is a great-looking man," Floyd told Charlene. "He's not Jewish-looking. He's redhead, 5'10" tall, slender, a good dresser, loves Italian Cordovan penny loafers; he has a pair of old rare pennies worth lots of money that he keeps polished and wears in his penny slots for good luck. They are Lincoln wheat pennies 1909 San Francisco mintmark VDB that he takes out to polish once in a while. I saw them up close once when he was visiting. He places them securely in those loafers, looks down to admire them frequently and tells no one of their value. He has to be unique," Floyd raved, assuring Charlene that he knew a great deal about rare coin collections and the value of certain coins. Realistically everything he told her about Frank was positive, though there was always a reference to *money*. Charlene knew Floyd prized his friendship with him, in part because they felt the same about money.

Her mind became a computer, mechanically sorting and saving everything Floyd told her; the good friends file became dominant in rank and greatest in size and number of segments. He talked about both close colleagues who had often helped Floyd when he needed advice and the reliance of a buddy.

"Someday I'll have the bank account these guys have," Floyd swore. "I can reach a million, maybe even surpass it. There's nothing like having money, a lot of it. It buys anything you want. Whatever you want, money can buy it."

"How do people make so much money?"

"Getting into good money-making pursuits. Frankie likes to teach part-time, I think he likes to be around learning institutions, he likes the atmosphere. You know he is a brain. Both my good friends are into gambling. A career in medicine or law can lead to a six-figure annual salary, easily. But it takes time to get there. I go for the fast track. Many a fortune has been made on shrewd bets when you have big stakes."

Charlene would have assumed that there was no assurance of millionaire status in these careers, but Floyd thought so. She tried to visualize what making millions would entail.

"I can't understand Frankie some times," Floyd told Charlene in a later discussion. "The guy's got all these mutual funds and investment accounts pulling in a whole lot, and still he drives a Cavalier. And then he doesn't even buy it, he just leases it."

This could not compare with Floyd's black sleek Corvette. He had a passion for flashy cars, and he especially liked to get compliments about them from people who were envious.

"I needed friends after I divorced my first wife," Floyd went on. "We used her social security number to find out all kinds of things."

"Was it a bitter divorce?" Charlene asked.

"No, not really. She was okay."

"I think you are still in love with her," Charlene ventured.

"No, and I don't know if I ever was."

"You hold no ill feelings toward her?"

"No. She had a rough time of it. Only she should not have tried to force her religion on me. I told her I would not convert to Catholicism. She kept putting crucifixes up all over the place."

"Is that why you divorced her?" Charlene questioned.

Floyd never seemed a religious person. Why would he marry a girl who was? Charlene found herself getting into areas that were beyond her comprehension.

"No. After a while I was just not psyched for her. She put on some weight. Her body changed. She was not desirable. And she wanted a baby."

Floyd said he talked it over with Frankie before getting a lawyer and suing Pat for a divorce. He made a small settlement with her.

"She really loved me. She did not want to split up."

Charlene began to feel sorry for Pat, knowing that if Floyd told her one day he was not psyched for her, she would be totally devastated. She tried to put it out of her mind, but still she insulated herself for it. What he told her about Pat may not have been the whole story, and she did not ask more.

"Wanting a baby is not so unusual," she told Floyd. "Most women do when they marry. I did. I wanted children, and I love mine very, very much." Floyd stared off in the distance in a gesture that negated Charlene's belief that everyone loves children.

But Charlene knew Floyd loved her. Nothing else really mattered.

5

A Man Like No Other

Charlene waved good-bye to her girls as they left with Bart for a Saturday afternoon outing. Susie sat across the table from her, leaning over her steaming cup of tea.

"Well, tell me about Valentine's Day. He took you to the Adam's Mark for the weekend? What did your Mom say about that?"

"She's not a creature from the 19ᵗʰ century, Susie. She knows what's going on."

"Wasn't it romantic?"

"The most romantic time of my life. He gave me dozens of really great gifts, having hidden them in every corner, even under the bed, in a little game. But more importantly he told me I was his Forever Girl and wanted us to pledge to see only each other from now on. Well, I don't know about him, but I haven't thought of dating anyone but him since our first date."

"I don't want to get personal, Char," Susie prefaced, "but . . . er, how was the sex?"

"I'm only telling you because you told me about Will. I'd really rather not discuss it. I feel a little dirty about this."

"My curiosity doesn't have to be satisfied," Susie said, reaching for the teapot.

"I'll tell you this. He seemed to be trying to set a new record. Each time he asked me if it was good for me. He seemed to put great importance on my reaction to his performance. I couldn't complain."

"Where do you think the relationship is going?"

"He wants to move in with me. His lease is running out and he has to move somewhere."

"Is marriage in the equation?"

"Marriage and children seem to be something of a sore spot. But he doesn't dislike my kids."

"Is that enough?"

"I don't know yet. But I know if we ever part ways, I will never recover. I have to give him my answer tomorrow. Something is holding me back. I can't explain. I love him. I know he loves me, but there's a missing link somehow."

As she spoke, Charlene's mind wandered.

"You are so right for me; I feel I have known you all my life. We were meant for each other." "I feel that way, too."

"Suze, we are compatible, Floyd and me."

"So it seems."

"I will have to pass the approval test with Frankie; if Floyd talked over his possible divorce from Pat with him, he would certainly do the same about remarriage."

"Can you handle that, Charlene? It seems to me he is a man like no other. I think he is a little too close to this Frankie. Your commitment to each other should be enough, don't you think?"

♦ ♦ ♦

By the time Floyd's lease was up, Charlene had made up her mind.

"Thanks for this. You do know I love you, don't you?" Floyd said in a half-whisper on the phone. "This will be to your advantage. I'll pay your bills. I don't have much furniture. We can store what you don't want upstairs in your basement. I'll need space for my computer and business stuff. I might even sell some of my things to my mother, my sister or one of my friends."

Floyd began moving his living room and bedroom furniture into the basement right away.

"What's all this stuff down here?" he asked.

"That belongs to my brother. He was paying storage on it for a long time. I told him he could use my basement to save himself that money. He needs to save for his tuition."

"Well," Floyd stated flatly, "he'll just have to move it out. I need this whole area for my stuff."

It took some doing. Steve took some of his stored items out and Floyd sold some exercising equipment to his mother.

"She gave me $500 for my treadmill. I only paid $350 for it."

"You mean you made a profit off your own mother?" Charlene asked incredulously. "I would have just given it to mine."

"That's how different you and I are. I only took what she offered," Floyd bragged. "Who am I to refuse a profit?"

From what Charlene had seen Floyd's parents were not, by any standard she knew, wealthy people; they drove a rather dilapidated car, lived in a modest house that needed some repairs, were quite conservative when it came to spending and, admiring Floyd because he had accumulated quite a lot for himself, would gladly have accepted the exerciser as Floyd's gift.

"Couldn't you just give her the treadmill?"

"Hell no. My Dad taught me never to give a sucker an even break."

"Even your mother?"

"You can't let sentiment get in your way. My mother gives my sister money all the time. She's always hiding what my sister does from me. Do you know she had a baby and my mother didn't tell me? I saw the baby car seat in their car. Now who do you suppose bought that for her? Why shouldn't she pay me for my things?"

"I sense a little sibling rivalry," Charlene hinted. "Don't you like your family?"

"My mother's not fair. And she used to be a real YS."

"YS? What on earth does that mean?"

"Fat. I told her Your Shape is a disgrace. She went to Weight Watchers and lost a whole lot."

"And so now she needs your exerciser to maintain the weight."

"Enough!" Floyd announced. He was openly irritated with Charlene. He never lost control.

To counteract Floyd's irritation with her, Charlene decided to do something really special for him. She had to do something.

"Hello, Mrs. Mitleider? You know next Saturday is Floyd's birthday and well, I would like to give him a party. Can you tell me who to invite and can you come?"

The planned celebration turned out to be a success, even though it cost more than Charlene could afford. Floyd was surprised and pleased. He claimed he had never had a party given for him before. His parents beamed. Charlene could see that for them family get-togethers were rare. While they were all at the table applauding Floyd, his mother agreed to go out to dinner with them for Mother's Day the next month. That was followed by a Father's Day dinner date. Their families got acquainted. It brought Floyd closer to his parents than he had been in years. Charlene was content that maybe, just maybe, a cure for some of the family ills would be to Floyd's benefit and therefore to hers.

Acts of kindness slowly began to change things. Charlene hoped she was acceptable to his family. That included Frankie.

"I'm getting Jericha a bunny rabbit for Easter," Charlene outlined for Floyd. "Tracie isn't sure she'll like it."

"Don't expect me to like it," Floyd declared.

"But you do like pets, don't you?"

"I like Load. But he is a lot of trouble. Most dogs are. And I'm allergic to cats. In fact, I may be allergic to Load. I get these asthmatic attacks sometimes. My folks don't have the stomach to get rid of my dog. I pay his vet bills."

Not really fond of his dog, Floyd had only one person that he seemed close to. He always had praise for him. Floyd needed that closeness to Frankie; he needed a mentor. It was a reciprocal thing; Frankie likewise admired Floyd. They called each other almost daily and seemingly kept abreast of each other's activities.

Floyd did not have an abundance of friends in town. His mother could only name Tim and two others when Charlene arranged his party. A few others involved in Floyd's work were invited. Though the party had been good for their relationship, it had still shown Floyd's tendency to mistreat people. He told Tim to shut up a couple of times. Tim was too dense to realize he was being insulted and used, or that Floyd did not hold him in anything like high esteem. The way Floyd treated some people made Charlene wonder how he had any friends.

Charlene wanted to turn things around for him, but she made a mistake showing sympathy to Floyd for not having or keeping friends.

"I'm not ever going to bend over backwards in order to have friends. Either they like me, or they don't. Anyone who really counts does like me," he vowed.

He tended to brag and on one occasion went overboard talking about the women in his past.

"I have had plenty of girlfriends," Floyd told Charlene. "Nothing ever worked out. I always broke it off somewhere along the way. I gave them a shot at it."

Charlene learned his former girls were "too old, too young, too nosy, too fat, too unattractive" or he just got tired of them. He also invited in and later kicked out any number of male roommates; they had undesirable traits as well. He was unlucky in his choices. Floyd's self-reliance was aptly shown by such decisive actions; but that he changed his mind with the cycles of the moon did concern Charlene. It had always been hard for Charlene to change her mind, once it was made up. Quite the opposite for Floyd. What was hard was making up his mind and sticking to his decision.

Their personality and opinion differences were small, Charlene thought, and they were generally compatible. He seemed starved for a lasting relationship. Charlene wanted that too. It only bothered her that things always turned out diametrically opposed to the way she expected, especially from the way Floyd described them.

Floyd, for his part, was more amused at Charlene's efforts to bring his family into the picture than pleased. His intentions did not include being any more a part of any family than he was at the present. Her importance to him was a subject he discussed often with his mentors. And he cared for her more each day. Maybe in her case he would make an exception and keep his halo.

6

Measuring Forever

During the months of Floyd's living in Charlene's house, she began to see that Floyd was not always a man of his word. Paying expenses became a once in a while thing and because she was buying more steaks and expensive foods, doing his laundry and maintaining air conditioning colder than she really wanted, Charlene's resources began to wear thin.

"I don't have enough money in my account to pay this month's house payment," she told Floyd.

"Won't your Mom give you the money?"

Charlene finally dropped a bombshell on him. "Floyd," she blurted out, "I thought you were going to pay some of the bills. After all, you do live here. I expect you to pay something. I can't support you on my salary."

"But you get child support in addition to what you earn. And I've had to put out a bundle for these transplants," Floyd confessed, pointing to his bald spot, "and the insurance premiums on my vans have increased. Money gets scarce for me at times."

He made a series of pleas but finally Floyd reluctantly made one month's house payment.

There were other areas of disharmony and late night arguments. Charlene would not have discussions with Floyd if her girls were present. Floyd would tell Charlene where she might get some extra cash but would rarely give up any of his own. After every argument, Charlene felt ashamed to have complained about anything when Floyd sent her flowers or left "I'm sorry" notes which soon accumulated.

The worst part was that Floyd did not like Susie; he called Will the Pill to his face. He showed his animosity toward them openly.

"I do not insult Frankie; why should you insult my friends?" Charlene asked Floyd.

"There's nothing to insult where Frankie is concerned."

Charlene apologized to Susie repeatedly. "Maybe he doesn't want you to have friends for fear they might find fault with him while you do not," Susie told Charlene. She implied strongly that she did not like him.

Their friendship meant a lot to Charlene. It had endured since the third grade. "But you seemed to like Floyd at first," Charlene reminded Susie. "Floyd should not stand between us."

"You're right, Charlene," Susie declared. "You and I have been friends through thick and thin. I'm just a little worried about this guy."

Since she gave Charlene no concrete reason for this change of attitude, the subject was less significant.

"I have to give him a chance. I really care for him, Susie," Charlene confirmed. She had made up her unyielding mind, even though she could not understand the depths of the friction between Floyd and her best friend. Charlene was a pacifist and since she was Floyd's Forever Girl, she had to conclude that he wanted harmony and happiness as much as she did. That was the only way the relationship would be forever.

The crevasse became even deeper when Floyd came out of the toilet one day saying, "They are no better than my Suwills."

"What on earth are you talking about?"

"My Suwills," he laughed. "What I leave in the stool before flushing it."

This "little boy" side of Floyd was the antithesis of the "big man" Charlene had come to imagine him to be. She could tell he was at best still an adolescent in some ways, but because he was so vulnerable and needed her, she loved him even more.

From that moment on, he always referred to Susie and her husband together using his code. Charlene hated it and the fact that Floyd seemed so unsettled. She couldn't understand his need to do put-downs. But one day he came home bursting with excitement.

"Guess what! Frankie's coming to town. You'll meet him at last. He likes to get his dental work done here. We've got this friend, he's really an orthodontist, but he does regular dentistry for us. Of course we'll do lots of things while Frankie's here."

It was late summer of 1992 and the girls had been out of school for a while. Their grandmother took them on a trip to South Padre Island for a short vacation and they would be gone soon after Frankie's arrival.

"Good," Floyd said. "Now we'll have the place to ourselves."

"The girls do not get in our way," Charlene insisted. "They are well-behaved, obedient and easy-going, like me."

"Will you always be like this?" Floyd asked. He seemed to be expecting her to say that one day soon she would not be so endowed with gentleness.

"My kids are my life," she said instead. "I miss them when they are away."

"They are okay as far as MLK go."

"Translation, please."

"MLK. Moronic Little Kids."

When Frankie arrived, Charlene discovered as soon as she met him that Frankie had much the same charm as Floyd. An addictive tie between them, they were a matched set. Floyd just wanted to concentrate on Frankie. Charlene was not sure that was good or bad.

"Remember those days out at Parkway? When you transferred from Brittany to West County, you and I became friends."

"Yes, and on through our college days. I remember how much money we made on ticket sales to Florida that year during Spring Break. If the college office hadn't sent that security guard to stop our operation, no telling how much gambling money we could have made."

"So, you left Brittany when your folks moved out to the Parkway School District? I stayed on and finished high school in U. City."

"That's because your folks didn't have the good sense to move out. I hated those Lou brats who moved into our neighborhood and school system. They tried to take over our school, especially the athletics."

"You mean the Blacks, I guess," Charlene said, lowering her voice. "Why do you call them Lou?"

"That's our code. Ever hear of Lou Brock? If you've seen one, you've seen them all."

Floyd and Frank burst out in laughter. They seemed to enjoy their codes. In the course of a few days Charlene became acquainted with YB (your beard) which designated men with beards, YN (your nose) for people with large noses, YS (your shape) for overweight people, and YA (your age) for older people. They would point at and laugh about people they came across bearing those characteristics. It was obvious they felt themselves superior to other people.

"It's just our way," Floyd explained. "Frankie and I say these things so we won't have to give away any of our secrets. To you we'll say more because you are one of us."

"You know how we feel," Frankie explained.

"The masses are asses."

Their attitude was overstated superiority. Charlene wanted to know if there was any more room at the top or if she was part of the masses. She stopped short of tampering with the alliance and hierarchy of the two buddies. Strangely she felt if she said too much she would be expelled from the coalition and would never be "Load," a term in their circle for best buddy, not exclusive to Frankie.

Charlene was relieved when friend Frankie's free time was up and he had to go back where he came from. She couldn't explain to herself what about their friendship made her distrust Floyd. She considered that perhaps she was jealous of their closeness.

"Didn't I tell you she was perfect?" Floyd asked, standing in the corner of Charlene's kitchen with his back to her, telephone receiver in hand. "Yeh, we'll talk about how to do it. I'll be concentrating on finding a buyer for my routes. It may take a while to get a good price."

"Talking to Frankie again?" Charlene asked casually as he signed off. "He just got home, didn't he?"

"Yes. But he's going to visit Uncle Dave* in New York one week this Fall; maybe he'll stop over."

Even if Frankie was a means to getting to know Floyd better, Charlene could not help but wish the stopover would never happen. She sensed that this friend was a bad influence on Floyd. Besides she had never liked to have to compete. Charlene thought of Floyd's contrastive behavior and people he liked versus people he didn't.

Dusting his office corner in her dining room, a couple of folders fell to the floor. Underneath she found a rather battered autograph album whose embossed letters had half worn off. Flipping through it she realized it was a relic from Floyd's past. It had pages of autographs from big sports figures: Stan Musial, Hank Aaron, Joe Torre, Bob Gibson, Johnny Bench and Jackie Smith. It was obviously a prize possession, something a boy of eight or nine years old would have held dearly. She smiled, imagining a wide-eyed young Floyd holding up his book to those greats, until she turned to a page Floyd himself had written in juvenile cursive. It read:

Fealine

Roses are Red
Violets are Black
I'll come up to you
And stick a knife in your back

7

Drawing Lines in the Sand

Charlene's humble house was comfortable, though it had become a bit cluttered with Floyd's computer, business files and exercise equipment. It saw the comings and goings of the four of them and an occasional visit from Jericha and Tracie's father. Charlene drove to work in her Dodge Aries K during the week, but on the week-ends Floyd drove it. His Corvette and delivery vans were inappropriate to their going out, especially on the rare occasion when they all went out to dinner or to celebrate some occasion. Charlene thought their arrangement was fine, until one day out of the blue Floyd sprang news of another change.

"I was in such a hurry yesterday that I wrecked up the black van. I know of a place closer in that's for rent. You're so far out here," he explained. "I have to get up too early to do my routes. When I filed my 1992 tax returns I noticed I hadn't made as much money as the previous year. I think the added expenses of driving farther and spending more . . . ."

"Maybe 1993 will be a better year for you. It's not even half over yet."

Tracie cried when she came home from school and saw a moving van filling up with Floyd's things. Charlene thought Jericha looked a little bewildered, too, even though she was older and would not show her feelings.

Charlene did not know what to think or say about it. Floyd's changeability was upsetting their lives.

"He'll still be coming over," Charlene consoled the children. "It's not like the break-up with your daddy. Don't worry."

The second day after moving Floyd called early one morning.

"Charlene, I made a terrible mistake. I should not have moved out. If I can get this fool who rented to me to give me back my security deposit, I'm going to move out in a month and . . . back to you, if that's okay."

"I don't know, Floyd. This is very unsettling to my girls, and in fact, to me too. I think you should stay where you are."

"Some things you have to do no matter what your kids think. They can't rule your life. I'm moving back."

"Floyd, I have to do what's best for the kids. I'll never shirk my responsibility to them. I love my girls. They are counting on me."

They were at an impasse. But Floyd could not get out of his lease, so there was no room for negotiation. He then had a series of guys who stayed with him briefly, but none was permanent. Floyd complained about them.

"I had to pay the whole amount of the rent for this big house," he moaned. "Tim should have paid me more. He stayed here almost all last month. And Greg owes me, too. Screw'em."

Charlene did not know why he began talking about marriage; for so long he had been resolute. He would remain single, just like Frankie. But one day in the Fall he told her.

"We should plan on getting married."

Floyd was surprised when Charlene hesitated. "Did you hear me?" he said raising his pitch. "I want you to marry me."

Charlene did not want to make another mistake in her life. She held her ground for a while.

"*Is my love for him enough? How can I be sure he is the one for me?*" Charlene asked herself. She decided she would let someone besides Susie help her at this crossroads.

"Mom, I don't want to bother you with my problems," she began, "and I know you thought it was over between Floyd and me when he moved out, but . . . ."

"I have seen you pretty despondent several times since you've known Floyd. I would like you to be ecstatically happy over this proposal, not lukewarm. But you do what you think best. I will respect your decision."

Charlene knew Floyd would not wait too long for her answer; he would move on. He had done that with others in the past.

"I can't just up and leave."

"I know. The kids. They come first."

"Floyd, they have to."

Ups and downs, pros and cons, arguing and making up continued. They considered themselves engaged.

"You know my sister remarried," Floyd began, "and, well, this guy she married is pretty well-heeled. She signed a prenuptial. She'll probably try to rip him off like she did the first guy."

"I was so shocked that we didn't even attend her wedding."

"I was busy running that marathon. That was more important."

"She didn't seem too upset," Charlene added, not venturing too much opinion that Floyd might not like.

"My mother thinks I should get you to sign a prenup, too," Floyd said sheepishly. "I'll have my lawyer draw one up before we get married."

"Don't bother," Charlene returned angrily. "If we are going to get married on a dollars and cents basis, we might as well just continue living together. I am insulted. I will not sign."

They never talked about this any more.

♦♦♦

The tree was up, the lights glowing on Christmas Eve and a fat-free dinner was in the oven. Floyd kept up a dietary regimen which, even when holidays requiring rich foods came, Charlene managed to honor. The children and she were expecting him, peering out the front windows, when the phone rang disrupting their anticipated festivities.

"Hello, Charlene. Is Floyd there?" Floyd's mother asked. She explained that Frankie's uncle had called and wanted Floyd to go immediately to Atlanta.

Frankie had been involved in a very serious car accident, she said, and Uncle Dave knew Floyd would want to be there with his buddy in this trying time.

"Have him call me the minute he gets there," was her final word.

Her attitude was different, somehow. She was all business, excluding Charlene from the family, wanting nothing from her except to put Floyd in touch with Frank. She was unsympathetic to Charlene's concern and frustration that Floyd might be gone over the Christmas holiday. Floyd's parents showed great fondness for this Frankie. At this point they did not seem to care as much for the girl their son wanted to marry.

It was an unheard of idea, in Charlene's opinion, that a man would fly off in the middle of a marriage proposal to be with a buddy rather than enjoy a convivial time with the woman he professed to love. Her girls and Charlene were disappointed, and matters were worse when Floyd's mother called her very late to say Floyd had left.

It would have been so easy to do what had to be done, end this relationship, if Charlene did not love him. She cried all night because of her failure; she would have to start all over again and she would always regret letting this one get away. She kept seeing a white sandy beach where a long deep line had been drawn. In the middle of it stood Floyd, his arms folded and an enigmatic smile on his face, looking like a genie. On one side of the line were the Mitleiders wielding strange indistinguishable weapons, flanked by the redheaded wonder; all of them beckoning to Floyd, urging him to come over. On the other side stood Charlene, feet imbedded in warm moist sand, holding hands with both girls, paralyzed and unarmed. She tried, but was unable to cross the line or move back. "Come home to me," she called out. "The sand is better here. It feels good oozing up between our toes. You can have this comforting feeling, too. Don't listen to them. Come to me."

8

Another Lie for the Holidays

"I'll be back for New Year's Eve," Floyd said. "Call some place, any place you like and make reservations for us."

"What did you say? Our connection is bad. How is Frankie? You say you're coming home?"

Floyd thought it was a good sign: she couldn't hear, thought they had a bad connection. Perfect. He would simply hang up.

He returned to their suite in the Paradise Island Hotel.

"Did you talk to her?" eagerly asked the man sitting at the phone table.

"Yeah. Everything's cool. She doesn't know we're here. That story we told her about Frank's accident worked out fine. She bought it all."

"Are you sure? I hear you had a little tirade and move-out. You're going to blow this thing!"

"God, don't keep mentioning that. I couldn't help myself. I needed my girls. I couldn't take all that sweetness and light. I needed some action."

"If you blow this, you're out $750,000. We've always dreamed of a way to get quick cash. We need to keep our plans straight. The YN connection in San Diego is ready with the front and we can tie in the Bees after we get the business started."

"I'll have to take your word for this. I wish I really had gone to Atlanta to see Frankie. But he is there safe and sound. The accident story was pure bull. Is the YN you're talking about an Arab? Big noses can mean anything-Roman, Palestinian, Iranian, Iraqi, Jimmy Durante," Floyd guffawed.

"He's a Palestinian. I know we can trust him. I like to make money as much as you do."

"Can we go for a midnight swim? I'm missing my work-outs. My joints are stiff."

"In a while. I'm waiting for a couple of calls. We still have some wrinkles to iron out. And I want to go back to the tables. We need to make enough to cover the cost of this trip to the Bahamas."

"Okay," Floyd agreed gulping down the last of his quart of orange juice. "But I still want to return to St. Louis day after tomorrow. I want to get things straight with Charlene. She's a little mad, you know."

"Tell me you can handle her," the companion said, looking up from the page filled with figures and stock symbols. "She can't be all that uncomplicated."

"That's the beauty of this whole plan. She's a very big challenge. You know, Load, I really miss her, more than I can say."

"Don't call me that! I hear that's what you call your dog! And, don't get sentimental on me."

9

New Plans, Old Problems

Charlene had enough time to decide if she ever wanted to see Floyd again. He called upon his return. Charlene was bitter about having been left in a second place position. Her frame of mind was not good.

"I have made other plans for New Year's Eve," she told Floyd. "I'm not sure I ever want to see you again."

Floyd laughed mockingly. "*I* decide when this relationship is over. And I say it will never be over. Why are you acting this way? Frankie is my best friend. I had to be there. Don't start acting like a nagging wife. End of subject!"

"I am not going out with you tomorrow night," she maintained. The hurt was too deep to be so readily dissolved. "We're not really engaged anyway. I say this is the end of it."

"Just because you don't have that engagement ring doesn't mean we aren't engaged. I told you you would have the biggest and best money can buy; a stone to dazzle everyone who sees it. It'll make Susie's look like the eye of a needle. And if you think for a minute you're going out with anyone else, you're wrong. I'll beat him up. You are my girl and no one else's."

He made her look foolish. He changed her. She was not a real person, but a convenient possession. He commanded. She jumped. It bolstered his ego when she accepted what she did not find acceptable. Charlene longed to be the person she used to be before Floyd came into her life, but with Floyd in it. She was confused and unsure of herself no matter how deep into her soul she searched.

"You've been talking to Susie again, haven't you?" he accused.

"Sure. She is my friend. You have your best friend, I have mine."

"I want you to stop talking to her."

Floyd threw back his head and cackled like a farmyard chicken. "You can never be as close to her as I am to Frankie. What does she do for you? I rushed to Frankie's side because I knew he would do the same for me at the snap of the finger. You and Susie are there to cry on each other's shoulders. The Suwills don't help you when you need it and have to keep out of our business."

"I'll talk to Susie whenever I please," Charlene said defiantly.

"No you won't. We will change your number and make it un-listed."

He was strong and easily convinced Charlene whose weaknesses were always exposed. She had to believe in someone; it had to be Floyd.

The wound began to heal when he told her he had sold his *Post* routes and was seriously considering buying a liquor store in San Diego. At last he could get away from St. Louis, he explained. They would start a new life, he said. He showed her a check he'd been given in the sale and bragged about the deal. "When you're self-employed, you've got the perfect way to knock off half of what you earn for IRS purposes. Not only that I got ole Larry to pay me $50,000 more than we originally agreed. I got that in cash."

Floyd was flying high. Charlene could not bear to bring him down to reality.

"I can thank my good friend for the tip on this liquor store. A good friend of his, some foreign guy, assured him I would make a pile of money if I invested in this business. And we get San Diego besides."

"Aren't you worried about an audit by the IRS? I always heard they check carefully. My Dad, ..."

Floyd interceded. "They catch Nerds like your Dad. I've been getting away with it for the last ten years. I've got a great CPA. No-body can catch me. We know how to handle these things."

"Frankie cheats, too?"

"I told you. He never gets caught, at anything. He's nobody's fool," Floyd nodded.

Floyd leaned back in his chair, smiling contentedly, as he thought out his plans. "You know if this store makes the money I think it will," he babbled on, "and I keep all my mutual funds just sitting around drawing interest, we'll be able to retire in five years. Your parents will croak in a few years and we'll have all their money, too."

Floyd's plan lacked humanity; it was extreme, like his entire aura. Money was supreme to him. It had been a problem for Charlene. It was a tempting idea not to have to worry about earning enough to survive. But love and devotion, respect for God and family, decency with one's fellowmen were all priceless. He would see that someday.

Their romantic times were enhanced by Floyd's exalted plans for the future. They loved to dance and had their favorite music, that of Engelbert Humperdinck. Their disagreements, mostly still unresolved in Charlene's mind, slipped into the past and became dim when they danced to Engelbert's *I Love Making Love to You*. Charlene loved him and knew she always would. She did it Floyd's way. She missed having her own friends, having Susie to call when she needed a boost, getting together poolside at her parents' place. Her world had become limited, but the more she loved and respected Floyd, the more decent he became. She knew she was having a good sway over him and he was coming around. It was worth her sacrifice. He would soon be the brave knight who rescued the distressed damsel.

"San Diego is the best city in the whole world," Floyd proclaimed. "When I visited Frankie there a while back, I did not want to leave, ever."

"Frankie?"

"Yeh, he used to live there. He loved it. He had some business there."

"And moving there will make you happy?"

"Why wouldn't it? The store makes money, we have nothing but good weather. Year-round cycling, running, working out. Frankie even recommended a good place to live, La Mirage. Why should we hesitate?"

"What will happen with the girls? I have to clear a move out of state with their father. They'll need things like health insurance. He'll have to continue supporting them."

"Of course. But you won't have to work when we get out there. What little you make will not help. You say you have always wanted to be a stay-at-home mother. This is your chance. The child support will be enough to pay their health insurance and expenses. If there is a problem, we'll just waive the child support."

"I'd like my girls to be my junior and only bridesmaids," Charlene added excitedly.

"Oh no, you don't," Floyd retorted. "If they are going to be there, so are my friends."

"Family is different," she faltered. "No other friends would be likely to attend our wedding if we marry in Las Vegas like you're planning."

"The answer is simple, Charlene," Floyd persisted. "It's our wedding. We don't need anyone else there."

Floyd did not think an engagement ring would be a good idea. "The store needs all my available funds at first. We'll get you an extra fancy wedding ring."

So it was on June 14, 1994, at the Silver Bells Chapel, they became husband and wife.

"Dumb Lou," Floyd said as photos were being taken. "Of all the ministers this chapel has, how did we get a Lou?"

"It can't matter or spoil our day, Floyd," Charlene begged. "This is our special day." The fragile heart frame under which they were standing for this pose swung slightly as the camera flashed.

"You finally snagged me," Floyd said as they left the chapel. "I always knew you would." Charlene's guard was up. Only her good manners and modesty inhibited her from saying: "*You have made a spectacular deal for yourself. You get me.*" Just having the thought satisfied her.

Their wedding night. Floyd sat beside her on the edge of the ample bed. His kiss was deep and lusty, but he released her abruptly to talk, and this amazed her.

"I want to tell you before we go any further. You know I am not eager to be a father," he started, matter-of-factly. Actually she did not know this before, but they had discussed the issue and decided against having children together.

"Yes?"

"If you get pregnant, you have two choices, the two A's," he pronounced firmly. "Abortion or adoption."

Charlene was too into the moment to be openly upset at this new threat. He was more serious than she had imagined about not wanting children. His attitude concerned her. How many times was he bound to say the wrong thing? He could not exist without his alphabetical sayings. This was not the time nor the place. It made her wonder how he really felt about the two children she already had, the two children he at one time said he wanted to adopt.

This new edict was another power play, part of his personality and pattern: happy to sad, yes to no.

One thing was a constant: their love, and they were what the minister declared: husband and wife.

The glitz of Las Vegas did not deter Floyd from his single-mindedness about their ultimate destination. "We can jog the track every day," he urged, "and get the business going better, the big money coming in. The La Mirage pool makes your parents' look like a fish-pond," he bragged, rambling. "I can't wait for us to get into it. And I have been missing my bike rides."

Charlene's idea that the city or the business were not equal to what was in their hearts for the success of their marriage was not considered important. She had to promise she'd do whatever he wanted.

It was too late to waver any more. While Floyd talked, a desperate last-minute call to Charlene's mother ran through her head.

Should I marry him? If you love him, go for it. I am only thinking of all these upsets you've gone through. He goes so hogwild—I can take it.

Charlene's mother was not completely comfortable about this marriage, but being the grandchildren's advocate always gave her a skeptical perspective. It was Charlene's decision and she had confidence in herself. Charlene could make the marriage work. This was their honeymoon, she would make the marriage last, concentrate on the loving, always reassure herself that it would never end. *After the*

Lovin' resounded in her head; she resolved to please. Being with Floyd was paradise to Charlene. So what if they had their differences. They were unimportant.

10

Where Paradise Begins

The U-Haul van chugged up the long and winding road to the hillside complex whose enormous sign LA MIRAGE was seen a mile away as they approached on Friars Road. The mauve stucco buildings on the high perch looked more mysterious than exquisite with the sun beginning to set behind them in a reddish haze. This summertime view was more impressive on June 17 than it had been in March when Charlene first visited Floyd there. That had been a reassuring moment. Floyd, having pioneered the place and purchased the liquor store, had told her: "I know I have been selfish in the past, and you're going to see a different Floyd from now on." That was what she needed. He was coming around, growing, becoming thoughtful in ways she had not foreseen, without gifts or coercion. This was the real Floyd inside that solid body, the other moulting away. She would build on this new Floyd and his pledge.

"Did you hear that newscast at the restaurant in Barstow today? I wonder if the police caught O.J."

"That Lou is guilty as hell. Why else would he be running?"

"They say he killed his ex-wife Nicole and a young man, Ron Goldman. How could he have done such a thing?"

"I don't know why he would want to. He has plenty of money. He's got everything."

"A great athlete, too."

"But he's just a Lou," Floyd countered, yawning, "I'm too tired to talk about it any more."

"At least we had a stopover and diversion in Vegas," Charlene mused. "Bet you wish you had won $100 in the slots like I did."

"I've won thousands before," Floyd swelled. "And who gave you the money to play?" he asked childishly. "You should split the money with me at least," he pouted.

"Here," she said, reaching in her purse for the $100 bill they had given her at the cashier's window. "You can have it all. What's mine is yours, and . . ."

"We're here," Floyd interrupted, putting the bill in his shirt pocket. "I'll let you in, then go to the rental office phone and call Nick." As the door to 5116 opened, it squeaked badly like in a haunted house. But the anticipation of making a new home in this place inspired Charlene. Neither Floyd's gesture of stinginess nor any other concerns about money could stifle her delight. He would take care of her.

Charlene looked at the nearly empty rooms of their townhouse and the sunny balcony at the back side of the place where Floyd had put his bicycles and some large boxes. Her footsteps sounded hollow-into the foyer, through the open space having a dining area on one side and compact kitchen on the other, and the long living room ending at the balcony. The split stairway leading to the bedrooms was off the foyer, making their new home quarters complete. It would not be long until her furniture added to his would make this a warm and homey abode, she calculated. Missing was the merry sound of Jericha and Tracie's giggling and speaking or singing for their Barbie dolls. Nothing could take their place. Charlene wanted them to get there soon.

As Floyd returned, the fax phone on the kitchen bar rang.

"Hello, hello," Floyd answered. "Yes. We just got here," he said, turning to Charlene awkwardly. "I can't talk right now."

If he expected her to ask who was calling, then accuse her of nagging, he was in for a setback. The new Mrs. Mitleider knew who it was and didn't care. After all, Floyd married her. He loved her.

"I'll drive the van close to the front walk to make it easier to unload. I got hold of Nick. I'm going to pick him up in the Marquis after that."

The delirium of the moment drumrolled. Here she was in a beautiful place with a magnificent though mystifying man. She picked up the phone, dialed her mother's number and within minutes was talking to her precious daughters. This concluded the rhapsody in her heart, measure for measure.

It was a great day. Charlene could think of almost nothing wrong with it.

11

Life with Floyd

"I do for you with pleasure," Nick said, looking to Floyd as if he needed a clue. "I like wuking for this guy," he added. His accent was enticing, and his trouble with r's noticeable. "Floyd is smart man. Especially in picking out wife," Nick grinned.

"We appreciate your help," Charlene insisted. "Oh, that wardrobe crate is so heavy," she warned. "Can you both carry it up the stairs together?"

"No need," Nick assured, taking the whole, huge carton to his shoulder and lugging it to the upstairs level in a few steps.

"I can't believe how strong you are!" Charlene remarked. He did not really look muscular; his build was only average, but he had a super strength. She did not expect that from a man who wore an earring in his left ear.

"I could've done it," Floyd flashed back.

"Of course you could," Charlene agreed.

"Yes, bossman has muscles like wocks," Nick admitted, coming back down the stairs.

Charlene spent most of her time fixing up the girls' room, regretting only that they had to share a room; in their house they had become used to having their separate bedrooms. A small sacrifice, she thought, and with their own private bath and the new pink ruffled curtains and bedspreads, the room looked as if it belonged to two pretty girls, aged 9 and 12.

After they had gone out to eat with Nick they took a swim in the La Mirage pool, even though Floyd was tired. Floyd was right; it was a terrific pool with an unusual meandering shape that seemed to go on forever. The stress was gone from Floyd's body in no time.

Next day, Floyd picked out a short skirt and halter for Charlene to wear. "Come on. We're going to my store."

Sam and Issa were working. "This is the wife," Floyd told them.

The two were polite, but gave Charlene a thorough visual examination through the dark eyes of Middle Easterners. The store was small, but elongated with an enclosed section at the rear for employees, a toilet and storage spaces. There was a small cage-like area to the side as one entered. The cash register, money orders, Lotto tickets, bus passes etc. were kept there. Also a gun. Only a few weeks earlier there had been a robbery. Floyd was still upset about it, reported $40,000 had been taken and only a small part was covered by insurance. He had tried to con various people into giving him a few thousand dollars here or there to make up for the claimed stolen amount. He even wanted Charlene's parents to lend him $40,000 to recuperate the money. He could not abide having a loss; it consumed him. The gun was added to the inventory, in case robbers ever came again.

The shotgun-style store had an imposing supply of bottles. They were of all shapes and colors, looking very impressive. Whiskey, wine, liqueur, aperitives, mixes. On the wall opposite the cage was a series of pictures of bearded men. Some were odd-looking, resembling historically significant men, others looked religious. They did not add any particular decorative attraction to that wall of Hillcrest Liquor & Checks Cashed 1%, Floyd's store.

"No, you wouldn't want to work in this neighborhood, girl," Floyd answered when Charlene offered to work. "Hillcrest is known for homos, Spiks, weirdos of all kinds. We do business with anyone. The check-cashing part of this store accounts for a lot of revenue. None of these low class people have checking accounts or know anything about handling money. They live off the government."

"It does not look like very hard work."

"But doing money orders, cashing checks and doing all the state reports is not easy. That's why I have Yusuf staying on. He's been running the place for the last three years. I'm learning from him."

"Yusuf?"

"We all call him Joe. Just about all these guys have an American name besides their Arabic name. Sam's real name is Sarmad. Atta goes by Allen."

"I am wondering why Joe wanted to sell," Charlene murmured.

"See that guy who was coming in the door when we were going out?" Floyd asked as they headed for the car.

"A sort of dark guy with slicked-back black hair? Kinda effeminate looking, pretty tall, good-looking?"

"Yeh. Right after I took over the store, one of the guys told me the guy's one of our typical weirdos. He cross dresses, he lives with men sometimes, but married a Spik woman here in Hillcrest. He cashed a check in the store once or twice. Name's Cunanan, Andy, I think. We hear he's a gigolo."

"I can believe that. He's got a handsome face. Doesn't look like such a bad character," Charlene mused. "But then who's to say? You have to candle an egg to see if it's rotten. Too bad we can't candle people."

"That's what we have to put up with here in Hillcrest."

Life with Floyd was absorbing, full of bombshells, but when Charlene's parents arrived a few days later, she was thrilled to have the familiar, the normal, back. She could be herself again. Jericha with her pet rabbit Kimber first jumped out of her parents' van, followed close behind by sleepy Tracie. "We're finally here, Mom," they exclaimed. "We were getting tired of mountains, rocks and highways."

"I'm glad we took the northern route. Your mother and I tried to make this as educational as possible. The girls now know what the Rockies are."

The scenery through Colorado and Utah was spectacular. Here, too," Dad explained. "We went clear downtown accidentally. I parked at a meter and we walked around, got our bearings and found out how to get back on the freeway."

"Sorry you had trouble," Charlene told them. "It's a little confusing out here."

"No, it wasn't bad. Your directions weren't bad. I love those jacaranda trees down on Ash Street," Dad said. "Blossoms are about gone now. The bird of paradise flowers are just lovely."

Tracie had perked up and was trying to follow their conversation. "There are lots of flowers in California, aren't there, Mom? Most of them smell good. A skunk sure don't," she said as an afterthought.

"Doesn't," corrected her grandfather. "And you are quite right."

"Can we go to Sea World again?" Jericha asked her grandmother. "Last year when you brought us out to Disneyland and we took the bus there to see the dolphins and whales, we didn't get to see all the shows."

"Maybe we can see some different sights here in San Diego before Grandpa and I have to go back home. Eventually I'm sure there will be another Sea World visit."

Charlene's mother kept a watchful eye on Jericha and Tracie.

"They seem to like it here," she admitted. "I'm going to miss them terribly! I feel like I am making a sacrifice, letting Floyd take charge of you. You'll be so far away. But as long as you're happy." "And all of us will miss you, too," Charlene told her. When the time came, it was a tearful farewell. Charlene's mother hugged them all, told Floyd to take good care of her girls and to be happy. "We'll be fine," he promised. The skeptical mother-in-law did not seem to find him truly credible. She would talk about it with Phil on the way back home.

"Kimber says thanks for bringing her out, too," Jericha said, holding her pet up to her grandmother's eye level. "It was hard to take care of her along the way. 'Member when she got loose in that town in Utah? I was scared Bunny was going to run away and drown in the Great Salt Lake." Jericha stroked the black and white silky fur of Kimber's head and long ears.

"Did you say Bunny? I thought this was a Skunk," Floyd said, "a retarded skunk." They laughed, thinking this a follow-up to Tracie's playful observation.

But this was the name by which Floyd continued to call Kimber long after Charlene's folks were gone. Jericha did not like that, but, like her mother, she learned to say nothing.

"Aren't your parents going to give us a wedding present?" Floyd asked that evening.

"Well, I don't know. They have done a lot for us. I don't expect them to give us money, too. That's what you're talking about, isn't it?"

"A wedding present. You think that party they threw for us, that barbecue around the pool before we left, was enough? That didn't cost much."

"It was a great party. Mom went to a lot of trouble for us. Does it matter what it cost? The folks are taking care of selling my car and my house. Someone has to make my house payments until it is sold. I think we should be grateful for their help."

This was the beginning of a series of disagreements that foretold how difficult life with Floyd was going to be. He would not let Charlene have her own set of keys to the Grand Marquis. She had to ask, even beg, each time she needed to use it. She wanted a credit card, but Floyd said, "Pat never got one. Why should I get one for you? I can already tell you think money grows on trees."

"But Floyd, why do you want me to be inconvenienced? You wouldn't let me bring out my own car. I have to sell it. When the money comes, I want you to get me a car of my own. And what's wrong with my having a Visa card?"

"We'll see," he said, "but I'm not promising anything."

The girls did love to swim with Floyd and Charlene when he came home from the store every day. But he started going to work late and getting home late. Once they had already had their swim by the time he got home, very late.

"You couldn't wait one lousy hour for me?" he stormed.

"Okay," Charlene said soothingly. "We'll wait for you tomorrow."

As though the joy was spoiled by the disappointment on one occasion, a change in the original routine, Floyd never again wanted to swim with them, and in fact, they did very little together. He went with Nick to Jack Murphy stadium for games, did his jogging and workouts with whoever came along and he went to his store less and less. Romance was kept alive and they often went to the movies or dancing. They went late after the kids were asleep.

"I'd like us to do more as a family," Charlene confided.

"Family?" he sighed. "What do you think I've been trying to get away from most of my life? I have wanted to leave St. Louis and my so-called family there for years. Don't expect me to be a stepfather to your kids. I can't do it."

Charlene realized there were more questions she should have asked when they discussed marriage. In the master bedroom one afternoon right after the 4th of July, Charlene remembered she was supposed to call Susie back. She reached for the receiver on the extension phone. She was happy Floyd no longer found Susie a threat. Charlene called her frequently from San Diego. She felt disconnected from her previous life back home. She sensed an uneasy isolation.

As she lifted the receiver, she realized the phone was already in use.

"Yes, I think it's working," she heard Floyd say in a near whisper. "Our plans are going like clockwork."

At first Charlene thought he was talking about their marriage. She was exploding with joy.

"Remember to stay cool," the unrecognized voice was advising. "Leave nothing to be suspected of."

♦♦♦

The only way Charlene could have transportation during the day was to take Floyd to Hillcrest, then go get him when he was ready to come home. She missed having her Dodge and the freedom it represented. She needed to go to the California DMV office to get the driver's test booklet so she could then get her California license; in addition she wanted to look for a birthday gift for Tracie. When she got to Hillcrest, Floyd and Nick were carrying on like two little kids about the pictures of bearded men on the wall. They pointed to each one and said. "Wah Bee, Wah Bee, Wah Bee," exaggerating the first part by prolonging it and lifting up on Bee. Nick seemed to enjoy having this insider joke with the Boss Man and probably didn't even know what YB was. Their playfulness seemed highly immature, but at least Floyd was not stressed out, as he often was, on this day. When they got home, Charlene showed Floyd the gift she had picked out for Trace.

"How much did that set me back?" Floyd growled when he saw the Gymnast Barbie doll.

Charlene thought the miniature equipment and Speed-O clothes on the doll would intrigue him, and he would say , "Oh, how cute."

"It was $25.00."

"And Bart didn't send the check this month."

"Not yet, but today is only the 6th. The check will come."

"If we don't get it, you take the doll back. I'm not paying for this present. He's her father."

Floyd ignored her when she reminded him that Tracie's grandmother had sent a check for the girl's birthday. Floyd himself had deposited it in the bank. $100.00 was a generous gift, covering four Barbie dolls!

Charlene went upstairs and heard through the closed door to their room that Tracie and Jericha were playing Nintendo. They were content enough. From there she went into the master bedroom, threw herself on the bed and began to sob bitterly. She felt small, unimportant, a rug for Floyd to walk on. She had no say in anything, even birthday presents for her children. She had no money of her own. What she had had was now either in Floyd's personal account or a joint account on which she had to justify any check she wrote. She had promised to let him be the money manager, but she did not expect to have the status of a servant, an outsider.

"You deserve better than me," she heard Floyd by her side. "Can you forgive me?"

It had been a long time since he asked Charlene that question. A few kind words comforted her and renewed her spirit. She knew their problems were her fault. She had to find the way to avoid them.

The next time they went to Mission Valley Shopping Mall to get Floyd new sneaker socks at the sports center, he found swim goggles, as well as lights and reflectors for his favorite mountain bike. Then they went to La Mesa to buy him a new pair of Sauconys running shoes. He whipped out his credit card, paying high prices for each item. He loved to indulge himself and would not even consider depriving himself of anything. Charlene said nothing, not wanting to break the "good Floyd" attitude which still prevailed since his apology. He had been unmarried too long, she thought. In time he will appreciate having her and her girls for his family.

Tracie's birthday was celebrated at Disneyland. Both girls were electrified to return in such a short span of time to their favorite territory.

"We'll show you around," they claimed. "When Grandma brought us here last summer, we thought that would be the only time. Now we can do things we missed before."

"Thanks, Floyd," Tracie said running up to him. Jericha smiled broadly with her approval.

Joe went along with them. He was rather childlike and played with the girls as though he was really having fun. He sat with Tracie on the rides and chased her around in the open areas of Tomorrowland and Frontierland.

"We have to take the Monorail from here," Jericha told them. "We can get over to the hotel end that way and there's a good place to eat. Goofy comes out and acts, um-um, goofy!"

Joe laughed heartily. They ate ice cream and cake. Floyd pretended to stuff Joe's mouth with cake and it made the girls laugh as Joe feigned gagging on it. Joe was good with children; Charlene did not know if he was a father or not, but thought he was the right material for that role.

"Let's take the train to Adventureland. There is a man who says we are going to the Grand Canyon," Tracie proudly instructed. "And we get to see a dinosite egg."

"You mean dinosaur egg," Jericha said.

"Yes. A great big dinosaur egg . . . hatching."

Their own burst of laughter surrounded them.

The memory of that marvelous experience remained vibrant long after they got back to La Mirage-Floyd acting like a self-respecting father (even if he was only following Joe's lead)-the girls acting carefree and on top of the world. Charlene prayed to capture the feeling for always.

One night after Charlene was already in bed

Floyd woke her up, and talked to her in a sad tone.

"You know, Charlene, I think someone is stealing from me at the store. The cash receipts are always low when Joe and Issa work. I am sure they are ripping me off."

"You can find out, but don't jump to conclusions. You trust Nick, don't you? Call him and get him to watch for clues."

"Nick's moved and I don't know his new number. But I can tell you this: nobody's going to make a jackass out of me. Those guys have got to go."

"Don't you have a personnel card on Nick with an emergency phone number, next of kin etc.?"

"No. He was recommended. That's good enough. That's the way I run my business," Floyd insisted, getting huffy. "It's done that way out here. Loose, friendly."

But later Nick did help Floyd, declaring that both of the Palestinian brothers were truly taking Floyd's profits home with them.

Floyd believed everything Nick told him. He became especially close to him because of this incident. Charlene noticed a stronger attitude of camaraderie between Floyd and his Iraqi employee. Floyd fired Yusuf on the spot, but did it very cleverly. "Joe," he said calmly, "I really don't need your help any more. I release you of that part of our contract. I can take it from here."

All the employees were young men from the Middle East, the way Hillcrest Liquor had always been, even when Yusuf and another Palestinian had owned it before Floyd. Charlene was suspicious of them, not because of where they were from, but because she was afraid Floyd was out of his element. Charlene knew more about foreigners than he did, having been a part of the international club her parents sponsored. She could guess that these Middle Easterners did not like Floyd, a Jew. She reflected on some of the Indian, Bangladeshi, Iranian and Iraqi students her family and she had met. They often called each other "brother."

One of their commonalities was an inborn distrust of Jews. Charlene wondered how their feelings would clash with Floyd's.

Everyone said American families offering friendship were often "used" by these foreign students. Maybe Floyd was being used. She wondered if he could be duped. . He was sensitive to the fact some people did not like Jews and, justifiably took offense to that attitude. Charlene wished he would ask for her help. But he did not.

Nick seemed Americanized but to Floyd was very submissive (an un-American characteristic). Charlene had a feeling about Nick.

Floyd had him come to their apartment the next day when he got off work at the store.

"How did it go without Joe?" he asked Nick.

As he approached Charlene noticed a small filigree gold cross on a chain around his neck. He must be a Christian, she thought, rather than Muslim like the majority of Iraqis. Charlene's attitude was, then, that perhaps he was different. He was an enigma.

Floyd was flattered by Nick's constant subservient remarks about Floyd's brains and superiority. "Wight, boss. Wight away, no pwoblem. Not to wowwy. Nick do it for you." He said everything was fine at the store. Nick was like a Frankie with an accent and less reciprocation from Floyd.

Not long after Floyd's dismissal of Joe, Nick told Floyd that two $500.00 money orders had been stolen. The consecutive numbering of the checks gave away that a theft had occurred. He suspected Issa. Floyd immediately fired Issa and ordered him out of his store. Issa claimed total innocence and vowed to get even. Later he left Floyd a phone message. "You owe me money and don't try to get out of it. I didn't steal the damned money orders and you'd better not even consider getting me in trouble with the law. You're the one in trouble. The IRS would like to know about your dirty deals and unreported income. You could go to a federal prison. If you want to keep me from turning you over to the feds, get down to the store and leave me my check."

Charlene heard the message. She knew one of Floyd's deadly flaws was his bragging. She thought it was destined to get him in trouble.

Issa had spoken without an accent and as though he knew a thing or two. He was sharp. Floyd flinched at the mention of federal prison.

Charlene knew Floyd would take it out on her when he had business problems. She dreaded the consequences.

12

A Lesson in Self-Control

It was nearly time for schools to begin, all too soon the girls thought. They were preparing to start classes at their respective schools in Allied Gardens, a few miles from La Mirage.

Floyd continued to lift weights, bike, run or otherwise divert himself. Even though there had been trouble at his store, he rarely went to work. He seemed unconcerned, confident that the store would take care of itself.

According to him the business was not making money. The image of a successful man with plenty of money was fading. Charlene was taking grocery money out of his wallet and found that it was full of big bills: $100's, $50's and $20's. The wallet was bursting at the seams. She had to wonder where this money was coming from if the business was not making any.

Floyd purchased a Titanium racing bike of which he was very proud. Charlene knew it had cost Floyd nearly $3,000; her old dependable Dodge had sold for less.

When the kids were asleep, she asked Floyd again: "Are you getting health insurance now?"

"You won't give up, will you, you DC," Floyd yelled.

"Sh-sh-sh," Charlene warned. "Don't wake up the girls. It has been more than three months now. You promised you'd use some of the child support money to pay for the health insurance. You have the money my folks sent me when my car and stuff were sold; can't you take that money and get at least minimum coverage? Why are we broke? Where is all the money?"

"You'll have to take my word for it. I can't spend any more money on your kids. Enough!"

"Well, then, you are not a man of your word. Why did you promise things you never intended to do?"

"I said we will not discuss this any more."

"This isn't fair. You are keeping all the money for yourself. You are cheating me just like you cheat the IRS. I hope they catch you," Charlene said angrily.

Floyd came up to her chair and gave it a tremendous push backward. She fell on the floor with it and cracked the back of her head on the hard surface. He rushed to her side and put his hands around her neck. She cried out in pain and fright. His strong hands tightened and she could not breathe. She began to choke.

Floyd released her as abruptly as he had grabbed her. Gasping for air Charlene managed to get up and run to the privacy of their bedroom where she locked the door. She heard the familiar door squeak; he was gone.

Her neck was sore and she couldn't swallow right; she patted cold water on her face, remembering how he had hit her before and the splash had helped. Somehow she fell asleep despite the vision of Floyd, sitting at a massive desk, counting stacks of dollar bills. "Don't bother me now," he was saying. "I'm busy making my fortune."

He was sleeping on the living room couch next morning, wrapped up in his favorite brown flannel blanket. He was cuddling motionless with his face almost hidden in the back cushions and his body in fetal position.

The car keys were on the table. Charlene did not have to beg for them.

"Have a wonderful first day," she told each of the kids, trying to maintain her sanity. The kids knew something had gone wrong.

"I'll be back for you at dismissal," she promised. Charlene had hoped this day would be a very happy one; as it happened she was only glad to be alive. Floyd could have killed her. For a paralyzing moment she really thought he was going to. It could have been just like the O.J.-Nicole story, she told herself. The world would not have cared so much about Charlene. She was not a celebrity. But there would have been motherless mortified children, destroyed lives, unprecedented pain: the same elements of Nicole's death, Charlene thought, her mind going wild with the visions of what could have been.

Floyd was still in a long, deep slumber when she returned to the apartment. She went upstairs to the extension, called Susie and told her about the incident. She had to tell someone.

"I think you should come home. Don't let pride stand in your way. This has been just a mistake in judgment. Everyone makes them some time. You know I have been very worried about you ever since he threatened Will and me."

"When was that?"

"Never mind now, Charlene. It was about money. He wanted us to make a house payment for you and I mean he was really pressuring us, since we were close friends. He wasn't going to make it for you. That's when I began to see him for what he is-a man whose first priority is money. I've known the type, though not this extreme. But that's in the past. Let's get back to you and how to get you out of there."

Charlene sat alone after talking to Susie, trying to reconcile her comments with the heartbreak she now felt.

Floyd came to the dining table where she was having coffee. He was trembling as he looked at her with tears in his azure eyes. "I'm sorry; I don't know what got into me. I lost it."

"I can't take it," she sobbed. "I think I should go back home. It has only been a few months, and you already have fallen out of love with me. Lord only knows what you'll think of me in the months or years ahead."

"Don't go, please. Stay with me. Give me another chance. We've come this far. Don't give up on us. I still love you."

Because the girls liked their respective schools and were enthralled by the freedom and loose structuring of the school programs, Charlene vowed once more to try harder to make this marriage what she had dreamed it would be.

She thought of nothing else from that moment on. She thought that Floyd knew more than anyone else what control meant; he just didn't know how to apply it to himself. He needed a lesson in self-control. Had not his parents, or any of his role models, ever taught him? It would be up to her, Charlene told herself. Her resolve dominated her being.

Just as she was beginning to feel better, believing this incident to be a one-time thing, before the month of September was over, Floyd again turned against her during an argument about money.

"Everything I owned has been sold, except the house, and I have turned all the money over to you. Can't we get me that used car you promised? I don't like to have to beg for the keys to your car. Why is it your car? We are married. Can't this be our car? I hate the uncertainty. I have to take the kids to school and go to the market dependent on whether or not I may use your car. It is like 'Mother, may I.' Get me my own car and I'll never use the Grand Marquis again."

"If you don't stop whining about money," Floyd declared, "you're going to be sorry. I will take Tracie out to the edge of town or to Santee, some place far away, and drop her off. She'll never find her way back; she'll just fall apart, or someone will pick her up and do whatever they want with her. There are plenty of weirdos looking for an opportunity like this. She'll . . ." Charlene's heart was pounding in her chest and breathing was labored. Her gasping became uncontrollable ire.

"You are a sonofabitch," she yelled, totally out of character. "How does such a terrible thing occur to you? What has she ever done to you or what has any of us done to deserve this kind of treatment? If you ever even think of doing such a thing," she cried, unable to go on.

This threat conjured up the worst crime scenario imaginable, the brain child of a deranged man. Her young daughter out on the street somewhere, running, her long blonde hair bobbing up and down, terrified, quietly weeping, no one to help her. Where was Floyd coming from?

"I have no intention of doing what I said. I was just talking, and you were just talking, about money, about the IRS, about health insurance and needing a car, right?"

"I am talking about real issues. You are threatening the welfare of my child. It is not the same." Charlene was not in the mood to play Floyd's mind games.

She thought of Floyd's stated goals back when they were dating. He wanted to make money, plenty of it, because if you have it, you can buy anything. So what he wanted was whatever money can buy. . .for himself. He could not bring himself to spending money where he could get by without doing so. This had to be the reason he would not give in to any monetary demands.

Whether she feared his threats were real or simply that she hoped her love would somehow reverse this frightening existence with Floyd, she realized she had to stop confronting him. She would refrain from asking him for anything from that day forward. She had to trust in God that Floyd did not have a bite to go with his bark, and that he would somehow be purged of the demon within him, the demon who would not let the unselfish man he promised emerge.

And so his control over Charlene continued. Charlene turned her full attention to the two real loves of her life: the two innocent children who had faith in her and needed her. She didn't know what else to do. She silenced her own voice. She had passed the lesson of Self-Control herself.

13

Whatever Money Can Buy

The girls were making friends at school. Jericha wanted to have a friend come home with her after school. She was to call and arrange it the evening before.

"She's so cute, Mom," Jericha said, "with her long black braids and beads."

"A Lou?" Floyd butted in. "Certainly not. Lous are not welcome in this house."

"There are lots of Black girls in my room," Tracie said. "I like them and they are nice to me."

Floyd stared at all three of them and pronounced with authority that he would decide who could come into his apartment and that it would never ever include a Lou.

That night as Charlene passed by the girls' bedroom door, she heard the double sobbing of two young girls. Their hearts were broken, too. She knew her going in would only sadden them more; she had no words to console them. Her ability to mother her girls was usurped by a man who cared very little for them. His acceptance of them, Charlene feared, was based on the amount of child support they brought. They provided him with another source of income.

When Floyd asked Charlene to pick out a movie, she believed some thoughtfulness had returned to him. Her eye caught the new Sinbad movie out. "This one," she said right away. "He is so funny."

"What? Of all the movies showing you have to pick a Lou one?"

"Then, I don't really have the choice, do I. Okay, just go on without me. I don't really want to go anyway."

"You DC," he went on. "Can't you do anything right? Well, if you don't go with me to the movies, I will stay home too and I'll turn the volume up to maximum on my big screen TV and blast the kids out of bed."

"Just a minute," Charlene conceded. "I'll get my purse and we'll leave."

All the way to the movies Charlene thought of Floyd as a spoiled child, a brat, an undisciplined schoolboy. It was a strain on her to put up with such base immaturity as name-calling. But she had made up her mind to accept him and keep silent about his faults. She would not change her mind.

Tracie finally managed to find a friend who met with Floyd's approval. A quiet girl like Tracie, Lailani* was of Polynesian ancestry, a perfect playmate and friend.

"She'll break someone's heart, someday," Floyd told Charlene.

"Tracie looks too much like Bart and Jericha looks like you." His implications were obvious; it was something else Charlene had to ignore. Floyd's declarations as to her perfection had not completely left her memory, but they had left his.

Tracie had every Thursday afternoon off from school and on that day Charlene and she habitually stopped by Carl's Jr. for chicken stars and fries for Tracie. She delighted in this new "California" tradition.

"What is she eating?" Floyd demanded to know. "They are like chicken nuggets," Charlene explained, thinking he was interested in her nutrition.

"They probably cost about $3.00," Floyd exclaimed.

"$2.29. And I didn't buy anything for myself."

"That's outrageous," Floyd continued. "Next Thursday just bring her home from school and give her a peanut butter sandwich. Hear me?"

"Is $2.29 beyond our budget?" Charlene asked, half laughing. "I can't believe you'd object to such a pittance."

Charlene looked at Tracie who had put the chicken star she was about to eat back in the box. A big tear ran down her face.

"Go ahead and eat your lunch," Charlene told her. "Floyd was only joking."

The next week Charlene's friend Mary* brought her two young children over to their apartment. She was room mother to her daughter's class at school, as was Charlene for Tracie in Grade 4. They had seen each other frequently at meetings at the school. Charlene liked her and besides, she needed a friend.

Floyd came in from the workout room and Charlene introduced him to the guests. The moment they left, Floyd asked: "What's in it for you? What do you get out of it?"

"You mean my friendship with Mary?"

"Yeh. You entertained her, you gave the kids snacks and drinks. What did she do for you?"

"Nothing. And I didn't ask for anything. We have become friends. Do I need to charge her something for that?"

Mary spoke about her husband and how her children adored him. Charlene could not help being jealous. Mary had what she longed for: a man who loved her and her children unconditionally, a man who did not require her to report every penny she spent, a man who remained loyal to her even if money became tight.

Charlene's husband was a different breed. She had not compared him with *normal* men in a long time; to be a man like no other was not necessarily good. Charlene saw it clearly.

One day Floyd took her to Hillcrest en route to the DMV where she was finally getting her California driver's license. Nick was there. A bewhiskered customer came in and went to a shelf where he picked up a small pack of aspirins. Floyd and Nick pointed to him behind his back. As he left the store, Floyd said, "YB has a headache. Poor YB." They tittered about the pictures on the wall in a juvenile fashion. Sam stood by stiffly not understanding the humor.

Floyd revealed some new information. He arranged to sell his business in a short time. Allen (a man who had been sure Hillcrest Liquor would be a money-maker) and a newcomer to the scene, Tarak Mustafa (known to others at the store as Terry) were willing to buy it, he said. By the end of October, they had made their agreement. Floyd told Charlene very little, but she knew the terms because Floyd left documents concerning this negotiation on her table. She knew he would be collecting $10,000 a month plus a down payment of $20,000.

Now Floyd did not work at all. He went once or twice a week to the store which he still owned technically, he told Charlene. There was more time to spend at the exercise room. Charlene did not understand the arrangement. *I never know what's going on*, she told herself anxiously.

"You seem completely exhausted, Floyd. Why do you spend so many hours working out? Are you getting a lot of pleasure from that?"

"It's pure torture," Floyd said in a scratchy voice.

Floyd was jumpy, complained that he had a pain in the abdomen.

"You have given me an ulcer," he moaned.

He went to the store to pick up payments being made by Tarak on their sales agreement. Charlene heard Floyd mentioning this process and saw things he carelessly left lying around. Once he referred to Tarak's brother, Charlie, who now worked as manager of Hillcrest. The Mustafa brothers seemed to be in charge of the store. But for the most part, Floyd was very secretive, leaving Charlene out as though the whole thing had nothing to do with her just as he had always done.

Allen, who had the same last name as Floyd's attorney, dropped by the store occasionally, according to the rare word from Floyd. Charlene wondered if either of Floyd's buddies had anything to do with the disposition of the store and people who worked there. All she knew was that Floyd had daily conversations with them. No one told her what was going on; she was only guessing. Nick and Sam were the only holdover employees still working at the store. Nick came by the house with Floyd when there was a game at the nearby stadium. Floyd had season tickets for two. Nick was cordial but never said anything about the store to Charlene.

Although the handwritten or- typed official-looking papers Charlene saw were still her main source of information about the store, another interesting thing began. Their FAX machine began receiving messages almost daily. They were abbreviations and numbers, possibly dollar amounts. The long paper rolled up after transmissions and remained untouched until Floyd retrieved it. They were codes of some sort. Floyd retrieved the information, then made phone calls. This may have had something to do with the store. From Charlene's untrained observations she concluded Hillcrest Liquor was a very unusual kind of commercial endeavor; everyone seemed to have his fingers in the pie, and for the most part, like Little Jack Horner, each one pulled out a plum. So many people worked at this small business. Floyd said it was not doing well. The mystery of the FAXes was even greater, because if this was business, why did they come to the apartment? The FAX machine should have been in the store. She wondered why the FAX transmissions had started only after Floyd turned over the running of the business to Tarak. They must have involved something other than the liquor store.

Nothing that happened brought Floyd any contentment. He treated Charlene with some respect frequently but in between ignored or cursed at her.

As to finances there had to be money. If not, the business was just a community project, she mused, knowing well that stacks of large bills still bloated his wallet. Floyd found it easy to be untruthful. He had come to realize Charlene was not going to question anything he did.

She continued to keep her questions to herself but wondered what was troubling Floyd so deeply.

No sooner had Floyd made up his mind to sell the business and the transfer had been initiated than he came up with another unusual, preposterous idea. He told Charlene he was getting life insurance for them. She was flabbergasted.

"Where are we getting the money for this?" Charlene asked. "You have said we can't afford health insurance, except for you, so how can we pay for a $750,000 life insurance policy premium?" "Uncle Dave is getting a special deal for us," Floyd expounded. "He wants to issue as many policies as possible before he retires. The yearly premium is not that high. I want you to be protected."

"My girls should be beneficiaries, too," Charlene insisted. "If I were to die, they would need money for their education and future lives."

"Absolutely not. They are not my responsibility, at all."

They bantered the life insurance idea around for a couple of weeks. Floyd was thoughtful and loving during this period. One evening he went to the drugstore and bought a bottle of Anbesol to soothe Charlene's throbbing toothache.

"I hope this will make you feel better," he told her. "The insurance office wants to send out a health official to examine us before issuing the policy. What would be a good day?"

"I don't know, Floyd. I just don't see how we can swing this. If we can't afford to have me go to the dentist, and we have cut back on practically everything, the expense of a life insurance policy does not seem right."

"But a man should have life insurance for his wife. It should be based on his net worth. This is for you; I'm concerned for you."

Charlene had enormous doubts that he had such feelings for her. He had shown her how lacking concern for her had become the norm. He was conning her again. She knew it. She was afraid. She did not want to sign the insurance application, but she was more afraid of how Floyd would treat her if she didn't.

And as to Floyd's worth, maybe what he said was true. Maybe he was worth $750,000. But where is the money he is worth when you need it? When Charlene has to make school lunches for the girls and the pantry shelves are nearly empty; when the child support checks from Bart arrive, Floyd has her sign, then takes them to his personal bank account as though his life depended on them; and when the girls need new shoes but Floyd says their old ones are okay; when Charlene needs to go to a dentist for a severe toothache unfazed by Anbesol, where indeed is the money? Charlene's objections were unheeded. On her birthday in November, the policy was issued. Floyd triumphed and seemed very happy with his accomplishment.

Susie gasped when Charlene told her the amount of coverage. "Charlene, do me a favor. Watch your back. If you won't come home, at least look out for yourself."

After a few days of jubilation, Floyd again became unhappy and moody. It was his mind-changing mode again. Charlene thought he was sorry he had spent money on the insurance policy. She could not account for his attitude. He walked past the kids and Charlene without a glance or a greeting. He was like a robot feeling nothing, a robot without a heart.

He still thought he had an ulcer.

Charlene accompanied him on his doctor's appointment and through the procedure of the stomach test in which Floyd had to swallow a small camera. The diagnosis was almost disappointing to him: he had no ulcer.

When the distancing became too severe for her to handle, Charlene finally had the nerve to ask what was the matter. "Can I help?"

"Not when you're the problem."

"I don't know what I have done that is so bad."

"I guess you haven't noticed. You've put on weight. I am just not psyched for you any more."

What Charlene had not noticed was Tracie, standing in the foyer at the foot of the stairs, game box in hand.

"Want to play 'Nopoly with me?" she asked Floyd. Her desire to help, as she had on other tense occasions, was genuine. She was a quietly courageous little girl. Somehow she hoped to recapture the Floyd who had taken them to Disneyland a short time ago.

But now she was so upset with his behavior that she could not look directly at him, or at her mother. He brushed past her and went to the bedroom upstairs without even a grumpy "No."

"Want me to play with you?" Charlene asked.

"No," she answered. "I know you're busy. I'll be the top hat and the doggie. I'll play both. One will be sure to win. If this was real money, Mom, I would give it all to you. Nothing for Floyd." "Floyd probably doesn't need it anyway. He already has money to buy whatever he wants."

"What does he want, Mom?"

Charlene hesitated, searching for a response. "That's a very good question. I cannot answer it. Good luck with your game."

14

The Truth Hurts Every Time

It seemed like a miracle to Charlene. In December Floyd became human again. He received news that Frankie was coming out to San Diego to be interviewed by San Diego City College for a teaching position that had become available. Floyd made arrangements for him in an appropriately de luxe hotel. He smiled frequently. Jericha noticed the change and asked: "Does Floyd like us now?"

Christmas was again a rather exclusive occasion, with Floyd's minimal participation. He did come down in his underwear to the small tree he allowed Charlene to buy; he watched the girls open their presents. He unwrapped but quickly tossed aside an attractive shirt and vest his in-laws had sent him for Christmas. He was still upset with them for not giving them a wedding present. He had gone so far as to write his parents, lying to them that Charlene's parents had given them a generous monetary wedding present. Soon they, not to be outdone, sent a check for a matching amount. Charlene felt bad that Floyd had schemed his own parents out of an amount she knew they could not afford.

Charlene recalled Christmas the year before, every detail. She tried to find comfort that, this year. Floyd would at least be with them, if only in spirit. It was the day after Christmas when Frankie arrived. They all went out to dinner the first night.

"Now how are the newlyweds," Frankie asked, acting semi-apologetic to Charlene. She tried to read between the lines. Was he sneering, or did he genuinely care? He had a carefree, unruffled air, as though things were going his way. He was impressively dressed in a new-looking Versace Classic suit with a striped dress shirt and silk tie. The trademark loafers with highly polished pennies were dazzling as was his charm.

Floyd and he went out by themselves every night after that until Frankie's departure after New Year's Day.

One night they came very late to the apartment. Charlene could hear Frankie shouting: "Shit, I can't believe the luck! After putting at least $300 in that slot, I get up to stretch my legs and that clown sat at my machine, put one token in and ding-clang-drop trailer that ass won the jackpot."

Charlene crept to the top step to hear more distinctly. "Fuck!" Floyd replied. "I had bad luck, too, at the Black Jack table. Last night I won a bundle, but not tonight. Lost all I won and then some. I hate to lose."

"We'll go back, make a few bucks, I'm sure. Let's go to that peel bar tomorrow night. By the way how's the Bee scheme working?"

"They're just setting it up. It will look like a Hillcrest expense, but we'll get our cut."

The riddle of their discussion baffled Charlene but seemed in character for this duo. She wished she could ask questions or be included instead of just eavesdropping.

After the departure of Frankie, Floyd resumed his routine. So did the girls and their mother. They were playing cards at the oak table, enjoying their last day of winter break when Charlene went up to the bedroom to get her slippers out of the closet. Floyd was on the extension phone there. Charlene heard him talking: "You were right about her. She's only after my money. I shoulda made her sign a prenuptial like you told me. She's not like Pat at all."

Realizing that Charlene heard him, Floyd changed the subject and pretended to be asking his mother something about his rental properties in St. Louis. Again he put on a pleasant air. Apologies now took the form of a few days of decent treatment. Charlene never knew if his mother believed him, but assumed she did.

"If you only knew," Charlene dreamed of telling his mother, "how your son really felt about you." But Charlene continued her see-no-evil, speak-no-evil performance, realizing he controlled both

Mrs. Mitleiders.

It was the era for Floyd's friends to pay them visits. Within a week Tim flew out; Floyd was jubilant that Tim would be there to bike with him. It was business, in a way, because Tim was supposed to have been collecting rent and managing the rundown properties Floyd owned back home. But Tim played with the girls, and Floyd, probably thinking he would otherwise look very bad, followed suit once in a while. It was just like he had done for Joe's benefit before.

Tim, not prosperous enough to afford a hotel room, stayed in the apartment and slept on their sofa bed in the living room. He was under foot during the entire two weeks. The kids ate breakfast in relative silence and darkness each school morning because Tim was asleep a few feet away.

Before returning home, Tim asked Charlene what was wrong in their marriage. He was not as brainless as Floyd thought. Tim said, "I was kinda surprised when I heard you and Floyd got married. You know Floyd used to have all those girls come to the house. After they'd leave, I'd hear him call you up."

"Girls? Are you telling the truth?"

"Do you want to hear the truth? Floyd liked being with prostitutes. That's why he rented that house, the one where Greg and I lived for a while to help him with expenses. He had call girls regularly. He loved having those sex-for-hire playmates over. He always thought I was jealous that he had the money for that. Greg told me he acted snooty to him, too."

Charlene was shocked. "Why didn't you tell me this a long time ago?" she stammered.

"I honestly didn't know you very well. I didn't know you two were serious either. I realize now I should have had a talk with you. Floyd was not very nice to me, called me names. I let him get by with it because I saw something worthwhile in him. He gave me a job collecting rent from his North St. Louis property. I figured what he did in his house was his business."

"What was the time frame for all this?"

"Well, it was in 1993. In the summer. In the fall. I didn't live there very long. But Floyd had a 'lady of the night' at least once a week. He just couldn't seem to get enough. He is into everything. Even phone sex."

"I didn't know," Charlene blurted out. "Floyd didn't care that he was putting me at risk. We were going steady, or so I thought. He wanted me to marry him. Naturally I thought I was the only one."

"I didn't mean to cause trouble," Tim went on. "I can see you already are having plenty of it. I'm sorry. If you tell Floyd, I'll deny the whole thing. I don't want him mad at me."

Charlene tried to downplay her humiliation. Tim himself had been the subject of late night arguments with Floyd. Floyd claimed she was buying too much expensive food for Tim and that he ate too much. The novelty of having Tim with them had worn thin soon after his arrival. After what Tim had revealed, Charlene knew for what things Floyd preferred to spend his money, besides mountain bikes. Fantasy phone sex, call girls.

Meals for Tim were too expensive. So were Charlene's needs. Floyd's needs. Floyd's money. What kind of man was he?

Charlene was sure that Floyd would have been infuriated that she knew this secret about him. The truth was out, thanks to Tim's honesty. Charlene regretted knowing it. It made her wonder: what else? It added to the torment and hurt she was already suffering. She didn't know if there were more truths to come or if she wanted to hear them. There was no more believing. She had trained herself to believe a lie. She had learned to control her emotions and avoid out-bursts. Now she feared she did not know the simplest lesson of all: how to face the truth.

15

Prelude to Disaster

"Isn't it fun?" Tracie exclaimed as she showed Jericha and Charlene her Valentines. "I got one from every kid in the room. And here, this one is from Brian and it says 'I love you, Tracie,'" she giggled.

"Did you pack your bag for the sleepover at Lailani's?" her mother asked..

"I put it by the door," she said, just as Floyd unlocked the door and stepped in, tripping over it.

"Fuck!" he screeched. "First the retarded skunk on the porch and then this."

Tracie ran to move her bag, and Jericha went to the porch to see Kimber. The lop-eared rabbit was shaking and had a bloody paw that Jericha inspected; she came in to get a cloth to wipe off the blood and said, "It's all right, Bunny Kimber. I'll take care of you."

"I don't know what you think you are doing, all of you," Floyd said. "This shit is going to stop." "I'm sorry," Tracie said. "I'm going to Lailani's to spend the night. That's my travel bag," she explained, pointing to the tote.

"Mom's going to buy Kimber a hutch," Jericha said. "Then she won't be running around on the porch and we can bring her in when it's cold."

Floyd went to the fridge and took out a bottle of Evian water. He gulped it down quickly without really looking at the three of them, all in awe of what Floyd might say or do next.

"Nobody is going anywhere this evening," he declared. "At least not in my car. I have to be at the beginning of the trail in ten minutes." He went to the balcony and wheeled out his bike.

Tracie and Charlene discussed the transportation problem in the girls' room. "I'll see if Lailani's grandmother can come for you," Charlene promised. "Don't worry about it. And tomorrow I'll pick you up. I'll get the keys to the car. It'll be okay."

But Tracie's evening was already ruined. It was Valentine's Day, a time for love and words of love. Jericha too was shattered by the thought of Floyd's having stepped on Kimber. She rather thought it might have been on purpose. "He didn't even say he was sorry, Mom," she lamented. Both girls were fighting back tears.

"Why doesn't Floyd like Kimber?" Jericha continued when Floyd went upstairs to change clothes. "He keeps calling her Skunk," she pouted. "I don't think she understands his words, but I wish he wouldn't say that anyway."

"Well, you know," Charlene tried to explain, "Floyd has funny names for people and things. He calls his own dog 'Load.' A load of what? Back home they have an organization called Loyal Order of Alley Dogs, or L.O.A.D. Only Floyd would use this name for his pet. It's one of his dumb codes. We have to try to understand Floyd."

Their laughter alleviated the burden of the moment. They got to talking about what it used to be like in St. Louis: the Easter Jericha got Kimber, the trips to the park to feed the ducks, the train ride at the zoo, the sensation of being in space at the Omnimax theater at the Science Center, playing games over at Grandma-Grandpa's house. "Remember those big heart cookies Grandma baked for us last year?" Tracie recalled, calming down from her Floyd encounter.

"Speaking of Grandma, I forgot to tell you a package came today from her."

As the girls tore open the package and found plastic compartment boxes filled with red and white candy hearts, they heard the squeaky door closing They breathed a sigh. The self-made monster had left.

Very late that night Floyd returned, gift in hand. "Here," he said, extending it to Charlene. She looked surprised. "Well, it is Valentine's Day, isn't it?"

It was as though nothing that happened earlier was real or important to him. The cycles of the moon again: prest-o change-o.

Her task in holding the marriage together was almost an impossible dream. Like Don Quijote, she kept on dreaming; Floyd, like Dr. Jekyll and Mr. Hyde, kept on changing, back and forth.

He had transformed so much that she could not recognize him at times. *Who is this man?* She asked herself. The mood changes were too close together. Charlene could not recover from one incident until there was another. Like hitting a moving target, it was hard to find this changing person, let alone understand and please him. Charlene told the children to be especially sweet to Floyd, that he had business problems and they should not worry him too much about anything. Charlene tried everything.

"Why don't you go out to the games more, Floyd?" she had told him a few days before.

"I'd rather just watch them on my big screen," he said. "If you would just bring me my meals on the tray table. I'd like that. Nothing good's been on since the Super Bowl."

"Sure," Charlene said. "I'll do that."

"I know how my old man felt when I was a kid. He'd hole up in the bedroom where we had a TV set. Mom brought him in his food and drinks. He would come out once in a while to go to the bathroom, during commercial breaks. I could hear him yell, 'Way to go' once in a while. He'd give out a loud cheer now and then. But if I went in the room to see him, he'd say: 'Get outta here, kid, I'm busy.'"

Charlene imagined that he had not had a truly ordinary childhood. He had a confused role model and hadn't bonded strongly with anyone. His transformation from child to man was still taking place. No wonder he showed hostility like his autograph album rhyme, *Fealine*, at so young an age he did not even spell correctly; he was trying to show strength by aggression. He had probably become greedy and incurably selfish even then. It led to more cruelty and deviant instincts. How far the cruelty would go was a troubling thought. Considering all that had been happening in these few months of marriage, Charlene could only wonder what other hurdles lay ahead and if she had the ability and the energy to clear them.

16

A Dilemma Not Unlike Scarlett's

It was only a few days later that Charlene began daydreaming about the Old South with its genteel manners and traditions. *Gone with the Wind* portrayed this life in the era of the Civil War so amazingly. Rhett Butler was a man of action, she mused, with a streak of unkindness which brought Floyd to her mind. Rhett did not give a damn and neither did Floyd.

"When the check comes," Charlene's mother advised, "open a bank account of your own. I don't want to start trouble, but neither do I want you and the girls to suffer because of his minginess. Then get that tooth taken care of."

"He'll explode when he finds out. He claims I owe him money. Ever since we made that trip to Hawaii before our marriage, he has told me I had to pay him back."

"What? Why would you have to do that? Was the trip your idea, your treat?"

"He has mentioned it so many times when we have a fight. Then later on he'll say 'That's okay,' and acts like he has forgotten. He says he made my house payments when he lived with me, but that's not true. He has faulty memory. He used to buy groceries occasionally and pay some bills, but after all, he lived there. He only helped me out once with the house payments in the whole time he lived with me."

"I'm sorry he has turned out to be this way. It can't be a very pleasant existence for you. It seems everything has only a monetary value to him. Didn't he take over the child support money? And you gave him the balance in your bank account when you got married, isn't that right?"

"Yes, yes. But he is the money manager in the family."

"It should not mean you have no access to any of it."

"He wants me to take less for the house so it will be sold finally. I think he expects to get that money, too."

"But he is not making the payments or fixing it up. We're doing that for you. If we could say the money is yours, like in yours and his, fine; but I can see that any money that comes close to him he grabs and it is his, and no one else's. Then it's a secret what he's doing with it. If we sell your house and send you the money, will you never see a penny of it again?"

Charlene was in a predicament like she'd never known before. She didn't want to be a weakling, run to "Mommie" with her problems, come back home to her family in complete humiliation. She still held out hope for their marriage even though Floyd's lies were exposed. If she contributed to their finances, maybe that would help to bring them together again. Floyd would respect her if she contributed the equity money from her house to the total coffer. But she was determined to have access to the family money; after all it was at least in part hers.

Floyd was there when she received the letter from her mother, check for $3,000 enclosed. He saw and took it. "Well, finally. I'm getting the money you owe. Here, sign it."

"Only if you put it in our joint account. I am going to buy the rabbit a good cage and get my tooth fixed. You can have all the rest."

She thought she had made a very generous offer, but when Floyd came back and sat down at the table, she saw the Grossmont bank receipt where Floyd had a business account. Their joint account was at Bank of America.

"You didn't put my check in our joint account, did you? You are not going to use my money for your business expenses!" she shouted, grabbing the check he had just written. "Pay them with money you get from the store."

"You DC," he barked. "What do you know about anything?"

He pulled at her blouse until it tore and began punching her chest and side. His eyes were glassy and his jabs hard, delivered in rapid succession as though coming from a machine that could not be turned off. Charlene cried out and stepped back but he reached even farther to strike her shoulder with his fist one final time.

"You're hurting me," she cried out again. "Stop it! You stole my money and now you're hitting me? I should be hitting you! I have been waiting for so long to have money to call my own, and now you've taken it," she sobbed.

"All you do is nag. I'm going out now and when I come back, you'd better not have used this phone." He took the receiver off the phone and slammed it down on the bar. "If you do, I'll hurt you and your retarded MLKs too. Do you hear me?"

Where shall I go? What shall I do? were questions repeating themselves over and over as Charlene flipped through the telephone directory. San Diego Police Department, Eastern Division, Traffic, Drug Enforcement, Domestic Violence. This was the number to call.

She lost her nerve trying to press in the number. She had to do it, but couldn't. A deadly silence fell in the apartment with only her rapid steady heartbeat resounding in her ears. "Girls, are you okay?" she projected from the second step up to the upstairs, feeling pain from the blows to her upper body.

"Yes. We're playing," was the tranquilizing response of the two soft voices.

At the phone again, Charlene lifted the receiver and touched in a long distance number familiar to her.

"Hello, Mom," she began, choking the words out. "I don't know what to do."

"What's wrong? What's going on?"

"It's Floyd. We just had a big fight about the check you sent. Do you know he deposited it in his personal account?" "He did what?"

"He made me sign it. I was going to be able to draw on the money as I needed it, but he didn't deposit it in our joint account. I can't use a penny of the $3,000 now. We argued about it; Floyd hit me, called me names and threatened to hurt the kids when he comes back."

"Charlene," said the voice. "I only know one thing to do. Call the police. This man's unreal. How do we know what he'll do when he comes back? No telling. I am afraid for you and the girls. You can't deal with this alone."

Charlene was sobbing violently and her mother's voice was weak and shaky. She gave her mother the number to call. She could not do it herself.

In a matter of minutes Charlene got a call from Domestic Violence. They wanted to confirm everything her mother had told them.

"Yes, he is still gone, but I think he'll be back very soon. I am afraid of what he'll do. He said not to call the police," she whimpered.

"You have done the right thing," said the police officer.

"We are on our way. If your husband returns before we get there, call 911."

Charlene checked to see that the girls were still okay in their bedroom. "Lock your door," she ordered frantically. As she went on down the hall to the master bedroom, she heard the front door opening with its heavy squeak. She slipped into the bedroom and locked the door. Picking up the extension phone there, she dialed 911.

"Don't hang up," said the operator. "Stay on with me at all times. Tell me about the apartment complex where you are."

"It's called La Mirage, and is a large series of buildings. Ours is on Ambrosia Drive as you come up the hill. Number 6522, Apartment 5116."

"Charlene," Floyd called out gruffly. "Open this door. I want to talk to you."

She froze against the rough wall as far from the door as she could squeeze, still clinging to the phone. "You didn't give me a chance to apologize," Floyd continued.

Thump, thump, thump. "San Diego Police. Open up."

"Charlene," Floyd pounded on the bedroom door. "What's the meaning of this? Why did you call the fucking police?"

"Yes, he's here now," Charlene told the 911 operator in a muted voice. "No, our doors are locked. He can't get in. I'm a little worried about my girls. They must be scared to death."

Again came a thundering thump, thump at the door. "Open up now," the police ordered.

Floyd ran down the stairs, across the living room and to the balcony on the back side of the apartment.

"Go back," shouted two armed police officers standing under the balcony in the street. Floyd stepped back, knocking down storage boxes and bicycles to the cement floor. Guns were pointing upward. Floyd was trapped.

"Ma'am, the officers are getting a key from the management office," said the 911 voice. "Do not open your door under any circumstances."

"Tell them to go away. This is all just a mistake, tell them," Floyd screamed.

Charlene heard the front entry door being pushed open and the rapidly moving footsteps of people shuffling in. Floyd had backed into the living room. There was no other place to go. Things were out of his control, a position in which he had rarely found himself.

"Hands up and turn around-slowly," shouted an officer. He put Floyd's hands behind his back and handcuffed him, giving him official notice he was being arrested. "You have the right to remain silent... ."

An officer came to the bedroom door and asked: "Are you in there, ma'am?"

When the frightened woman answered, the officer told her to unlock the door and step out.

"Whose room is this?" asked a female officer, pointing to the other bedroom. "My children's"

The officer entered and talked calmly to the girls reassuring them. They were white with fear. Charlene gave them a hug hoping they would believe everything was all right. The officer bent down to them, writing notes in her pad of paper. The girls seemed less tense as they answered her questions.

"What's wrong with Floyd?" asked Tracie. "He came in our room and looked out the window."

"He did?" Charlene gasped. "I thought your door was locked."

"He didn't talk to us, just went over to the window."

"Like he was going to jump out or something," Jericha added.

"Oh, my God. He is desperate."

The female officer took Charlene back to her bedroom and looked at her blotched pink skin and torn top. She took polaroid pictures.

"These spots will be purple in a few hours," said one of the officers. "Now, ma'am, I have a few questions to ask."

"I didn't do a thing to her," Charlene could hear Floyd shouting downstairs. "Ask her. I just pushed her a little bit."

"Sorry, man. But there is evidence you did more than push her. And you made threats. You're going downtown with us."

"I didn't mean anything. She knows that."

"Ma'am, are there any weapons in the house?"

"Yes," she said. "Somewhere in the master bedroom there is a gun and ammunition. It's a gun they used to keep at the store."

When the officer located the .38-caliber special Smith and Wesson gun, it was put in a plastic bag along with a box of bullets. "This will be held in custody," he declared.

This was good news to Charlene. She had never liked the idea of that gun in the apartment.

"Where are the car keys?" she asked shyly as she came close to Floyd.

"On the bar," Floyd said grudgingly as though he knew he would have to answer. "Don't let them take me," he begged. "You know I didn't hurt you. It was nothing."

"Nothing?" Charlene wailed.

"Ma'am, you don't have to talk to him," said the officer. "He may think twice before hitting you again after spending a night in jail."

Bright rotating lights of the squad car flittered around in the covered passageway just outside the apartment door. They were dancing lightly on the greenery of the walkway as if to cheer Charlene; but the handcuffed man being hauled toward the stone steps exit and her pounding heart dominated her being, and she was far from being cheered.

She called her mother to tell her what had occurred, and the worried mother tried to give her daughter some comforting words and offered to come out to help her. But in her mind the familiar words of Scarlett O'Hara resumed: *Where shall I go? What shall I do?*

17

Another Promise to Break

Charlene knew that things would be worse when she saw Floyd the next time. In such a short time the anticipation of a wonderful life with Floyd had changed into a sickening nightmare. She knew he would not be subdued for long. He would be a raging bull piqued by the happenings of the last few hours. Things would never be the same.

The hours passed and Charlene, exhausted to the bone, had found no answers to the questions of what to do and where to go. The girls had dropped off to sleep swiftly after a cold drink and a brief talk; they did not ask questions, though Charlene could see in their eyes they had many. But they gave her quiet support; they trusted her. She had let them down.

Tired, so tired, she put her head on a pillow at the head of the couch. On the table by her ear was a small acrylic clock ticking, louder and louder. Her distressed thoughts could not make it stop. She turned to face the back of the couch hoping to drown out the sounds. Tick, tick, in precise fashion, never missing, the disturbance continued. She could not sleep; she could not even rest.

The phone rang, jarring her from her pessimistic thoughts.

"Come and get me now," Floyd's strange-sounding voice said. "I am making bail with my credit card. I need a ride."

"I don't think I should."

"What's the matter with you anyway?" Floyd queried innocently. "I'm not staying in this place. Everyone here knows I don't belong here. There's nothing but dirty, smelly Lou and Spiks."

"You said you were going to hurt my girls," Charlene defended. "I will not let you do that. And you're not hurting me any more either."

"Listen to me, peon. You know I say things I don't mean. I wouldn't touch your MLKs. They're just a nuisance that you spend all your time with. I won't hit you again. Just come and get me and we'll talk."

"I think you need help, Floyd," Charlene said boldly. "You keep changing your mind, about everything. I don't know why you wanted to marry me and bring me out to California, so far from home. You treat me like the lowest form of life. Why didn't you just go away and leave me alone?"

"I said we'd talk, just come and get me before I change my mind."

The trip downtown was long and terrifying in the middle of the black night. The freeways were nearly bare and ghostlike, stripped of their usual bustle like a partially clothed body. Charlene was so alone. The ride home was strained, Floyd's offer to talk having been immediately forgotten. He pretended to be sleeping while she drove.

At last he came out of his reverie. "You shouldn't have called the fuckin' police. No wonder I have an ulcer," he groaned. "What are you trying to do to me? I can't own and operate a business if I have a felony offense against me. Then where would I be?" Considering only himself, he did not say where *we* would be.

"I didn't really call the police. My mom did."

"So the police said. But you called her. It's all the same, the old YA biddy should mind her own business."

"Officer Chelby says I should press charges against you. I think I should. It'll depend on how well you keep your promise."

"To go to a marriage counselor? Is that what you expect?"

There was hope... a way out of this mire.

"You said we'd talk," she reminded him. "I am willing to try to resolve our problems."

Floyd said nothing, but as the transmitter opened up the iron gate and they pulled into the lower level parking garage under their apartment building, Charlene saw that enigmatic smile crawl over his face. A few hours in jail had not altered him in any way. The bad side of him was never going away.

The next day Officer Chelby came by. He could not believe Floyd was off on a bicycle affair. "This was planned days ago; I already paid the fee," was Floyd's simple explanation.

"Are you going to press charges?" Officer Chelby asked.

"I don't know what to do."

The dilemma had no answer. Floyd became even more detached from them. Instead of showing gratitude for getting him out of jail, he taunted her. "Are you still here?" he would ask. He offered her $500 and a bus ticket home; someone else would have to pay for the kids. How had she changed from his "forever girl" to a "DC", from the kind of woman Frankie would love to a woman he couldn't stand? His female attorney who had handled his business dealings left him a message on their machine. Charlene heard it first. "Call to make an appointment so we can discuss the divorce." Charlene had no choice. She needed an attorney to represent her before Floyd kicked her out. Every minute of every hour she thought of Floyd's past actions and how they grew out of his selfish ways. His mother was blinded to his faults; his father had ethics like a branch of P. T. Barnum's. He wanted to get away from them. He thought he was nothing like his parents, but he was wrong. He *was* his parents.

Contaminated by his outlandish codes and his assumed position of superiority, Floyd just could not stay on a straight path. He needed his connection with Frankie, because he was a constant in his life, someone who acted like him, thought like him, lived like him.

"You know how people say NOT at the end of a sentence? Everyone does that these days to be dramatic and cute. But Frankie and I invented this. We say INT, but it is the same idea and we had it first. We ask people, 'How are you doint?' because we don't really give a shit. It's a disguise, because if we openly insult people and then later need their help, we won't get it. This way our 'I don't give a damn how you are,' routine goes unnoticed."

It was true. Charlene had heard Floyd and Frankie doing their clever negatives and laughing about it later.

The Floyd-Frankie formula lived on; they were one. So now Frankie had probably advised: divorce her. She felt almost relieved, but in the depths of her heart, despite abuse and disappointment, she still had her love for him. It was a tragedy, not entirely his fault. Something had gone wrong and caused her Prince Charming to fail.

She saw Floyd in a daydream; he was a master of ceremonies at some big event. People were crowding around the platform where he took the microphone in his hand, everyone applauding, whistling, acclaiming him. "Good evenint, everyone," he began. "I'm . . . No, no I'm not." The crowd did a collective, negative "Oh, oh," a sign of disbelief. "Is he for real?" someone asked. "Is he going to be our leader or not?" Frankie quickly appeared like an apparition out of a crack in the floor. "Let me present to you all the Master of all Ceremonies. He's goint to talk."

"But he just told us he wasn't? Who can believe him?"

"All this time I've been believing in you," someone in the crowd said to the MC. "Tell me the truth, like you promised."

Charlene looked around to see who it was. It was she.

18

The Tables Are Turned

Floyd called his attorney on the phone downstairs. He did not know Charlene was listening from her top step roost. "She knows about the sales agreement with Tarak and my income from investments... Yes, I took the MLK's money. She may have sold her house. I heard her talking to her mother about it. Yes, I think she forged my signature on some papers. That's against the law!"

Floyd, making things up, trying to make Charlene look bad, was fuming. Frustrated and afraid, Charlene held back. She had an appointment with her own attorney within a few hours. He was her only hope.

"When was your husband arrested for spousal abuse?" asked the paralegal in the conference room of Dunne's* office. "Did you press charges?"

"It was earlier this month, and no, I decided to trust him once more. He said he would go to counseling. I believed him."

"I think I have all the facts now. I will write this up for Mr. Dunne and he will get back to you. Is that all right with you?"

Charlene prayed this attorney was qualified. He was recommended by a women's law center she called. She knew nothing about him. The girls and Charlene left his office and headed for home. "Can we play for a while before dinner?" Tracie asked. "We didn't have time when we got home from school."

"If you have finished your homework," Charlene promised. "But that has to be done first."

"I hope Floyd isn't there when we get home," said Jericha. "He is acting so mean."

As they got in the car parked at a meter on "B" Street, Charlene saw a parking ticket plastered to the windshield. She knew they were keeping her too long in the lawyer's office.

"I didn't really need this, God," she said under her breath, wondering if all the cards were stacked against her.

Floyd was not in the apartment when she unlocked the door. A heavy sigh of relief came over her as they entered. Charlene checked on Kimber. "She needs more pellets, Jer," she noticed. The girls stroked her where she huddled on the cool front porch, open except for the 3-feet stone enclosure and wrought iron gate.

Dunne's office called the very next day, February 28, the last day of the shortest and saddest month of the year 1995 for Charlene.

"It's going to be a problem today to get the car. Floyd may be home and I'll have to think of a good reason to take the car."

"Don't worry, Charlene. It won't be long before this man is out of your life for good. I know it has been tough, but you are about to get some satisfaction, and some money, too."

Charlene was nervous in Dunne's office signing papers until near 5:00 in the afternoon.

"I must hurry home with the car," she exclaimed. "He is waiting for it. He'll be very angry."

"You stupid bitch," Floyd yelled as they entered the apartment. "You've made me late to my meeting. I told you to be back in an hour."

"I'm sorry," Charlene lied. He would be furious had he known where she had been. "It couldn't be helped. Now that you're late anyway, don't you want me to fix you some pasta or something before going?"

It was a delaying tactic that worked; as he sat down to the plate of food, the doorbell rang. It was a process server with the paper Mr. Dunne told Charlene about.

"Floyd Mitleider?" asked the server. "These are for you."

Floyd snatched the batch of papers and began reading frantically:

You are hereby ordered to... you will vacate the premises in the next 24 hours, leaving the 1994 Grand Marquis in the custody of your wife, Charlene Mitleider. You will surrender the vehicle immediately upon receipt of this document. You are restrained from...

"What?" Floyd burst out. "You're never getting my car," he vowed, grappling for Charlene's handbag, dumping out the contents and extracting the set of keys she had just been using. "Not my car, not anything of mine are you getting." Charlene was terrified.

She ran out into the walkway and stopped two foreign-looking men who lived in a nearby apartment.

"Help me," she begged. "My husband is about to abuse me."

The two men stood by motionless. Charlene ran back, picked up the scattered contents of her purse and dashed to the end of the walkway toward the pool. She called from the pay phone there. Mr. Dunne was still in his office.

"Tell Floyd he has been ordered to turn the car over to me," she implored. "He won't believe me even though the papers have been served on him."

Floyd listened and without speaking to the attorney, handed the keys back to her, throwing his arms in the air in contempt.

Charlene heard him call Frankie from the same phone as she was walking away. "Let me tell you what she's doing now. She's upsetting things. This is not working out. I'm going to need your help. Dumb bitch."

After Floyd had finally accepted his fate, he came back to the apartment. "Let me in," he yelled. "I have no place else to go."

Charlene had never seen the serious, uncocky Floyd. "You shoulda told me what kind of a person you really were, Charlene. You had me completely fooled into thinking you were quiet, caring, understanding. Things have happened all along that you let go, even when I..." he hesitated, reeling. He was shaking his head.

"Me? You are the one who has done a complete turnaround. Had I known how you intended to treat me, there would never have been a wedding. This marriage has brought me only a brief happiness. The rest has been hell," Charlene sobbed.

Floyd hung his head like a child about to be punished. He was unable to respond. He was again trapped. He had lost his control. Charlene had been too quick to forgive in the past, allowing offenses to go unpunished. Few times in his life, she thought, had he been brought to account for his actions. Now he was forced to face the fact that he had done something wrong. The real world was closing in on him all at once. He was defeated.

A feeling of strength and triumph invaded Charlene's being. That long-awaited sensation of vindication was potent; it felt even better than she had imagined. The car was hers. She was in charge. The tables had turned. But almost immediately he made her feel a little evil to have gained this momentary revenge.

"You're enjoying this, aren't you?" Floyd said bitterly, his crooked smile returning. "Don't like it too much. This isn't the final score. If this is a game, you lose. When I am back in control, you will be sorry, very sorry."

19

Life Without Floyd

What bothered Floyd most was that Charlene had filed for divorce first. His attorney also filed for him. There was a flurry of legal papers back and forth. Charlene's was the lead case. She soon realized Floyd was steaming that he had not discarded her like he had so many other people; this time, he was discarded. This just couldn't happen to a superior person!

Mr. Dunne had paralegals on his staff trying to digest the fact that Charlene knew little, almost nothing, about the family finances. It was immediately evident that Floyd was not going to be rushed to comply with any orders. And he was going to proclaim that he was the one to end their relationship.

"You were supposed to move out yesterday," Charlene told him on March 2nd.

"I can't help it. They don't have a place for me yet," he said. "You'll just have to wait until they do."

"No. That is your problem," Charlene insisted. "You were ordered to leave within 24 hours."

And she did not like the idea that his move out of their apartment was merely to be a matter of moving to another building in the complex. He would still be just down the road from her.

Charlene had the locks changed on their apartment door. He squirmed at this change and the difficulties it caused him.

"Here is $40.00," Floyd said. "I closed our joint account and this is your share. I am going up to take a shower now."

While Floyd was showering, Charlene noticed his fat wallet had been thrown, but not far, under the bed. She took out some money. $40.00 was not going to be enough for gasoline and even a few groceries. And how did she know that was all there was in their joint account? And what gave him the right to close it? He should not have been allowed to close it out. She would report this to her attorney.

When Floyd found out about the parking ticket, he told Charlene she would have to pay it.

"Okay," she agreed. "Here it is."

Charlene laughed inside; this $40.00 came from Floyd's wallet, not from the money he had just given her. She loved fooling him even if in small ways; after all he had fooled her in enormous ways. She had to do whatever it took to survive; that meant money from whatever source, until her parents could get funds to her. It was unbelievable that she had no money in any bank account. Floyd had taken it all.

Mr. Dunne called about the business of the divorce.

"Where are his accounts? Which banks?"

She told him all she could. Mr. Dunne said Floyd's attorney had stated that Floyd was living off his credit cards. "If so," she told Dunne, "it is his choice. He has been receiving money from the business, my money, child support payments and interest on mutual funds. He sold his paper routes in St. Louis for a whole lot of money. He closed our joint account."

"Without your permission?"

"Yes. He did it today. And he hasn't moved out yet."

"Call the police. It is a violation of the restraining order not to leave as ordered."

The call at first made Floyd very angry, but then he calmed down.

"Charlene, stop treating me like this," he shouted. "You can't put me out on the street."

The police did not respond quickly. The restraining order was not yet on the Sheriff's computer; Officer Garvey joked around with Floyd and they talked about the scores of last week's games.

Feeling secure Floyd told Charlene, "Get one of our Humperdinck records and play it on the stereo. One last dance," he begged.

"No way," she defied, still shaken by the police officer's failure.

Officer Garvey left without knowing the panic she was in. It was not a matter for joking; she feared Floyd only needed a little jostle to become abusive again. But he surprised her by calling the rental office. "I need that apartment tomorrow," he urged. "I'll take anything, even second floor. She is not going to give me a break."

Charlene remained in her locked bedroom, imagining what Floyd was doing downstairs, sleeping on the sofa. His dreams were of her as hers were of him. The Charlene of dreams showed compassion; but she knew the Floyd of dreams was conferring with one of his mentors and planning how to get even with this bold new Charlene who would not give him a break. Early the next morning Floyd came into the kitchen while Charlene was fixing lunches for the girls to take to school. "I've been thinking, Charlene, all night... about us... What on earth are we doing, getting divorced? Things are bad for me right now, things we are into, finances and all, but when I get it all together again, I will come for you and we can remarry."

"You think we can go back to the way it used to be? I know we can't, I can't. This is the end for us. Don't try to con me or deceive yourself. It is over. but," she hesitated, "we don't have to hate each other."

Floyd grabbed her and tried to kiss her. "Just one last time," he begged. "I can't face life without you forever. You are all that's good about it. I can't let you go."

"I wish it had worked, Floyd. But it didn't. Your life cannot be dependent on mine, because if we continue on the path we've followed so far, mine will be over. You can't expect me to sacrifice my life. I have two kids. And you change your mind so often I can't keep up. For once, stick with the decision: to be divorced."

Floyd bristled, released his wife abruptly and cleared his throat. "Well, I gave you a last chance. You know no one else is going to want you now. You'll never find a man willing to marry a woman your age with kids."

"I won't be looking. I don't think I'll ever want to marry again. I am not ready to think about it. What I have to give will always be there for someone. Your opinion doesn't matter to me," she said looking away from him, "I know how to love and I thought you were the one to love. But you weren't... I will survive." It was all she could do to counteract his pessimism. What she really wanted was to fit into his arms again. Instead she bravely resumed her speech.

"You may find yourself in the same situation you're predicting for me. Who will ever fall in love with you as I did? You don't know, do you?"

"And you don't know what is in your future."

20

Revelation in a Passport

Charlene took the kids to school and Floyd waited for Nick. They were moving things out when she returned.

"How you doing, Chawlene?" Nick asked as he began taking out lamps from the first floor. He seemed kindly, even likeable, but she knew from Floyd's description of his store employee that Nick was a lawless type. Nick had a sparkle, a devil-may-care disposition that seemed genuine and somehow suitable to him, like his heavy gold earring that caught the light when he walked past the fluorescent fixture in the kitchen.

"Where is he from?" Charlene had asked when the same Nick had helped them carry her furniture in from the moving van last year.

"I don't know," Floyd had replied. "Iraq, I think. There are a bunch of Iraqis in San Diego. He used to live in Detroit with his parents, but they've all lived here a long time. That Nick. He knows how to take care of things. He does things for me. He's even killed."

"Killed?"

"Yeh," Floyd beamed in awe. "During sex once, he knived the woman in the back. And that was the end of that problem."

Charlene imagined this was a made-up story. It was something that sounded good to Floyd.

Though eager to chat a short time ago, now Floyd was agitated and caustic about his move-out. He said only three words. He sneered at Nick's inquiry as to how things were going for Charlene. "Feelint good?" Floyd asked.

Not really, she thought.

By late afternoon after the hectic day of leaving, returning, leaving and returning again to a cluttered apartment with most familiar things missing, the young mother thought at least she had seen the last of Floyd. There was infinite consolation in that. The apartment was left in an empty silence without much furniture now. She thought of all hers left behind or sold for peanuts when the move to San Diego came. At least her oak table and chairs were still there. She had fought to keep them. Floyd had started to take them to his new place.

Strewn papers on the master bedroom floor were too many to be left until later. She began to pick up. In the corner near where Floyd's chest of drawers had been she noticed a small leather case. She unsnapped it and found inside a pocket a U.S. passport, Floyd's. Flipping through the pages she came to the last entry. December 24, 1993. Christmastime, 1993, she began to recollect. Yes, the year before last, the year of Frankie's near-fatal car accident, her distress at Floyd's leaving her for Frankie, his indignant response to her complaining. Their near break-up because of Floyd's behavior was a vivid memory. It came flooding back as she kept on inspecting the passport pages. ENTER was stamped, along with the date, OFFICE OF TOURISM, Nassau, Bahama Islands; on the same page EXIT December 29, 1993, OFFICE OF TOURISM, Bahama Islands. So now she had an answer to a question that had plagued her: how Frankie had recovered so quickly from his *terrible accident* and why Floyd defended his action in rushing to Frankie's side so vehemently. A trip to the Bahamas-there was no car accident! Floyd had gone to the Bahamas. He did not go visit Frankie! Just because his mother called and said he was to go to Georgia and later confirmed that he had left did not mean that's what happened. His trip to the Bahamas was a fact told by his passport. It did not tell her enough. Why the big mystery, the lie? And why did he need a fabricated story to go to the Bahamas? Did he go with one of his buddies? This passport only showed where Floyd had gone. Charlene felt the world against her. Now she only knew that this trip had nothing to do with Frankie.

She sat there among the scraps of paper and tossed clothes and pondered what she should do with the new found evidence. Her anger at finding out what really happened that year before their marriage veered logically into contempt and then rapidly into hatred. Floyd's pious indignation had caused her sleepless nights and a strong feeling of guilt that persisted for months. She had searched her soul to find a way to forgive him for going to Frankie's side; now she knew she was a fool twice over, once in believing Floyd and again for blaming herself. He scored two marks against her with that incident: deceit and condemnation. She began to shake as she sat with the passport in her hands. Through cascading tears she repeated over and over, *I hate you, I hate you.*

Her mind swept through the unending list of Floyd's offenses. She had been duped in so many ways. This revelation cut deeper into her heart than even Tim's bombshell about Floyd's sex habits.

Now the thought of Floyd nauseated her. She could never look at him again, never see him as a real person. Now he was a phantom, a devil who took pleasure in torment. She feared this imposter. He was a man whose mind and spirit belonged to two different worlds. In his aspiring mind he proposed they should get together again in the months or years ahead. That rang out in her mind. But his spirit pulled him back into his other world: never concede anything to this bitch , make her suffer, make her pay.

Haven't I paid enough? Haven't I tried? Charlene asked herself. *Please, God, let me find peace.*

Suddenly she became aware of the sound of the old creaky front door and Nick's voice calling up to her.

She quickly snapped the leather case shut and stuck it in a shopping bag beside the door.

"What do you want?" she asked, too frightened to move.

Nick explained, "Floyd send me to return this suitcase to you."

"I thought the door was locked. How did you get in? What did Floyd do to it? I'll have to have Maintenance look at it again."

"I knocked at door. It was not locked, but I fix for you, Chawlene. No pwoblem. I fix the big squeaks, too, I get some oil for hinges. But Floyd say here is your suitcase we took but not Floyd's," Nick said. "He say to look for a bag of clothes he left; needs new shoes he just bought."

"What did it look like?"

"Boss say things in a Running Shoes shopping bag."

"I think I know where it is," Charlene told him. "Wait here. I'll get it."

"No pwoblem," Nick repeated.

At last Nick left and the door was secured. Charlene was not afraid of him no matter what Floyd had said. Nick was a gentle soul. It was good that the oiled hinges cured the annoying squeaky sound. It was peaceful that it was gone, like the peace of not having Floyd around, calling her names and deceiving her. Charlene thought God was beginning to answer her prayer.

21

The "Conmaniac"

"Mom, it's just us girls again," said Jericha the next morning as she prepared for school. "Look at the room we have now!"

"There's something I have to say to both of you," Charlene began with much vacillation. "I am so sorry how things have been. When I married Floyd, I thought it was going to be good for all of us. He made me a lot of promises. I know this has been a bad experience, but let's try to forget it quickly and let things get better for us." Her heart was aching as she looked into the wide eyes of the girls. How she regretted this, another upset, they had to endure.

The comforts of having all the mountain and racing bikes and sporting equipment removed did not compensate for the financial pressures. This was an expensive townhouse apartment, out of Charlene's price range. Paying for things until they could get back home made her dependent on her parents. Their small television sets were dwarfs compared to Floyd's big screens. They made Charlene feel small, like them, and like Floyd made her feel.

Mr. Dunne's office called and said there would be a hearing on April 5 regarding the car. She knew Floyd would get it back sooner or later.

"He is mad as a castrated rooster," Charlene told Susie. "He passed me in his rented car this morning and stared at me with such loathing he almost went off the road."

"I'm looking forward to having you back home," Susie told her. "We know how to start over, don't we?"

Charlene's Mom arranged to come out and Charlene met her at Mission Valley Shopping Center. The plan was for Mom to get there a few days before the hearing and for Dad to drive out later with a car for Charlene when she had to give up the Grand Marquis.

"You can use our old Caprice. It's in good shape and has low mileage for an '88. Now that we're retired, we don't really need two cars. Dad will drive it out for you."

"It will only be for a short time. As soon as school is out, I'm leaving San Diego."

"And what's the news on the divorce?" Mom wanted to know.

"All I know is Floyd is not cooperating. You'd think I could at least get some of the money he's been taking from me. I don't expect much, but I gave him all I had. He has taken my money from all sources. Dunne is investigating just how much money was earned during our marriage. He says I am entitled to half."

"It's bad enough that he has disrupted your life and the girls' too."

Floyd was sullen and hostile at the hearing in Family Court. For hours Charlene and her mother just sat around while the lawyers talked at the benches outside the courtrooms.

Charlene was afraid and relieved only superficially that her mother was with her. Her glance at Floyd on the other side of the room made her uneasy. She wanted her attorney and Floyd's to come to some agreement that would bring her some financial relief.

She began to regret that she had not reinstated the charges against Floyd for abuse. The abuse continued, now in the form of non-support. Her regrets included seeing her parents writing out checks for her. There was no other way. The kids needed to have the basic necessities, including food. She felt Floyd would have to pay eventually.

Floyd stared at her at first, then looked off in the distance with a face full of pomposity.

Their respective lawyers were talking and making decisions. Charlene felt completely powerless.

Finally Floyd walked by Charlene's bench, leaned down toward her and said almost inaudibly: "The lawyers are taking care of things. It's up to me to take care of you."

His tone was sarcastic and his smile faked. He seemed confident. If only he had made his statement a sincere one, rather than a
threatening one.

Charlene became wobbly as she scooted to the edge of the
seat. Her dilemma was far from over and she knew it.

"This is going to be a battle to the end," she reported to her
mother.

Charlene had to comply with the stipulations of the day. She
would return Floyd's car on April 14 and he would pay temporary
spousal support of $1,500 a month until they were divorced.

Then Floyd went into action. He had had Tarak file a declaration on March 29 stating that the divorce restraints kept the escrow
documents for the sale of Hillcrest Liquor signed in January from
going through and that Floyd had not received any income from the
business since November 1994. There was also an Income and Expense Declaration (likewise filed March 29) that had falsified information on the finances of the business and unsubstantiated dollar
figures, in every case lowering Floyd's financial worth. Strangely since
the time of application for the $750,000 insurance policy, his worth
had mysteriously declined. It was to his advantage to be a poor man,
net worth zero.

"He'd do anything to get his car back," Floyd's attorney declared.

Charlene was depending on her attorney to take the right steps
to make Floyd keep his end of the bargain. After everything that
happened, she was pessimistic about everything. She pictured herself
in the middle of the ocean in a rowboat without oars, barely alive.
Now the rowboat began taking on water. She felt like yelling for help
but no sound came out of her mouth.

No one could see what a high-class con man Floyd was.

"He is a maniac of sorts, Mom," Charlene complained. "To
coin a new word perfect for Floyd, he is a 'conmaniac.' And I am at
his mercy."

There were even problems with the agreement to return Floyd's
car and he became so impatient that he entered Charlene's parking
garage, an act which was another restraining order violation, and

drove his car out.

Charlene was in such distress over Floyd's erratic behavior that her parents were reluctant to leave for home.

"Don't worry, Charlene. It will not be long now until this whole thing is over," promised her mother.

"And it won't be a minute too soon."

"Well, I don't like the idea of his living so close to your building," her father said. "He can easily spy on you. Just watch yourself."

"What did he say when you met him out front and returned my set of car keys?" Charlene asked.

"I shook my finger in his face and told him to leave you and the kids alone," Mom reported. "I could tell by his reaction that he is not to be trusted. He looked at me haughtily, shrugged his shoulders and said, 'Who, me?' He tried to appear totally disinterested, but we all know he is a bastard, the way he has treated you and the way he is lying. He loved giving me cause to worry."

"Dunne says Floyd has to pay all the legal expenses of this divorce," Charlene told her parents. "I feel so bad that you have spent so much."

"All we want is for you to be safe," Dad said. "Don't worry about anything else."

"This guy does not even seem like the same person you married. I am so mad at this poor excuse for a man," her mother went on. "I wish his mamma would spank him," she laughed.

"In his family, he did the spanking," Charlene added. "That is a big part of his problem."

Charlene's parents tried to imagine what they could do to help. They were concerned that dealing with this recalcitrant man was going to be difficult.

"I keep getting this feeling that someone is watching me," Charlene told them. "I can't help it. I look around all the corners, I inspect the elevator to the parking garage carefully before we get in and . . ."

"Don't get paranoid about it, but do be careful," Dad warned.

"I don't think I should leave you," Mom said.

"Now, what good can you do?" Dad asked. "Hopefully the lawyer will take care of things, like Charlene's legal needs etc. and she'll be home in a couple of months."

After her parents were gone, Charlene's hopes ran high that her attorney would soon work things out with Floyd's attorney and get her the divorce. Floyd's attorney seemed to be willing to do whatever Floyd wanted and that included helping Floyd hang on to his assets. It was such a puzzle as to who owned the Hillcrest store and how, if ever, they were to get the information.

Charlene watched the O.J. trial nearly every day. The defendant looked smug, determined, victorious. The prosecution's introduction of the 911 tapes brought tears to her eyes. Nicole had suffered horrible abuse. Charlene felt for Nicole because she was gone and could not feel for herself. There was an alliance between them; the parallel was strange. Whatever Charlene felt, she had no power over anything. She just wanted to get out of San Diego and leave the conmaniac to his friends, if any existed. They would live happily ever after as far as Charlene was concerned.

May 22, 1995

Floyd rushed to Union Bank College Center Office when he got the call.

"Finally," he announced to himself triumphantly, "I'm going to get that money and get it out of here."

The sun nearly blinded him as he flew along the freeway. He groped for the visor and jerked it down with a drunken brilliant flash. In the far right lane his car momentarily swerved to the shoulder where his rear tire cracked over a sharp boulder making a buzzing pop. "Fuck!" he snapped, believing he had punctured the tire, then, realizing it was nothing more than a loud intrusion, continued his trek clinging doggedly to the steering wheel.

The bank parking was filled and the pay lot more than two blocks away. He considered parking illegally at the street by the yellow curb. "No," he convinced himself. "I don't need a parking ticket or an encounter with the fuckin' cops."

Holding the leather brief case close to his thigh, Floyd entered the cool building with a skip in his stride and advanced straight to the manager's desk. There the bank officer handed him an approval ticket and pointed to the last teller's window.

"Good," Floyd muttered. "No one at any of the windows on that end. And they are ready for me."

He watched as the tall stiff-haired man carefully placed banded stacks of bills in the case. The man closed and latched the carrying case when the last stack was counted and placed in the last remaining spot in the corner slot. Then he slid the case across the window to Floyd's trembling hands.

The exuberant businessman jaunted through the doorway, his knees weakened by the adrenalin drain from his body. He wanted to stick the briefcase inside his shirt to conceal it, but realized it would do nothing but make him look deformed and his purpose obvious. His mind pictured the look of despair and disappointment Charlene would have when she found out. He tried to laugh, but he was too excited as he hurried down the street to the parking lot.

"*Only a few more minutes*," he told himself. "*Once in the car, you'll be safe.*"

He pulled a roll of bills out of his trouser pocket. "Dammit," he sputtered. "Is that the smallest I have?"

Reluctantly he handed the attendant a ten and got quickly into the car, pushing the case on the seat beside him.

"Thank *you*, sir," said the young greasy-faced attendant, unaccustomed to such a tip for a ten-minute parking.

"*You dumb ass*," Floyd's inner voice shouted. "*You get ten and I get my $157,000. The masses truly are asses.*"

♦ ♦ ♦

Floyd told his attorney that he had taken $100,000 in cash to Vegas in an effort to wager the money and have it grow substantially. But he had been unlucky and lost all the money. He also told her that he wanted to have an amicable divorce from Charlene. He was willing to give her the car.

These were only words. Nothing ever developed from them. However it seemed to Charlene that it was not proper for him to withdraw money from the bank accounts because he was supposedly restrained from doing so. Floyd filed a declaration stating that he was trying to salvage a failing business and was unable to pay spousal support in any amount. He had no money, he swore under penalty of perjury.

When Charlene was informed of this quite some time later, she knew there was definitely something fishy going on. Whoever was advising Floyd was just like Floyd. Above all was the money and how to hold on to it. That was paramount. Charlene imagined she had a crystal ball and she was staring into it. She saw the face of Floyd's coach, a man she imagined was his mentor and money manager.

22

Who Hates You, Baby?

Charlene's existence in the La Mirage apartment was one of bad dreams by sleepless night and apprehension by eventless day. From her apartment door to the boxlike elevator in the middle of the airy walkway, she always checked behind every bush and plant, glad to reach her parking space in the garage below without encountering anyone. And upon her return through the security gate, up on the elevator, the walk through the passageway and to the entry into her apartment she was relieved to have come back safely. She had begun to dread each trip to and from the schools, but twice a day every school day, she drove the maroon Caprice with its Missouri license plates, hoping time would pass smoothly and without incident.

It was a Friday night in late April, exhausted from the week's routine and having taken out loads of trash left from packing for the return home, she went to bed very late. It was stuffy in her bedroom and her back was aching from sleeping on couch cushions, her quasi-bed since Floyd had taken their bed, so she opened the windows and shut off the AC. There was total silence. The sweet-smelling San Diego spring air felt good with the gentle breeze it brought. She stood by the window drawing the mellow air into her lungs. Suddenly she heard a piercing, blood-curdling scream. It filled the whole open area. It was a long-lasting shriek ending with a cry of pain.

Charlene looked out the window in all directions and saw nothing. She was immersed in radical darkness as she stretched out on the cushions.

The still silence was interrupted as she closed her eyes. She continued to hear the high-pitched bellow resounding in her head. She started to believe it was she. Finally she convinced herself the whole thing was one of her nightly bad dreams.

The next morning Jericha was petting Kimber on the porch. "Mom," she called, sticking her head inside, "can we bring Bunny in? It is really chilly out here."

"I guess so. Since we don't have a cage, better put her in the downstairs bathroom again. It's easier to clean up her little marbles there. I'm trying to keep the place neat as possible so we can get the deposit back when we move out."

"Up on the second floor," a husky voice was calling in the walkway just beyond their entry door. It came from a man running, followed by two other police officers.

Jericha came in carrying her furry bundle. "I wonder what that's all about. Did you see the policemen?"

"Yes, I did. I was wondering why there were flashing lights shining in through the balcony's sliding door." Jericha, joined by Tracie and Charlene, quickly went to the balcony and looked down at a San Diego Police squad car. The officers did not know the complex very well or they would have parked in front of their 6522 building. There was no access to their building on that, the back side. The squad car moved out and around to the front.

They were sitting around the oak table when an ambulance, siren blaring, pulled up in the driveway in front. Curious, Charlene went out to take a look near the front security gate. She saw a couple of paramedics and a policeman from the top of the stone steps which connected the building to the front drive and parking lot. She could see only the gurney's end where the feet of the unfortunate patient raised up the sheet. But this patient was a corpse. The sheet covered up the face.

Later in the day on a newscast there was a report that a woman in their building had been murdered: names and a few details mentioned meant little to Charlene; in this complex there seemed to be few who would call each other "neighbor," but this victim lived in an apartment on the second level. Charlene could tell by the number given in the news report that she lived just above them. Someone had called the police this morning, but the victim had been dead for nine hours.

Charlene realized she wasn't dreaming last night. That was a very real scream she had heard.

On Channel 10 they were saying the police had no suspects and were asking for help from the citizens in solving this crime. Charlene didn't think her having heard a scream would be of any weight in solving the case, so she didn't say anything. She never knew who the woman was, how or why she was murdered, but she thought about it.

23

June Means More than Honeymoon

La Mirage Apartment 5116
June 1, 1995

It was a Thursday afternoon and Tracie having no classes to attend was doing her homework at the table. It was a clear, warm day, reminiscent of the June day Floyd and Charlene had moved into the place. Tracie wanted her mother's help with a history report on the Californios. Charlene promised to assist her younger daughter after her call to Mr. Dunne came through. "Okay, Mom. I'll start it with what it says in my California History Book."

"He did it. He called me about 9:15 but only breathed. So I used *69 a minute later. It called him back; I recognized Floyd's voice if only from a 'hello,'" Charlene told Dunne. "Isn't that in violation of the restraining orders? And I have been getting lots of hang-up calls. That's why I got the *69 function put on my phone."

"Call the police so there will be a record of this," Dunne advised. "This is definitely a violation. This guy doesn't play by the rules, does he?"

"He doesn't think he has to," Charlene offered. "Rules do not apply to him."

Officer Bruno answered the call and wrote up a report. "Too bad *69 can't tell you calls yet to come so you'd know if he was going to call you again."

"I'm just glad it told the past. Now I want to know how he got my number and why he was calling me."

Then Tracie and her mother sat down in front of the opened books and encyclopedia to work on her project.

"Will you be glad when we get back home?" Tracie asked when they were midway through their research. "We won't have to be bothered with Floyd. I like it in San Diego, but I have been missing our old house."

"Me, too, honey," Charlene confessed. "But you know, we don't have our house any more. We'll be living in a different city, too. I'm sorry about this."

"Oh," Tracie sighed. "But I don't care, Mom," she continued sweetly. "Long as you, me, Jericha and Kimber are all together. Can we get our own cat? I love cats."

"We'll see."

June 4, 1995

In the evening after supper, with the kids in bed and contemplating a new week at school, there came a knock at their door. Charlene tiptoed to the peephole. A rather tall medium dark-skinned heavy-built Black man, dressed in a green satiny sports jacket, stood there obviously impatient. He rapped again, shifting his weight from right to left and reaching into the pockets of his jacket, then glancing back at the heavy door, fidgeting. He was looking at someone or something in the corner of the porch, which Charlene could not see well from the peephole.

She was too frightened to keep staring at him. She imagined he could see her through the same peephole. He looked staunch and resolved to get in, even if by force. Charlene did not know this man and could not begin to understand what he might want. She was terrified. She trembled, standing as motionless as possible, frozen, afraid to swallow the saliva building up in her throat. She decided to wait it out, and after a few minutes and a third knock, he went away. She thought about reporting this incident, but opted against it. It wasn't a crime or even a violation for a strange man to knock on her door. She was still thinking of the incident the next day, wondering.

June having started with a bang, Charlene and her girls realized not much time remained for their stay in San Diego. They had decisions to make. One concerned Kimber. Instead of spending lots of money for a large cage or hutch for the bunny, they decided to send her back home in advance of their return in a simple portable carriage. All they needed was a health certificate and an air ticket. She would be shipped by air cargo. Jericha was going to miss her pet but was consoled by the fact her bunny would be back home in the good hands of her Uncle Steve, waiting for her.

"I am sorry to disillusion you," said the veterinarian examining Kimber, "but calling this bunny She is incorrect. This is a He bunny rabbit, and a handsome one he is."

"All this time we've been wrong," Jericha was telling her sister. "Remember to call him He now. We don't want to insult him."

"But what can we do 'bout already 'sulting him?" Tracie asked. "Do you think he cares?"

"Probably not," Jericha concluded. "Animals and even people sometimes are not really what they seem."

"You are so right," Charlene added, acknowledging this phenomenal wisdom.

They dropped Kimber off at the cargo dock. The children were sad waving their good-byes until a smartly uniformed pilot came along, stooped down to pet Kimber in his cage, and could be heard saying, "Come on, furry one. We're going to have a good flight to St. Louis."

24

Not a Good Day to Die

June 6, 1995

An old Kojak episode was on TV. Charlene watched from across the room, a glass of Pepsi in front of her. She rubbed a dusty spot from her old oak table, looked at her watch and then glanced back at Kojak. He had a sucker in his mouth and his trademark grin slipped out one corner as he asked, "Who loves you, baby?"

"I do," came a voice, "I do love you." It was Floyd's voice from the past. A million "I love you's" from their courtship blotted out reality in an ethereal circle flashing around her head, making her dizzy, making her ill. She stood up abruptly and pounded her fist on the table. "No. It's not true. You don't love anyone!"

She closed her eyes trying to see his face, but it would not appear. Only the voice activated his spirit, not his being. *Forever. You are my Forever Girl. I love you. I do love you.*

She heard his Hello on her call back a few days ago. That is all she had heard since the April hearing.

Why had he taken the chance? It was sinister how he used his power to do whatever he thought he was entitled to do. His self-proclaimed superiority was again rearing its ugly head. Charlene remembered.

"Lou are inferior; they are smelly, dirty people and should have been sent back to Africa a long time ago." "We have to put up with Spiks, homos, weirdos of all kinds down at the store; the masses are asses." "Your folks suck. They didn't even watch the Super Bowl on TV, they're always into some stupid educational program. When they die we'll get their money."

Stop! she yelled. She covered her ears, refusing to listen to any more. Didn't anyone teach him anything about the world? Has he no appreciation of the diversity of the peoples of the world; color, religion, the ethnic factor are all insignificant. He doesn't try to understand people, because he thinks he has an inborn wisdom. *Who are you to judge? Who are you, Floyd Mitleider?*

"I am the man you're going to marry," his spirit spoke out; "you are beautiful enough for me. People will watch us when we go to the dance floor."

He worked out to keep his body trim; he fought his battle with the bald spot . . . transplants, treatments. He had eye surgery because eyeglasses detracted from his good looks; that failing, contacts. He was truly vain. He had never needed an understanding of the world around him. He *was* the world. There was room for Frankie in it, and for a while for her. But she did not measure up to his expectations; he had given her a chance.

Charlene's delusional conversation became tense. How can you say you love me? she questioned. You won't let love into your life.

"He has all the signs of an abusive personality," her attorney had said as they discussed her case.

"The isolation, the excessive secrecy about his affairs, the insistence on handling the money, the act of putting you in total dependence on him, the power play, the control. These are the things men who intend to abuse their wives always do. Believe me, I have seen cases similar to this in my practice, though none quite so severe. You should not be too concerned," continued Mr. Dunne curiously, "You're good-looking and you'll have men at your feet." Charlene was embarrassed by Dunne's remarks. She did not think this kind of consolation was appropriate. She just wanted a divorce and to get home.

"He never got you and the girls health insurance nor allowed you to have a credit card. Do you know how many credit cards he has in his possession, Charlene? My God, his line of credit is astronomical. I cannot understand why he charges everything. Even his car is being financed. People with money don't usually waste it on high interest installment buying. Promising you the car is a joke. It is not his to give."

"When will discovery be complete?" Charlene asked. "My mother and father have been spending so much on this divorce. They told me a St. Louis-based private detective is looking in on his finances and his past. It seems in his first marriage Floyd treated his wife much like he's treating me; he filed for divorce after two years and settled with her for a very small amount of money. She was in therapy for years after her marriage. I am positive he mistreated her, too. I am not looking for a fortune, but I did give up my worldly goods to marry him and move to California. He made promises he never intended to keep."

"Have the detective furnish me with whatever relevant information he comes up with. Meantime we are trying to find out as much as we can about his business and his assets."

"And he has never paid any more spousal support. My parents are paying my rent and sending me money. What are you doing about the agreement he just signed?"

"He is filing to be relieved of that commitment now. He says he can't afford it."

"What happened to his money?"

"Reports show he might not have as much as he claimed."

"What reports? You know he has money. I gave you those papers which showed he was getting $10,000 a month on the sale of his store. He has all the money he left St. Louis with—I saw a six-figure check before he came to San Diego. And of course, he has all my money, too. This is not making sense. He is manipulating the accounts just as he does his income tax. This is his specialty."

It was about time to pick up Jericha, then Tracie.

Charlene took the Caprice keys and left the apartment a bit earlier than usual. The cautious trek to the centrally located elevator and on to the parking garage, Charlene began her afternoon routine. It was early enough she could stop by the Bank of America ATM machine and withdraw some cash from her meager account. She had to be very budget-conscious. Floyd's genius for having and hiding money was on her mind.

The parking lot was nearly void of parked cars and she felt very much alone, like on a desert island. Noting the hour she realized she still had more than half an hour to spare before Lewis School dismissal time; she decided to bypass the school and go on to a Wal-Mart store to buy a congratulations card for Susie and Will whose new baby had just arrived. There, too, was an eerie abundance of parking places. The shopping public seemed to have disappeared. That suited Charlene. She was in and out in no time. It was as though she had this place and the whole world to herself.

Charlene backed into her usual parking place at the school where she would be able to see the kids coming out seconds after the final bell rang. There was a FedEx truck parked in the drive directly in front of the school office . . . a man was unloading some cartons. It was an unhurried day.

There was some time to wait. Charlene reached for her Wal-Mart bag, took out the card and a pen and began to write. "Dear Suze, How wonderful to have a new baby boy brought safely into the world. Congrats! After your difficult pregnancy, it must be a tremendous relief to... "

Suddenly Charlene was aware that a dark gray car had come swiftly into the driveway which passed in front of her parking place, and had stopped directly in front of her, creating a shadow in her view and drawing her attention. As she looked up she saw the three black occupants of the car openly staring at her, one on the passenger side beside the driver leaning out of the window. He was pointing a gun at her. The sun's rays ricocheted a glint from the barrel of this instrument of death into her face, blinding her unbelieving eyes. She panicked, frozen in fear, unable to control her shaking body. "My God, he's going to shoot me! I'm about to die!" He fired a thunderous shot.

Duck down! Duck your head! I'll save you!

She did not know what the bullet had hit. As the voice suggested, she struggled to get her head down to the empty seat, hindered by the still fastened seat belt her hands would not reach.

Her torso bent over and her head tilted as far as it would go beneath the dash, she heard another deafening shot, a slight pause, then two more rapidly fired shots closer to the right door. A screeching sound and the smell of burning rubber made her realize she could now raise up her head. Through the windshield she could see a dusty film rising from the driveway and scattered small gravel settling as she unfastened her seat belt with violently shaking hands. She cautiously but rapidly jerked open the door and began to run to the school office door. Two workers from the office had stepped out and took hold of her arms, nearly dragging her, to help her get inside. The bell had rung. The school children were huddled around the double exit doors nearby and were clamoring to get close to Charlene. Among them she saw the colorless, pinched face of Jericha who had tears in her eyes that were begging Charlene to let her out so she could be with her mother.

25

Money vs. Angel

"Is that your mother?" "Who is she anyway, a movie star?" "Jericha, tell me why they were shooting at her." "Is she in a gang?" The excited kids were swarming around Jericha, crushing her.

"I don't know. I don't know. Yes, she is my mother. Leave me alone." Her tears of confusion were bravely contained.

"Let her pass through," said Mr. Elgin* the school principal. Behind her was a uniformed guard, a law enforcement officer of some kind.

"Come on in," they were saying. "Sit here in this chair. The police are on their way."

Jericha touched her shaking mother's sleeve and Charlene put both arms tightly around her neck.

"I'm okay," she peeped. "Just shocked. I'm shaking all over."

Officers swung into action as they arrived, taking statements and looking for witnesses. The FedEx truck had taken off down the street in an effort to follow the offensive car. The driver was just returning.

"I thought I could follow and get the license number," he puffed. "But they disappeared a lot faster than my truck could go."

"I need to go to Foster Elementary and pick up my other daughter," Charlene told the police officer nearest her.

"I couldn't let you go," he said. "We'll go for her."

"She won't go with you, you're strangers. Take my daughter Jericha with you. Tracie will come if she sees Jericha."

While they were gone the police continued to question Charlene.

"Why would there be a drive-by shooting with you as the target?" they were asking.

"If you think it was a typical drive-by shooting," she began, "you are mistaken. My husband and I are going through a divorce. This shooting can't be anything but an attempt to kill me because my husband wants me dead. I am getting sick of calling the police and getting nothing for my trouble. I have been abused, ignored, laughed at, hassled by a man who doesn't know what a restraining order is, and now this. And you don't believe me!" She heard herself wailing, worse than the shooters' car had. She looked around and incredibly the officers were all at attention listening to her. Among them she saw a familiar face, that of Officer Bruno.

"Why doesn't anyone believe me?" she shouted. "You never believe me!"

"We do now," Officer Bruno assured, taking a step forward. "We do now."

"I don't know, ma'am, exactly what's going on here," said another of the officers, perhaps less convinced. "But we will of course look into it."

The brief facts of the troubles with Floyd and the slow progress of divorce were related to the police.

"There is no one else who would have or could have sent thugs out to kill me," Charlene repeated.

"Did you recognize any of the men in the car?"

"No. And I only saw them for a half a second. I know they were all Black guys. My husband despises Blacks. My daughters cannot even invite a Black friend to our apartment."

Officer Bruno was shaking his head. "These guys were not friends, I imagine. And he didn't do them any great favor, getting them involved in this, if that's what he did. Is your husband a man of means?"

"Yes he is."

"Well, there is your answer. Money buys anything. And there's not a big pool of hired assassins out there to choose from. I don't think he hired the world's best sharpshooters, but he got whatever money can buy."

"He's not noted for the best hiring practices," Charlene said, desperate to find relief from the awful tautness of her body with a little humor.

"From what you've told us, one thing for sure is you know how and where to duck down. That's why you are alive."

"What else could I do," she said in half-whisper. "Something told me to duck and I did."

"Ma'am, these officers will take you to your apartment and stay with you while you pack your bags, then they'll take you to a new location. You cannot go back to live in your place. Are you going to be all right?"

Charlene felt a surge of relief, as though this was what she had been dreading and it was over. It was like taking the final exam that she had not prepared for properly, knowing she would do poorly, but walking out of the testing room afterward feeling freed of the burden. She knew she had to remain strong for the sake of the kids and there was no room for self-pity. Since the police had picked her up, Tracie would not let go of her mother and Jericha stayed close by. They were trembling and so was their mother. They clung to each other barely able to shuffle to the car.

"Are you okay, Mom?" "Are you really okay?"

The brave woman touched her head, shoulders and slipped her hands over the rest of her body in a stupefied gesture to check to make sure no holes were there, no blood gushing out. Finding nothing like her fantasy dictated, she answered, "I *am* okay. I am not physically hurt at all."

Nearing the Caprice she realized the same could not be said of the car. Four large glaring holes lay open, two on the hood and two on the right side. The police were picking up bullet fragments and taking polaroid shots of the car from every angle.

"The car is hurt, but I am not," echoed in the chambers of Charlene's mind as they moved toward Friars Road. She wanted to believe it, but she soon realized that hurt took many diverse forms. By definition, she was hurting. Tears clouded her vision. How had she cheated death, she asked herself, with shots fired that close? She remembered the melodious warning of her guardian angel. *Thank you, Angel. Thank you. Stay with me.*

26

Good News, Bad News

"Yes, I said shot at, right in front of Lewis Junior High. Someone shot at me. Yes, we're all okay."

"What do you mean someone?"

"It was three guys in a dark gray car," Charlene recounted. "They fired four shots and then drove off. One of them might have been a Black guy who came to my door night before last. I think it was."

"Well, we know who sent them, don't we? I'm going to inform the private detective, Brach*, about this. We just hired him yesterday to do a background check on Floyd since the divorce seems to be going nowhere, and he got us a partial report right away."

"No question in my mind about why these guys were trying to kill me. No doubt Floyd paid them a lot of money, or promised to. He believes money talks and buys anything you want. My being dead would simplify his life."

"You're sure you're all right? Are the police protecting you?"

"They are taking me to a new place. We can't stay at La Mirage any more. But they are not exactly convinced that Floyd is the one who did this to me. I'll let you know where we're going to be staying."

"Ready now?" the officer asked. "Where do you want to go?"

"It will have to be some place cheap. I just paid my rent here and I don't have much money. This is terrible. We'll be eating all our meals out. It's going to cost so much. Where are we going to get the money?"

The police offered no solution. They took Charlene and her two hapless girls to a Motel on Adobe Road not far from La Mirage and the schools. Location seemed irrelevant now since the police would not let them go back to either. The girls would have to miss the end-of-school parties and seeing their friends for the last time before their departure from San Diego.

Their room was dull and lifeless, matching Charlene's deep despondency and horror visions. Stale cigarette smell permeated the place. She was struggling to stay normal and alert, getting the girls some snack food out of a machine in the corridor and pretending to enjoy the food. Her head was a pounding aching entity which seemed severed from the rest of her. Over and over again in her mind she felt another bullet lodging there. Would she survive the next moment, or would it be her last? She could see Jericha looking inside the car, gasping at the sight of her blood and the horror of her death; she fought to sit up but something pushed her back down in the uncomfortable half-bent position. She fought and clawed the seat, finally succeeding in reviving.

Exhausted from the struggle she came back to reality. She knew why Floyd had chosen this scenario for her murder: the total terror Jericha would have felt, the flamboyant payback to the DC by the MC. There was a new meaning for DC: Deceased. That's what he wanted, Charlene deceased. The shooters had two better chances to kill her if they were following her. At the ATM machine and at the Wal-Mart shopping lot they had a clear shot at her with no one around. But at Jericha's school, this place where children were at risk and the effect more dramatic, would be his murder site of choice. In his twisted mind it would hurt Charlene even more that her children would be traumatized and horrified. It would hurt her even though she were dead.

When they went out later for a meal at Burger King, Charlene shuddered at the sight of the mutilated car. They would have to take it though the car and its bullet holes stuck out like the proverbial sore thumb.

Her parents immediately made arrangements to send her money. Her mother was making plans to come out and stay with them. Brach had found a place for them to stay where a bodyguard could protect them.

Very early before they were up, Officer Chelby came to their room and rapped on the door. "Why are you staying in his drug-infested motel?"

"I don't know. No one told me where to go. I had to choose."

"Your parking place is matched to your room number. Any one could find you. And that Missouri license plate on your maroon Caprice with bullet holes. You couldn't hide from a blind man!"

What he said was true, but she had been given no other option. The officers who brought her there gave her no advice or promise of protection.

Charlene didn't like this officer's attitude. It was as though she had committed the crime. It was bad enough that she was in shock from the crime; she didn't need a scolding too.

"I'll be checking out tomorrow. My folks have arranged for me to stay at the Handlery and I'll have a rental car. Until then, I have no other transportation and no other place to go. The officers thought it would be safe here. How could the shooters know where I have gone? The police officers said there are hundreds of motels in San Diego. Why are you making me feel worse than I did when the shots were fired? I can't just disappear into thin air," she said desperately. "Have you come to help me or just yell at me?" she asked hysterically.

An afterthought hit her as she saw the two sleepy girls rub their eyes to wake up. "Have you arrested Floyd?"

"We can't do that without something to go on. Who is to say he is responsible for this anyway?"

"I am."

"Naturally there is an investigation. But you say you can't identify the shooters and no one seems to have gotten the license number of the car. I talked to Floyd about the *69 call. There is probably no connection. He was shaken that you did that call back on him, I could tell. He claimed he just wanted to know how you were."

"Meanwhile I have to worry if they'll track me down and try again."

And worry she did. Chelby gave her no reason to stop.

The day did not get better; nothing could erase the memory of the gun pointing at her, the loud discharge it made, the endless time she spent hunched over.

They ordered in meals for the rest of the day; Chelby had added to Charlene's tension and preoccupation. The confines of the semi-clean room were like a cage where Mama Bear paced around and passed the two Baby Bears playing games on the floor. Mama Bear kept trying to forget for even a minute the worst day of her life just 24 hours before.

Maybe when they transfer to the new hotel it'll get better, Charlene thought. It can't be worse.

"What if it wasn't your husband?" quipped Gordon*, the body-guard Brach had found. A security man at their "hideout" hotel, Gordon had an opinion about this case. "People going through divorce say all kinds of things about their spouses. Something like this looks bad for him, but there is no proof he is to blame for what happened to you."

Charlene did not like Gordon. If Chelby were not enough, now Gordon was making her uneasy. But the Handlery was a resort hotel with a lovely pool and enchanting surroundings. The move lifted the spirits of the three girls gone underground, despite the openly sarcastic pessimism of Gordon. They swam morning and afternoon, drove the new rental car to Fashion Valley Shopping Mall, lounged on the balcony of their room and pretended they were on vacation.

Charlene could not truly be carefree or feel secure even momentarily. She imagined she saw Floyd or Nick under every downturned hat or bowed head they encountered. She didn't know from whom else she should be hiding. There would be no peace for her until the police arrested Floyd.

"Oh, do you really think Floyd had something to do with this?" Mr. Dunne inquired.

"Do you think he didn't?"

"I didn't imagine he was such a bad guy," Mr. Dunne stammered. "We have a hearing with him in a few days. Maybe we can get this thing settled for you. You know if Floyd is convicted of this crime, a civil suit against him will be slam dunk."

By the 12th when the plane bringing the victim's mother landed in San Diego, the three uprooted Missouri girls had become routined to their new surroundings. Jericha thought she recognized the same small birds around the pool each day. She had names for them and when she called to them, though they were wild, they seemed to respond to her. If California birds were unique, like the swallows returning to Capistrano, it did not astound Charlene. Everything was unique, even this nightmare.

Jericha shared her enthusiasm with them when they congregated around the juice machine. "See, Grandma," she was saying as they sat at poolside. "That's Mary Ann and over there, the bird with the white streak on her right wing, that's Brenda."

"You're really sharp," her grandmother told her. "I can't tell one from the other."

"Can we get my yearbook from Lewis?" Jericha asked. "They were supposed to be ready yesterday and kids were going to sign them at a party. I won't have anyone to sign in my book," she remembered sorrowfully.

Gordon agreed to have someone go for it. This made Jericha happier. Tracie was pleased that Charlene was able to talk to Lailani's grandmother and arrange for her special friend to come to the hotel and swim in the pool. Lailani was like an island girl, almost amphibian. This visit helped make up for missing the last days of school. For both the girls it was clearly cruel punishment to end their school year and their "California year" so abruptly.

They all had to find small things to make them content, because the bigger picture was nothing but grim. Charlene started her series of dental appointments as soon as her mother got there. She had brought money from the sale of Charlene's house and she could watch the girls for her during the long appointments: the abscessed tooth at last was treated by root canal therapy and other work on neglected teeth was done. It was stressful, but so different from the mental anguish the pain was almost welcome.

Gordon arranged for Charlene to have a personal bodyguard when she went to court on June 16. This paladin stood beside her with his arms folded scarcely taking his eyes off her. Floyd was sitting on the other side of the aisle; it was like a wedding arrangement with his parents on his side. Charlene could feel their eyes on her, but she never looked at them. The hearing was short. Floyd's attorney repeated that Floyd's business was failing and he could not pay spousal support. Charlene was sure this was not true. Dunne stalled them. Nothing was resolved. Floyd's attorney made some very eccentric remarks to the court, claiming Charlene was muddying the waters with the allegations of having been fired on. Charlene had to sit there barely across the narrow aisle from a man who wanted her dead. Why was he still free? And why did his attorney imply Charlene was the one who had done something wrong? It was beyond her comprehension. It gave her a sinking feeling.

"Someone has surely beaten up on him," the bodyguard told Charlene. "Floyd's face was red and puffy. I'd give a silver dollar to know who did it to him."

"I'd give him the silver dollar to do it again." Charlene wouldn't look. Her face was swollen, too, from dental work done earlier in the day.

Gordon knocked on Charlene's door late that night. He knew the insurance policy was about to be cancelled. It was a strong motivation for the shooting.

"I say let's not be too hasty about cancelling this policy. Someone out there just might bump off the other insured party, Floyd, and then who would be the beneficiary?"

"I can't believe my ears. Are you telling me you might actually believe Floyd, insurance policy and all, had something to do with the shooting?" What Gordon hinted would be veritable poetic justice. If Floyd were to die, Frankie would be right in there trying to stop the payment of any insurance benefit to Charlene. It was an intriguing idea.

A newly assigned detective named Al Rushing from the San Diego PD called Charlene on the 18th. He told her he was working on the attempted murder case now because there was another related crime that had occurred on June 12th, that of a stabbing.

"The victim of the stabbing incident has changed the picture entirely," Al said. "His identifications are going to make this case." Charlene heeded Al's every word. Everything he said was reassuring.

"There have been interviews with some people and they're helping with this investigation," Al told her. "I can't give you much information about this yet; but basically Floyd is in some trouble with people he hired to do a job for him. They'd like to get his phone number which, incidentally, Floyd has changed. He's trying to avoid the inevitable and not just from us."

"I was told he looked as though someone beat him up," Charlene remembered. "Maybe he is getting a dose of his own evil medicine. This is sounding like a police investigation out of the movies," she said sincerely. "I guess you just have to know where to look."

"That's the truth. We found one suspect through a photo album in a friend's house," he admitted proudly. "We are getting some breaks."

"I hope it continues to go well."

"We made an arrest last night," he told her with enthusiasm, "and we had already arrested one suspect on the 15th after having him under surveillance. These guys are probably two of the three in the gray car who shot at you. Don't get your hopes up too high, but I believe we're on the right track now. Hang in there."

"I am so anxious to go home knowing Floyd and anyone involved in the crime against me are behind bars. Thanks for calling me."

What a contrast talking to a caring police officer was after Charlene's experience with Officer Chelby. He hardly admitted there was a crime, though he knew of spousal abuse and the *69 phone call. He only upset Charlene, criticizing her for being in that motel and driving the bullet ridden car, but offering no help. Charlene remembered that her mother, in her concern, had tried to contact the San Diego police to inquire as to their safety right after the crime. They gave her no information; Chelby told Charlene to tell her mother not to call the police any more. He seemed to think she was trying to intimidate him! She was seeking accurate reporting that she thought could only come from the police. He missed the point entirely.

Charlene had begun to feel that help from the police was totally lacking in her case. But here was a man as gentle as others were crude. Rushing was a soft-spoken man with a certain lilt in his voice that gave her confidence in him. She believed he was going to be the one to unravel Floyd's scheme and dirty dealings. Good news at last.

27

Trouble Ahead

The Handelry Hotel was not home, and trying to pretend it was only lasted a short time. The not knowing when or even if Floyd would be arrested made Charlene apprehensive.

"I guess we should just go ahead with our plans to go 'home.'" The expense of living in a hotel and eating three meals a day in a restaurant was a strong motive to get away from San Diego.

"We'll have to be on separate planes," Mom said, "now that you've decided where you're going to live. I can understand why you don't want to be in St. Louis. That certainly could not be classified as 'in hiding.' By taking Jericha and Tracie with me I'll give you time to get settled in before we bring the girls to the new place."

They kept their plans as secret as possible and Charlene changed her name for her return ticket. Caution was in order.

"Where shall we eat tonight?" Mom asked. "Where is that place Lailani's father recommended?"

"It's called Ricky's. It's just across the way."

"Sounds good. Tell Gordon."

As Charlene wrote a note for her bodyguard, she thought for the millionth time how awful it would be to be shot at again. She knew she would not survive a second attempt. The first one had followed a route and a plan based on what Charlene did habitually. Now she was determined not to give shooters any such advantage.

Yawning as she parked in front of Ricky's where they all unloaded, Charlene glanced out the large front window as they went in and waited to be seated. She noticed a late model white Cavalier pull up in the same lot. The driver was a tall redheaded man of slight build who got out of the car and walked over to a public telephone located between Ricky's and a convenience store. They waited quite a while for the hostess to find them a table for four. The man returned to the car before they sat at a table near the back. He opened the door and just sat at the wheel looking attentively at the front of the restaurant. As they were ordering their meals, Charlene began to recall what Floyd had told her about Frankie and the fact that he always drove a Cavalier. She wondered if it could possibly be he. She panicked. He could have been following them. He could be fulfilling his role as Floyd's protector. Charlene had a hard time eating and she wondered if he were still there in that Cavalier. They were not at a table where she could see that area. What would she do if he followed them when they left? Charlene said nothing; but was formulating a plan of action.

Her mother had just given the cashier up front her credit card to pay their bill when Charlene saw a San Diego city police car pull up in front right beside the white Cavalier. An officer and Gordon got out! The Cavalier immediately backed out and sped to the street.

Gordon waved to them when he came in. "I got your message," he said, "my friend Len and I were going out to eat, decided to come to Ricky's, too. I haven't eaten here in a while. How was your meal?"

"It was okay, I guess," Charlene answered, "I thought I saw a friend of Floyd's outside, in a white Cavalier."

"You mean the car that left when we came in?"

"Yes, that one."

"Len is not really working on this case," Gordon said. "He is a friend of mine. He is active in Crime Stoppers here."

"Glad to meet you," the officer said. "Gordon has been talking about maybe putting out some reward money to speed up the capture of the conspirators in your case; he's filled me in. It might be worth the money."

"We'll see what we can do. Mom, what do you think?"

"If it will help, of course we'll try to come up with some money," she told them. "But, please," she went on, "find out what you can about this buddy of Floyd's. In combination with Floyd he may be poison."

The pair did not make any promises. Gordon had not been very sympathetic or supportive to Charlene. "I'm not going to stroke you," he had said. But this time he was there when she needed him. She hoped that if it were Frankie, the police car had properly scared him away. One thing he could never deny was his involvement in the insurance policy, arranged by him in a highly unusual manner. Nor could he ever deny that he was so close with Floyd that he would be tempted to assist Floyd in any way he could: Floyd was in trouble. Logic told her he was up to something, but she had to remember her father's advice: don't get paranoid.

28

Investigations

Charlene was afraid nobody was going to stop Floyd, ever. He was getting by with hiding his money, not paying what he promised, signing declarations "under penalty of perjury" that were lies and he was doing as he pleased. This had become second nature to him. Only briefly had this been reversed, when she was in custody of the car and he was forced to obey the restraining order that demanded he move out. Since her brief show of power had now expired, he had snapped into action and done what he said he would: take charge again.

The private investigator sent reams of information about Floyd and gave his reports to the San Diego Police Department. He reported that Floyd was signing escrow papers to sell Hillcrest Liquor. This was a surprise to her because she thought Floyd was blocked from selling his business under the provisions of the restraining order.

The FBI became temporarily interested in the case because of the unsolved attempted murder and the shady nature of the liquor store. Charlene was never told what became of this superficial investigation. It may have been a figment of Brach's imagination. He kept telling her things but never showed her any proof.

Private detectives in St. Louis and San Diego could never convince the Feds to investigate the dirty dealings and possible money laundering going on at Hillcrest Liquor. They had to rate lesser cases of unlawful business practices as not worth their effort.

"They regard this as small potatoes," Brach reported. "They would see just how big the potatoes are, if they would only look into it," he indicated ominously.

For some reason it seemed to Charlene neither the investigators nor the attorneys cared really whether this odd business was ever
investigated, but to Charlene and her parents it was essential to un-
covering Floyd's real part in it, where he was hiding the money and
his crime against Charlene. He needed to be punished and if the
punishment meant his losing some of his precious commodity-money
-even better. His love of it got him into trouble; he should not be
allowed to use it to get out of trouble.

The police were not effective either. Brach told his clients he
thought some of the police officers were too afraid to get into this
investigation seriously. There were truly bad "dudes" to contend with.
These trigger men who tried to kill Charlene were a very real threat,
not just to Charlene. Some people in the police department preferred
to stay clear of them, according to Brach.

According to Gordon everyone involved in the criminal case
was getting timorous. His bodyguarding skills were in demand. Even
Charlene's attorney was given protection, and Gordon saw to it that
he got home safely after the court hearing. Now he appreciated how
Charlene felt; he should have believed Charlene when she said she
was afraid! Charlene was confused about the money that was being
spent irresponsibly. Her parents agreed that the bills coming in were
out of line. But they were not about to let up.

Charlene put her faith and trust in Al Rushing. He seemed to
be the only one she could count on to investigate tirelessly. She could
tell he was as stubborn as her parents and would not stop short of
solving this crime.

In the course of surveilling Floyd, Gordon saw the suspect
withdrawing money from an ATM machine outside First Interstate
Bank. Charlene wondered what Floyd was doing there. He was ap-
parently doing whatever he wanted with his money in different banks.
Again the restraining orders against him did not faze him. He was
not up front. He was devious. Getting spousal support was out of
the question.

Gordon also reported: "I think the friend of Floyd's you were
worried about may have left. According to one of my contacts, it is
possible he flew out of here late last night."

From the hotel rooms that had become their temporary home, the four worried "girls" continued day after day to find some enjoyment, some purpose in being there.

"I just had to see how you and the kids are," Charlene told Mary.

"Oh, I am so glad you called. I couldn't believe what happened to you when I heard. The kids at Foster have really been missing Tracie. You'd be shocked to hear what the room mothers and some people have been saying, speculating about what happened that day at Lewis."

"I think I can imagine."

"There were so many rumors floating around. 'What kind of family could this be anyway?' 'That Mitleider woman was involved in something like drugs to have people shooting at her.' 'Good thing it didn't happen over here at Foster.' Those were things I heard."

Mary defended Charlene but was not happy with people spreading unfounded rumors. "Gossips are such trouble-makers," she declared.

"They should have made an effort to know you better, Charlene. They were glad for you to do book orders and have parties for the kids."

Mary was a true friend not influenced by Floyd's rudeness. Thankfully she had not heard his assessment of their friendship. She continued to be that "ship big enough to carry two in fair weather" and both of them, not just one, "in foul."

Charlene's foul weather had no immediate forecast of anything better to come. And the investigations, for whatever they were worth, were ongoing.

29

Arrests

Gordon was in the lobby of the hotel when the weary four-some went down to breakfast.

"What's up?" he asked. "I understand there is a new SDPD detective working on this case now." Gordon had an *in* with the police because of the nature of his work and his participation in Crime Stoppers.

"I'm expecting to hear from him before long," Charlene told him. "I think they have already made some arrests."

"What if they don't make a connection with Floyd? I haven't heard anything about arresting Floyd," he jeered in his usual pessimistic vein. "They have to come up with some evidence."

"They're working on it," Charlene retorted, trying to make Gordon curious.

"You know," Gordon went on, "I am still doing surveillance on Floyd for several days. I have to admit I have seen him in his car, the black Grand Marquis, riding around with some guy. How many of his friends are you worried about? I took a picture of one of them night before last. But I didn't know who he was, and now another has left San Diego."

"We can attribute the insurance policy to one of them, through a relative. There is a lot I could tell you about him. But since we're not sure he was the one I saw at Ricky's, I won't bother. I am glad he has gone."

◆◆◆

Handlery Hotel
June 21, 1995

It was another uneventful day through lunchtime and an afternoon swim; Charlene's mother had gone to the laundry downstairs, trying to get things ready for packing. The girls had been watching *Beauty and the Beast* on TV. When it was over, Charlene changed the channel to watch the O.J. trial briefly. They were examining evidence from the police lab. Defense attorneys were trying to prove the evidence was improperly gathered and blood samples were contaminated.

Even if they find enough evidence to arrest Floyd, Charlene kept thinking, there will be a trial and someone will try to get him off, just like they're doing for O.J. Accused people always got good defense attorneys, not necessarily paid for by themselves, she thought. They were entitled to more protection and representation free of charge than victims were. Charlene was becoming too embittered to think clearly about American justice, but she knew it leaned toward the criminal. The victim was expected to feel grateful that assailants and arraigned felons were brought to trial.

"Jericha," she called, "run down the hall to Grandma's room and ask her when she wants to go to dinner.

In a half-minute, Jericha was back. "She says whenever you want to go is okay with her. I'm going on back to her room to stay with her a while."

"I'm going, too," Tracie announced. "See you later, Mom."

Charlene's phone rang as they left and she realized it was later than she had thought, almost 7:00.

"I have some exciting news for you, Charlene," was the beginning of Al's report. "We have just arrested Floyd Arnold Mitleider for conspiracy to commit murder."

"You're not kidding me, are you?" she responded.

"No-ho," Al said in a half-laugh, half-word. "We got him dead to rights."

"Can you give me any other details?"

"Well, let's see now. For one thing, his parents were there when he was arrested."

"I'll bet they told you he was innocent."

"His mother followed me around as we did the search. I finally had to ask her to go sit down. She said she wanted to go with us when we took Floyd to jail so she could make his bail."

"He can get out on bail?"

"Not for a major violation like this. That's what I told her. The father sat down in an armchair and began to perspire and look real sick. Felt kinda sorry for him."

"Was there anyone else there?"

"No. We searched the whole apartment. There is some evidence, however, that someone was trying to help Floyd get out of the country."

"Really? I'm glad that didn't happen. We'd never see him again. He would have gotten off."

"He had tickets and reservations for July 1st, even a boarding pass. That's only nine days away."

"I guess you got the evidence you wanted or you couldn't have arrested him."

"Yes. We've got CW's and some solid evidence that he hired these guys to kill you. They had a picture of you with Floyd; it looked like a wedding picture. There was a large heart-shaped wreath or trellis in it. I am sorry, Charlene, but I am afraid you married a scumball."

"Thanks so much for calling me. I'm going out in the hall to do a few cartwheels."

Al laughed raucously at her planned celebration. "The Deputy District Attorney Herb Bowman will be calling you, probably tomorrow. He'll need your statement and some other things have to be settled before you leave."

"Mom, Mom!" Charlene yelled as she ran down the hall. "Guess what. They've got Floyd in jail. Let's go to a special place to eat tonight."

Dorothea popped open the door and mother and daughter hugged each other. "What a relief," Charlene's mother sang. The girls took hands as for ring around the rosy and joined in the gala.

"This may be the beginning of the end for Floyd," Charlene thought aloud. *If this is a game*, she thought in her heart, *you haven't won yet, Floyd.* His prediction was pulling away from the walls of real events. You are not winning, Charlene sighed.

The festive lights of Horton Plaza were illuminating not only the buildings, stairs and passageways of the radiant shopping center but also the spirits of the group. Dinner was more inviting than it had been for long days before and Charlene felt relaxed and un-stressed. It dawned on her as they were finishing dinner that Al had mentioned the wedding picture with the heart-shaped impression. The scene of the wedding itself and the arrival of the photo proofs came into consciousness, and it occurred to Charlene abruptly that the picture referred to had been sent to Floyd's parents. There were ten poses offered to them as proofs but not finished pictures. Charlene had sent three to her parents, three to his, three to Susie and kept only one for them. Choosing who would get which proofs was a process she would not forget. Floyd's parents got the heart one. How in heaven's name did it get in the hands of the shooters? Only one way. Probably Floyd had to have asked his parents to return the wedding pictures to him. Did they ask why? Did they know his plan? Surely they were not gullible enough to think Floyd wanted photos of her to admire; they knew the couple had been separated and they were getting a divorce.

The otherwise happy night out in downtown San Diego was spoiled by her inquiring mind and strong suspicions that the two strange parents of Floyd had now become even more devious than Charlene had imagined. She realized it was only a suspicion, and she hoped it was not true.

Dunne accompanied Charlene to Herb Bowman's office and she answered his questions for a half hour. Herb asked her about the Arabs and she wasn't sure whom he meant. He seemed to be using the term collectively for Floyd's business associates and employees. He did say that two of them were intimately involved in this crime. She was there to respond to his questions and did not have a chance to pose any of her own, except one: When will the trial take place?

The process is slow, he told her, and they still had to locate the third shooter. She knew from Al that they had arrested two of them.

"Who identified the shooters?" Dunne asked finally.

"The other victim."

Mystified as Charlene was, she could at least leave the prosecutor's office knowing that soon there would be a preliminary hearing and that the prosecutor was sure Floyd would be bound over for trial.

"Although we never know how a jury might find, it would be my guess that statements made by Mr. Mitleider himself are enough to have a jury find him guilty. As to others involved, their convictions might be a little harder to obtain. There is a lot of circumstantial stuff."

Charlene felt good about Mr. Bowman. She could see he wanted a victory for justice here and would work hard to achieve it. He was good in collaboration with Al. If only there was no slip-up!

"Your whereabouts will be kept strictly confidential," Bowman assured her. "I understand about this Frank person, and I know all about the origins of the insurance policy. I agree that you should keep a low profile. There is strong evidence that he is attempting to help Floyd. It may get him in trouble, but not so far."

At the airport and on the plane when Charlene was alone, she began to recall Floyd's motto: Frankie will do anything for me. All I need to do is ask, Floyd had sworn.

Charlene knew she would have to melt into the scenery of her new place which would be a hideout until this whole ordeal was over. That was the problem. Would it ever be over? There was no safe place for her. How she desired to be back to her life before Floyd. If she could be Dorothy she would quickly click the heels of her ruby slippers together three times and, closing her eyes, wait to be transported to that place, home, because she had learned there's no place like home. Home is safe; home is happy.

30

The Other Victim

While Charlene was a victim because of her great misfortune in marrying a conmaniac, Muaid was a victim because of his association with a fellow Iraqi named Imad.

"Come to California," Imad had urged him when Muaid needed a place to live. "I will help you."

Muaid was happy that he could continue his political asylum with an old friend like Imad. Being an orphan, he had been lonely most of his life and defecting from Saddam Hussein's Army only partially relieved his anguish. His meager wages and his lack of English language skills made life in America very complex, but then his life in Baghdad was not uncomplicated. When he arrived in 1995 and began to share Imad's small apartment, he socialized and drank alcohol just like the rest of the circle of acquaintances, some Iraqi and some American. These practices were strictly forbidden by their Muslim religion. It was a new era for Muaid, now twenty-three years old. One of Imad's friends was also twenty-three and worked at nearby Cliff Brown Automotive with Imad, whom he called Andy. This friend was James Ray Smith, Jr., a Black, whose live-in girlfriend Linda Brown often joined in their outings to El Torito restaurant, Club E or simple get-togethers at their Georgia Street apartment in North Park. These friends were all neighbors almost within shouting distance from one Georgia Street apartment building, 4450½ to the other, Muaid's, 4512 Georgia Street, Apartment 6.

June 12, 1995

Muaid was alone in the apartment at about 8:30 watching television. He was postponing things he had to finish before reporting for the midnight shift at work. There was a loud knock at the door. Standing there was Imad's heavy-built Black friend from work, wearing a black T-shirt, black pants and black and white cowboy boots with snakeskin trim. Muaid was surprised by his presence.

"Michael, man, is Andy here? He's supposed to go to the drive-in movie with us tonight."—"No, I don't know where he is," Muaid said.—"May I use the bathroom?"—"Sure, you know the way."

Alone again, Muaid realized he was out of cigarettes. He walked to a neighborhood convenience store, returning with a cigarette in mouth and a decision to do a little laundry before going to work. He took a magazine with him to the laundry room downstairs and looked at it while those wonderful American machines, unknown to him in Iraq, whirred and gushed, washing and drying his clothes. He went back up to #6, folded his clothes, put them away and then turned on the TV to listen to the news. The phone rang. "How is everything?" Imad wanted to know.—"Fine. Say, your Black friend was here looking for you," Muaid continued in Arabic, "said something about your going to the movies with him and his girlfriend."—"I'll be home later," Imad finished.

Just settling in again, Muaid moved to the kitchen and got some lettuce from the fridge and started to eat it. Another knock at the door interrupted his task. He peered out the window and there again stood Imad's Black friend, half-turned and making eye contact with someone at the bottom of the stairs.

The big man entered, asking again about Andy and again going to the john, this time without waiting for permission. And this time again Muaid thought the Black man's visit to the bathroom was too quick, the running tap water over in seconds and the man's hands were not even wet. Muaid wondered what was going on, his heart beating faster. He did not trust Blacks and was suspicious of this man, remembering a rancorous encounter between the man and Imad about a week before. Disliking this trespassing man anyway, Muaid sensed that something was amiss. Gripped with fear, he noted how jittery was Imad's friend, who stood looking at the TV screen for a couple of minutes, then announced he was leaving. "I'll walk you to the door," Muaid said shakily, opening the door, as two tall Black men rushed into the apartment brushing him aside. Stunned Muaid watched as James closed the door quickly. The shorter[1] of the two tall intruders (Ivan Catlin) had short hair, a thin moustache, wore a glove on his right hand and was armed with a small caliber semiautomatic 9 mm. gun in his right hand and a knife in his left. Marvin (taller) was similarly armed.

Muaid, astonished and scared to death, asked, "Hey, what's up?" to which Ivan responded, "Sit down on the floor and put your hands behind your head." Marvin shoved his gun on Muaid's left jaw and Ivan hit him hard on the right jaw with his gun and asked, "Where's the money?" Muaid, blood spurting from his mouth, replied, "What money?"

James declared: "Do what you have to do."

Dragging Muaid into the bedroom, knife against his head, Ivan snarled, "Where is your roommate Andy? If you talk or yell, I will shoot you." James stayed away from the bedroom while Marvin put a gun to Muaid's head and Ivan said, "I'm gonna look for something to tie him up." Muaid was filled with terror. Ivan took shoe strings from a pair of shoes (Imad's) which he found in the closet and tied Muaid's arms and legs together leaving him in a fetal position. James watched from the bathroom as the two thugs bound up their prey. "The binds are too tight," Muaid cried out. Marvin looked at him sympathetically but did nothing.

Ivan searched the apartment, feverishly ransacking it, pulling out all the drawers and dumping the contents on the bed. He found $400 and then kicked Muaid in the face. Marvin repeated, "Where is the money? Your friend owes us $70,000. We are from the Mafia."

Then Ivan looked around the apartment and found some black packing tape. Marvin grabbed Muaid's head and gruffly stuffed a handkerchief into his mouth making him gag. With a flourish Ivan taped his mouth shut from sideburn to sideburn just as Muaid was about to vomit. Next he taped Muaid's hands and feet together. The

---

[1]Detective Al Rushing labeled the two unknown assailants as the shorter and taller to help Muaid describe them, because both of them were tall and he did not know their names. Ivan Darnell Catlin is 6'1" tall and Marvin Keith Brown 6'3" tall. Their names are used here to avoid confusion.

two intruders shoved their trussed victim into the bedroom closet and closed the folding door except for a crack through which the frightened Iraqi could see and hear. He heard James talking to Ivan.

Shortly after midnight Muaid received a pager message from his workplace. Marvin opened the closet door, thrust the device into Muaid's line of sight and showed him the number. "Whose number is that?" Muaid gestured that it was for him knowing that he was supposed to be at work. Ignoring the page, the invaders turned off the lights except those in the bedroom, forcefully pulled Muaid out to the side of the bed, and closed the closet door. Ivan glanced at Marvin and said, "Shoot him." Marvin hesitated. "Shit. I can't kill him. I can't shoot." Ivan, pumped up, pulled out his knife and began stabbing Muaid viciously in the back of the neck and right shoulder. Marvin, inspired by his partner, jabbed Muaid in the left side of the neck, the jaw and the shoulder and without restraint cut down his abdomen all the way to his penis. Meanwhile Ivan cut Muaid in the back and made a big thrust into his innards. Blood was pouring out from all the wounds. Then, outwardly calm, Ivan went to the kitchen refrigerator, took out a can of beer, opened it and drank it up in a gulp to bolster his endurance, leaving blood stains on the can. "Let's wash our hands in the bathroom," he said to Marvin. Removing their gloves, they wiped the blood from their wrists with a towel and washed their hands, using a second towel to dry them.

"Allah, yeh-mini! (Lord, protect me!)," Muaid prayed, feeling all his blood flowing from his body.

To save himself, he went limp, lay motionless and pretended to be dead, a tactic he had learned from his military training in Iraq. When Ivan and Marvin returned from the bathroom, they saw Muaid covered with blood and not moving. Blood was quickly filling the space around Muaid's body. Trying unsuccessfully to avoid the oozing blood on Muaid's neck Marvin leaned down and touched him there. "He's not breathing," he reported. "He's dead." Then he wiped the blood from his finger on Muaid's blood-splattered white pants. "Let's go," Ivan ordered. They turned out the bedroom lights, left the apartment and closed the door behind them.

Muaid gasped for air, his bloody chest heaving. His face, though sauced with gushing blood from multiple sources, had a satisfied look: *I did it, I fooled them, it worked.* He felt like a gravely wounded soldier on the battlefield, something for which he was prepared. He heard the security gate clank as it was closed. Then he began kicking the wall furiously with his feet and making muffled shouts. With his tongue he managed to loosen the tape from his mouth. Wounds pained him throughout his body and he was groggy, not knowing how the thugs had punctured him. He yelled out, "HELP . . . ME! HELP ME! I've been shot. I am going to die."

PART TWO

HOW TO BELIEVE IN CRIMINAL JUSTICE

31

Behind the Scenes

San Diego Police Department
June 27, 1995

Before Al and Deputy District Attorney Bowman could begin the interview with Nick, Al had to ask some preliminary questions. "Can you say your name for us, please?"

"Name is Najah Sitto. I go by the name Nick."

It had been only six days since Nick, wearing a wire and conversing with Floyd in a corridor near his apartment, risked his life to help the police. He was afraid what the ramifications of being a CW would be. He was glad he had cooperated and was sorry for his part in this bad thing. With each question from his inquisitors he remembered vividly the circumstances and how he wished they had been different.

It was back in May of the previous year that Sarmad Eram, Floyd's manager, had called Nick, a fellow Chaldean Christian, to see if he wanted work.

"What kind?" Nick had asked.

"You know what a stockboy does: sweep, mop, clean up, fill up coolers."

"No pwoblem," Nick had answered. "This guy Floyd, is he a pretty good man to wuk for?" Sarmad switched to Arabic and told Nick the truth. "The man's a rich jerk, insults people, acts superior, brags about pulling some deals, has some money-making schemes on the side, but what can we do, we all need work. He says he's getting married next month. Must be a saint of a woman."

Nick got the job and he and Floyd began doing things together. In a way, Nick liked Floyd. He also knew that the more he
complimented Floyd, the better treatment he got. Sucking up to him
became second nature. But he agreed with Sarmad. Boss was a fucking
jerk.

Nick admitted to Rushing and Bowman that he had no other
job and Floyd had no other businesses in town that he knew of.

Floyd had a beautiful wife, Nick recalled as they continued the
interview. He had helped the couple move into their La Mirage apartment and decided Sarmad was right: the woman who married Floyd
was a saint.

Nick had always regarded Floyd as a complete fool. He had
money, a wife and two lovely girls for stepdaughters but was not
satisfied with that. He had done his usual thing: change his mind.
Such a short time before, he had married this woman and so soon
became discontent. That was Floyd. No matter what the situation he
always changed his mind many times and he had no loyalty to anyone. Nick thought of his own child born out of wedlock to a Black
woman. When the mother needed money for diapers, he asked Floyd
for it. Floyd wrote out a check for "Baby Lou." That was Floyd:
dumb stupid names for people, making fun of them. Acting like he
was the Lord.

Bowman asked: "At some point did Floyd get rid of the liquor
store?"

"Yeh, on November 11, 1994. New owners were Mustafa brothers. I stay on and wuk for them. They did the inventory and got the
keys."

Nick recalled how between May and November Floyd was always asking questions about what goes on at the store. He didn't
come down often enough to see for himself. "He also used to talk
about the two kids his wife had. He not like kids. I met them. I
thought they were sweet, like their mother."

Floyd asked Nick if someone was scamming him, taking things
from the store without paying. He had already had trouble with Joe
and Issa. He had a thing about that. Even after the Mustafas took
over, Floyd kept coming to store and talking to Nick.

The time came in March of 1995 when Floyd asked Nick to help him move out of the apartment at La Mirage to which Nick had helped him move in only eight and a half months before. One evening between 8:00 and midnight Floyd talked to Nick at Hillcrest in the doubleface office (a privacy area where checks were cashed and Western Union money orders were sent) and asked Nick, "Would you like to make some extra cash?"

"Just find me someone I can trust and I will pay you $20,000," Floyd promised. - "I find him Priest," Nick said.

The DDA prodded. He wanted to know what Priest was like and what Floyd wanted him to do.

"Priest was tall, bald, half black, half white. Used to come to the liquor store to cash checks. Floyd trusted this guy, gave him $2,500, then the guy just walked away with the $2,500. Priest told me that Floyd gave him cash to buy some things. He told me Floyd wanted him to kill his wife."

Why didn't you just walk away from Floyd and his plan to kill his wife? Nick's conscience told him. He could not answer, except to remember he needed work.

Floyd was very angry about losing money, but kept on coming down to the store and kept trying to find someone he could trust, according to Nick.

"Why don't you just give her the money?" Nick asked Floyd, knowing that if he were rich and his wife wanted a divorce that is what he would do. But Floyd answered, "She is causing me too many problems."

It was a Monday in April when Imad, another Iraqi, came to work at Hillcrest. Nick could not recall the exact date. It came about because Imad worked as a mechanic at Cliff Brown Automotive. Nick met him there one day. Tarak owned the automotive shop as well as the liquor store and Nick was sent there on business to bring something to Tarak. Imad talked to Nick about wanting another job where he could make some money.

"He only worked for four hours; he worked for the person who was not there; he wasn't that good." Nick said, of Imad.

"How much time passed since Priest took the money and Imad worked for the store?"

"Two weeks. And Floyd came around there all the time, said he wanted to find somebody, somebody to work out his deal." Nick then explained that when Imad came to the store, he told him about what Floyd wanted.

The two of them decided they would tell Floyd they were ready to do the job for him, but they would just scam him-and take his money.

"Did Imad know that Floyd wanted his wife killed?" the DDA asked.

"Yes, but he doesn't know about the insurance."

"Did you know about it?"

"Yes. I heard Floyd talking to his friend on the phone. Floyd said, 'Yes, she signed the insurance application and we got the $750,000 policy.' I knew Floyd was talking to his friend whose relative was connected to the John Hancock Insurance Company. Another time he called the relative and asked all about how much insurance he will collect."

Nick had difficulty explaining everything. He wanted to be accurate and truthful and he wanted to save his neck. Ever since Muaid got stabbed, Nick feared for his own life, also Imad's.

He told the interviewers about the meeting Floyd had with Imad at La Mirage. Floyd took them to the running track. Nick said he acted as Imad's interpreter and introduced Imad as "Mark."

"Floyd told Imad that he had a wife who was causing him too much trouble. I told Imad to go along with anything Floyd said, so we can start getting paid. 'If you kill my wife for me, I'll pay you guys $100,000.' Imad wanted $10,000 in advance. Floyd said he would pay us when he sees a report that his wife is dead."

The DDA asked Nick to explain how Floyd wanted the job done.

"In a way so it will look like it was a robbery, or rape, or something else."

Imad recalled Nick's advice, to appear tough and say he had killed before. After the meeting he went with Nick to Denny's to talk about what the agreement entailed. Floyd had told them he wanted the job done in two weeks or ASAP.

Nick told the interviewers that he and Imad had decided to scam Floyd, but Floyd kept paging or calling Nick every other day to see why they had not done the job.

Only five days later there was a meeting at Hillcrest Liquor, Nick told his questioners. This time Floyd arrived on his bicycle. While Nick stayed at the cash register, the other two went into the small room in back of the store. Floyd told Imad $10,000 was too much advance and they agreed on $5,000; he also informed Imad he would have to lower the pay for the hit to $70,000 because he said some other guys would do it for that price. After the first meeting with Floyd at La Mirage, a week later, the $5,000 was given to Nick at the store in the backroom. He kept $1,000 and Imad got the rest.

Then Floyd began to question Imad's ability to do the hit. Nick told Imad to show Floyd somebody who Floyd would believe could do the job and to act like a killer. Floyd used Nick's pager to contact him. Nick knew Floyd's phone number. They met at the store a couple more times. Finally there was a third meeting of the three of them at Denny's Mission Valley. Floyd complained that Imad was not doing anything. Imad said if he had $10,000 he would do the hit with a friend. Imad talked to James who used to work at Cliff Brown Automotive and offered him $2,000 to help him follow a man's wife. James agreed. Imad introduced James to Nick so he could size him up. They went out for drinks. Then, Imad told Floyd okay, they would do the job based on the pay and conditions Floyd wanted.

Then came a second La Mirage meeting a couple of weeks after the first one there. Imad took James to meet Floyd. Floyd thought James was capable. Out on the running track the final agreement of $70,000 for the hit was made. James now knew what the job really was. Floyd told them to get the job done quickly because school would soon be out and Charlene would be gone. Imad was given a picture of Charlene and Floyd. Floyd gave them a code to use as a notification about the hit: "Give me a wah-ba three times message on my machine so I'll know she's been shot. That is our code for murder." Nick knew about Floyd's meeting with Imad and James because after they left Floyd called Nick at ll:00 p.m. He wanted to know who the Black guy was, including his name.

The DDA was interested in Floyd's instructions to the hired assassins. "Did he tell you his wife's schedule?"

"Yeh. He told me when she left the house to take the kids to school and one night he took me to show me the places where the schools are. He told me her morning schedule and then the afternoon one.

"The next night after the La Mirage meeting with Imad and James was when Floyd came to Hillcrest to take me to the schools. I drove around with him while he showed me where she goes to schools, the parking spots and where the kids are dropped off and picked up. He even suggested a possible place to kill her might be in the La Mirage parking garage."

"Did you show Imad and James?" asked the DDA.

"After, just after, I tell Imad. I had to, so that we could show Floyd that we're doing the job."

It was about three days after Floyd met James at La Mirage that Nick saw James at Imad's apartment early in the morning. James was wearing a green Guess jacket with a hood and was acting nervous. James did not know Nick was involved, but had already met with Floyd and Imad.

Nick also told the policeman and the DDA that on May 1st Tarak abandoned the liquor store from which he and others had taken all the merchandise they could. He alibied that he gave the store back to Floyd because he had lost interest in the liquor store business. Nick again worked for Floyd for about three weeks and also saw him at his apartment. Perhaps fifteen times Floyd talked about murdering Charlene, saying the divorce and the Hillcrest mess were getting to be too much for him.

Imad stalked Charlene alone on a Friday and the next week both Imad and James went on the route. The two wore track shoes for the running track to impress Floyd. There were times when Floyd sometimes talked to James. The two cohorts followed Charlene when she drove past Carl's Jr. on Friars Road and the Shell Gas Station at Zion Avenue and Mission Gorge Road, going on behind her to the schools. Imad socialized with James and his girlfriend (Linda) for drinks and dancing; they had a photograph taken of them at Club E and went on a shopping spree together after Imad gave James that $2,000 he had promised. Now James kept calling Imad about when they would do the hit. James called Floyd and left him messages. Floyd did not answer.

"Floyd only trust me," Nick told the interviewers.

James was not working at Cliff Brown any more but he came there and bothered Imad always wanting to know when they were going to do the hit.

About the last week in May, Imad told James he was not a killer and was backing out. James got upset and said, "Forget it." He said he was going to do it anyway with Linda's brother, a guy with long hair in a pony tail, who had just gotten out of jail six months before. Nick did not know him. Imad said, "Fine. Just leave me out." Next day at Cliff Brown, James visited Imad with the girlfriend's brother nearby. Imad again told James that he did not want to be involved. Nick called Floyd on May 30 telling him that they had killed Charlene. Floyd ordered Nick to meet him at the liquor store the next day.

Nick met Floyd at Hillcrest about 1:30 on May 31. They went to the bank and then drove to the parking lot at Hillcrest. Floyd gave $10,000 to Nick, insisting no one should be paid until he heard from the Police Department that his wife had been killed. Nick was to hold the money until the job was done.

Floyd called Nick and arranged a meeting at Denny's on June 1. When he arrived, he told the two Iraqis that Charlene was not dead. He knew because he had heard her voice on the phone that morning. He wanted his money back. Nick, always the trusted lackey, convinced Floyd to let him keep the $10,000 payment in order to give it to the hitters when they were successful.

"Is that the last time you saw him?" Mr. Bowman asked.

"Until later, when I did the thing for the police."

On the 6th of June Imad kept getting the Wah-ba code from James, but Imad did not respond. James came to the garage about 3:00 p.m. and said he killed Charlene, said he shot her four times and she fell forward. James was wearing a black T-shirt and was sweating.

James called Floyd and left him a message but got no answer. Imad called Nick several times. Nick left messages on Floyd's machine.

"And you heard your friend was stabbed, and that was back on the 12th?" was Bowman's next question. (he should have said the 13th).

"Yeh," Nick said, the question impacting him deeply. His remembrance of seeing the blood-soaked apartment on Georgia Street on the morning of the 13th silenced him with a sober note he would never overcome. *Poor Muaid,* he thought. *Those bastards have to pay!*

32

The Puzzle

It was a puzzling question to which the police had to find an answer. Who had attempted to stab this Iraqi victim to death and why?

When his neighbors at his building heard this mutilated victim Muaid, and called 911, there was extraordinary turmoil at that Georgia Street apartment. They watched wide-eyed as Muaid, still conscious, was carried out to the ambulance.

"I know one of the men who hurt me. Imad's Black friend (James) who is called Joey, I believe," Muaid muttered.

The police interviewed Miguel Garcia, the manager, and talked to other people standing around. The tenants were frightened and one in particular who lived in the apartment below #6 was afraid of jeopardizing her family and having to move. She told the police nothing. Later on she disclosed in a private conversation under the promise of anonymity that she had been horrified by the events of that night. Soon after the stabbing, she had seen blood dripping from her ceiling, grotesquely discoloring it drop by drop.

Muaid's injuries required six hours of surgery at Mercy Hospital's IC Trauma Unit. Dr. Dandan who treated him wrote: victim stabbed 32 times; one eight-inch puncture penetrated kidney; patient lost approximately ten pints of blood.

The police followed up on the crime immediately and Detective Al Rushing was in the thick of it, trying to protect the victim as well as solve the puzzle as to why these three men would have thought Muaid knew where their $70,000 was.

Only Floyd could have told him the real truth—that his hired assassins nearly assassinated him.

"Who has our money?" they screeched at the man who wanted his wife killed as they pinned him down on the now famous running track.

"You'll never get a penny if you kill me," Floyd pleaded breathlessly. "I'll tell you where to collect. Let me up," he ordered.

Floyd's face was hit hard and stung as he touched it. "Get the money from the Arab, but he isn't authorized to give it to you without a special message from me."

"What Arab?" they demanded.

"You know the one we met with," Floyd revealed. "I will only give him the okay when you leave. And then get the hell out of town!"

Thus Floyd averted his own demise. He flashed his crooked smile as he limped back to his apartment, thinking of how he could explain his condition to his parents who were visiting. His heart was thumping in his chest but he was sure these fuckers would never be back. Mark would call the police and these Lou would all be arrested and put in the stinky jail where they belonged. There was no way he could be connected to Mark or any of these low-life asses. The Iraqis and the Lou: they would have to take the fall. They fouled up royally, he thought. How could those idiots have missed when they were so close to Charlene? What asses they were!

The rest of the puzzle would have to be solved by Al Rushing and the San Diego Police Department. It was going to be very laborious.

33

Not Just Any Liquor Store

Nick gave Rushing and Bowman about all he knew regarding Floyd's insurance scheme and how the attempted murder had taken place. He filled in the blanks about Muaid. When it came to the liquor store, other than the fact it had been the scene of meetings and money exchange, he did not tell all he knew. He had stated that Tarak and Charlie bought the store from Floyd in November 1994, but details were never clear to him. Floyd acted like it was still his. He was rarely there, but that had been true all along.

Who really owned the store? Nick couldn't tell. He knew that Tarak was not the only one signing Tarak's name on checks. He knew money was going out of the store; he knew too many people were hanging around and getting a share of it. But Tarak's turning it back to Floyd in May 1995 was something Nick found strange. Tarak and Charlie told him to take a week off and while he was not there, they removed most of the store's inventory. Floyd took it over with hardly anything left to sell. Nick didn't understand anything any more. Still he probably knew more about what went on than Floyd did and he was only guessing.

Floyd was in a fog. Two big concerns took most of his brain space. One was the plundering wife whom he used to love, how she came into his life and how he could get her out of it. The other was how to stop losing money. Ever since the store had been robbed before Nick started to work there, Floyd had been deeply affected by a personal loss of money. How could a millionaire care that much about a few thousand dollars? Nick wondered. He had had trouble with Joe and Issa and Nick was instrumental in having them removed.

But Floyd's perception of problems at Hillcrest was secondary; what to do to Charlene took most of his time, energy and planning. This is what he talked with Nick about so much.

Floyd still remembered how Hillcrest became a major part of his life and the expectations he had.

♦♦♦

"It's the opportunity of a lifetime," Floyd had been advised. "Buy that store and we can both become millionaires in a short time . . . No, not from sales, from money coming in and going out . . . Don't play dumb. You know what the store would be a front for."

But in a very short time, since Floyd was not a well man, something told him everyone was out to get his money, especially Charlene. He struggled from the moment of his marriage until signing the "sales agreement" with Mustafa and Erikat in November '94 because even though he had pocketed a hefty sum, too many others were in on it, and were cheating him to boot.

He had to hide the money he received as payments in cash for fear the divorce action would, through discovery, force him to pay Charlene off.

Even Tarak would file documents to help him out; he would swear that Floyd did not receive any income from the store; the divorce action was hampering the closing of the escrow deal to sell Hillcrest to the new buyers.

But Floyd was in for even bigger financial problems!

♦♦♦

"This is your authority to sign checks on Hillcrest's business account at Union Bank," Floyd told Tarak. He just wanted the income and his cut in the Bee scheme and the eventual selling of the business to Tarak.

♦♦♦

"Omer, take care of this," Tarak told his kinsman. "I don't want this store. It is too much trouble. I just wanted to make a little money."

In January '95 Omer did sign escrow papers and Tarak and Atta were out of it. Hillcrest checks were being issued, many with forged signatures, to oil and gas companies, employees, friends of employees and cash for large sums of money. By April 1995 merchandise was being removed from the store. Nick confirmed this in court testimony. Floyd was being ripped off royally.

In addition a group of Middle Easterners sent several thousand dollars worth of money orders through the Western Union account at Hillcrest to their relatives in the Middle East. On April 28 a small truck backed into the entrance of Hillcrest Liquor and several employees began loading boxes of Hillcrest merchandise, the inventory. The store was cleaned out.

Nick summed up the Mustafa brothers' removal of goods from Hillcrest in April: "The Mustafas put one over on Floyd and cheated him out of lots of money." Since Charlie had told Nick to take a vacation from work next week (last week in April), Nick knew Tarak's declaration that he was no longer involved with Hillcrest Liquor's affairs after March 31 was a lie. Nick was suspicious. When he returned to work on Monday, May 1st, the shelves and racks were bare and the store closed. Nick phoned Floyd who was aghast when he saw what used to be Hillcrest Liquor, his store.

♦♦♦

During the three weeks in May when Nick worked again for Floyd, attention to the store was a joke. Nick was more concerned about how he and Imad would get out of the plan to do any kind of killing and still get money out of Floyd; he knew he was being used by Floyd as a go-between to carry out this insane desire to be rid of Charlene. Floyd was nervously awaiting the moment he would be free of the pressures of the store business and the claws of his wife. He made false court declarations that he had no money. At the same time he cancelled the escrow to sell Hillcrest to Omer. But his actions regarding his business backfired. He made himself liable for all the Western Union debts and late tax filings. He closed the store officially on May 24.

Near the end of May Floyd called Yusuf.

"Damned Mustafa who was buying Hillcrest Liquor from me robbed me blind, stole the inventory and then abandoned the store. I tried to make a go of it again this month, but I found out that Mustafa didn't pay the taxes for the first quarter of the year. I am going to lose my seller's permit. I paid off my loan on Hillcrest at Union Bank and don't owe anything on it. Do you want it back? You've still got the lease. I can recoup a little money and you'll get the store back for a song," Floyd proposed frantically.

Yusuf accepted. He filed with the San Diego Recorder's Office June 2, 1995, the initial document to repurchase Hillcrest Liquor from Floyd to whom he had sold the store in January 1994. This was Floyd's history at Hillcrest; his ownership was not only rocky, it was extremely short.

Floyd's arrest on June 21 came before he was able to carry out the plans that had been made for him. He was to leave San Diego on July 1 as John Roland. His unused ticket and letter of instructions were among the documents confiscated by authorities.

Although Floyd had had success in his money hiding plan and came out with a profit from the ill-fated liquor store business, he was not so lucky in his plan to escape the country. It was as though this Hillcrest Liquor store had sealed his fate. Still it was the DC Charlene he thought he hated most.

34

Too Hard to Forget

The events leading up to Detective Rushing's first call to Charlene were so rapid and dramatic that his notes and files became enormous, long before any resolution was in sight. He wrote down everything as a good detective like him would. Sometimes, he thought, details are too hard to remember.

As for Charlene it was a question of "too hard to forget." The crime against her, and especially the agony of having her life and her children's lives drastically disrupted and the waiting around to see some signs of justice consumed her.

Neither of them had knowledge of what Nick and Imad were going through. It would be only after a preliminary hearing in July that Mr. Bowman had spoken about to Charlene and an article in the *San Diego Union-Tribune* which appeared in December 1995 that she knew anything about Nick's participation in this affair, and Imad was a name totally unfamiliar to her. At the preliminary hearing she saw Muaid in a wheelchair and felt great compassion for him, but did not understand his involvement until much later.

As for Rushing, he began his investigation after his first interview with Muaid in the hospital. Through interviews with both Nick and Imad, Rushing found more and more details, incriminating not only to the three men who had tortured and left Muaid for dead, but to Floyd Mitleider as well.

He knew that Imad bought a car about two weeks after he got the $4,600 from Nick and that James assumed when he saw the car that Imad had been paid for a job that James and crew really did. It was the 12th of June. Imad got off work at 5:30, went home, took a shower and got dressed. About 5:45 he drove to friend Omar's apartment in Mission Valley. About 6:30 or 7:00 he and Omar drove to and ate at an Indian restaurant in Mission Valley. At 7:30 or 8:00 he dropped Omar at his apartment and drove to a liquor store off Balboa Drive where friend Mark Namer worked to talk to him about fixing his car. Then he drove back to Omar's and helped him clean his apartment and fell asleep there.

The next morning, the 13th, Imad went home. When he entered his apartment he saw it was all messed up with blood everywhere in the bedroom and bathroom. He called the 911 operator who told him Muaid was injured in a robbery and had been transported to Mercy Hospital. This information drove Imad and Nick into a frenzy.

It was on the 14th that Al told Imad about Muaid's having mentioned his roommate's Black friend Joey who had something to do with the stabbing. Imad reported that the only Black that both he and Muaid knew was James Smith. This facilitated the investigation.

As Rushing's investigation continued the next day, the 15th, he took Imad and Nick to the Georgia Street apartment. While they were packing Imad's clothes Rushing looked through a photo album on the table and found a photo of James. Detective Marino took the photo to the surveillance team at James' apartment. Then Rushing took Imad and Nick to James' apartment where James was identified by Imad and detained. A computer check showed two misdemeanors and James was arrested also for robbery. James signed a consent form to the police to search his apartment where they found between the mattress and box springs a blue-steel .25-caliber semi-automatic Lorcin handgun loaded with seven rounds. Marvin's implication in the criminal activity was soon found.

The police were sure that James Smith, Marvin Brown and a third assailant as yet unidentified were the perpetrators of the assault on Muaid. They needed more evidence to be able to charge Floyd for the solicitation and attempted murder which mounting evidenciary information showed he had committed. At this point Rushing made arrangements for Nick, as a cooperating witness and Floyd's "running buddy," to visit Floyd wearing a wire.

This was arranged for June 21st. And so it was that Nick told Rushing: "I went to Floyd's apartment and knocked at door. Floyd answered and told me, 'Let's take a walk.'" They went down the hallway.

The recording device was vibrating against Nick's skin and he was apprehensive. He hummed and whistled to relax and appear casual. After a few pleasantries they began to talk in earnest about the pressing problems.

Floyd: I went to fuckin' court yesterday because this fuckin' bitch . . .

Nick: Huh?

Floyd: Because these fuckers fucked up and didn't hit her.

Nick: Who fucked up?

Floyd: The guys who missed her.

Nick: How did they miss her?

Floyd: Three shots they missed her.

♦♦♦

Floyd: Yeah, because of this shit, she's filed papers against me in court yesterday. She had a fucking cop standing there like that.

Nick: Fuck.

Floyd: . . . They hired a private investigator. They're investigating everything. You. They're investigating everything and they think I've hired a hit man. So you got to get those fuckers out of town.

Nick: How? Because Floyd, they want to get paid.

Floyd: They what?

Nick: I know. They think they did the job. They did the job.

Floyd: You should've seen her yesterday.

Nick: So, she's not dead.

Floyd: No, I saw her yesterday.

Nick: Fuck, I mean, I'm willing to give your money back if you want. I have your $15,000.

Floyd: I'd like to have it back. I'm hurting for money.

Floyd's raving continued. He said "she not only hired a private investigator, she's trying to ruin me" because of this shit. He remarked "she's got the cops on my ass, has a vendetta against me, is checking into everything and everybody I know."

♦♦♦

Floyd: They're checking every fucking thing. The heat is on. Really, they might be watching us right now. You got to be careful . . . They probably got a tap on your phone.

He kept going back to the fact there was a private investigator checking things about him.

♦♦♦

Nick: Did she know, she know you the one who was hiring these black guys?

Floyd: That's what they think. They know about the insurance policy.

Floyd's panic was evident when he talked about his frustration with his phone, claiming he could tell when his phone was being tapped. He showed his vulnerability and total hysteria as he blurted out his concerns to Nick. He told Nick the police knew he was hanging around the criminal element and that there were certain lawbreakers at his store. "They mean you," he assured Nick

Floyd: . . . The cop told me, he goes, "I can, I can't tell you your arrest was imminent, but we have some good evidence." So. . . you gotta tell these fuckers this.

Nick: If they catch them, they catch you.

Floyd: Probably, if they squeal on me. These fuckers, if they wouldn't have missed, none of this would have happened.

Nick: If they wouldn't have missed, they would have killed her.

Floyd: The heat would have been on. But now it's worse.

Nick tells Floyd about the crime against Muaid.

Floyd: . . . from a knife? Oh, shit.

Nick: Mark's friend.

Floyd: Lou?

Nick: Yeh, Lou.

Floyd: The big Lou we met?

Nick: That who met?

Floyd: The Lou I met with Mark. I don't know what the Lou's name was. They didn't tell me a name. I don't know. Whatever, I don't remember.

Floyd thought of his encounter with the shooters and how close he came to being still another victim, but he knew better than to mention it to Nick. The bloody interlude this dumb Iraqi suffered was too bad, but, after all, it was his own damned fault for being at Mark's apartment

♦♦♦

Nick: They thought he had the money over at his house. They came in there and did it.

Floyd: Didn't you tell them the deal was not done?

Nick: They don't believe that. They just missed, Floyd. Anyway it doesn't matter now. The $15,000 to me, the $5,000 you gave Mark the first time, then the other $10,000 to me. If you want it, I can bring it to you.

Floyd again acted anxious to get his money back. He needed it, he said. Then he came back to his most strident concerns: Charlene and how she could hurt him.

♦♦♦

Floyd: She's got me by the balls. She can nail me for income tax evasion and all sorts of shit.

Nick: Income what?

Floyd: All sorts of shit I used to pull back in St. Louis that nobody knows about, that she knew about cause I told her. She wants me to pay her $30,000 for the divorce. I don't have $30,000 and I don't want to pay the bitch off. This is going to make it really miserable for me.

Floyd warned Nick several times to be careful, to speak Arabic and watch what he said and did. He said the restraining orders against him prompted him to take his money out. He got it out of the banks just in time. He was concerned that the sales agreement he had signed (under which Floyd was receiving $10,000 per month plus interest from selling Hillcrest Liquor) was known and the liquor license was under restraining order, that Joe would be getting the store back. But mostly he was incensed that everything about his life over the past five years was being investigated and Charlene was doing it to make his life miserable.

◆ ◆ ◆

Floyd: And I don't know if she moved out or not, but I haven't seen her around. You should have seen her yesterday at the court. I mean, she was like sittin' here, her lawyer beside her, her bodyguard, a real big guy standing in front of her. I was sitting there, and he was looking at me like this. My parents were here in town. They were with me. My mom said, "That's a fuckin' cop." They asked me to take a lie detector test.

Nick: Did you?

Floyd: No, not yet, because they will know. It makes me look as guilty as hell, but I can't take a lie detector test.

Nick: They know you pulled it.

Floyd: I know. I'm in deep shit.

Nick: You're in deep shit. We in deep shit. Plain deep shit.

Floyd: Those guys should get out of town.

Nick: They have no money.

Floyd: You didn't pay them anything?

Nick: I didn't pay them anything.

Floyd: Fuck'um. Mark knows where I live, doesn't he?

Nick: Mark, yeah Mark knows where you live.

Nick asks Floyd if he is looking forward to trying again to kill Charlene. He answers that "the heat is on," but maybe when it cools down, later on maybe, yes.

♦♦♦

Floyd: I wish you could tell those guys what happened, that they missed.

Nick: Fuck, I can't get ahold. If I get ahold of them, they get me.

Floyd's desperation was not helped when Nick told him he wished he had never met him.

♦♦♦

Nick: I wish you never came to me and told me, "Nick, you want to make extra money?" Fuck, just wanna make some money. Fuck, man.

Floyd: Yeah, I even called, before this happened, I tried calling the Priest.

Nick: The Priest? What happened to him?

Floyd: Nothin'. I put a call . . .

Nick: Do you know his number?

Floyd: Uh.

Nick: Priest number?

Floyd: I have to look it up. I don't know, it's not in my head.

Nick: Can you give it to me?

Floyd: When I find it, yeah. I don't know where it is. It's an eight hundred number.

Nick: You met with him more than twice. One time when you gave him that $2,500 tip.

Floyd: Oh, yeah, that's twice.

That Floyd was confused was obvious. He referred to three shots and that his lawyer found out from Charlene's lawyer because of this shooting the authorities are tapping phone lines. He was being investigated thoroughly and so was everyone who knew him. He said she filed papers against him because of the shooting. That was pure imagined chimera. No new papers were filed; only the old ones for dissolution. His mind was ablaze with horror for himself that came out of nowhere.

He was seething not only with anger but with absolute fear. After the SDPD had sent a police officer to question him he had become unraveled and had convinced himself they had much more information than they really did. He thought, for example, that the police had a partial ID on the license plate of the vehicle driven to kill Charlene. They did not.

Floyd was suffering from painful paranoia.

Nick was good. He got Floyd's involvement with the first "hired hit man" and the amount Floyd paid to Priest on tape. He got him talking about the details of his hit order and money paid. His comments about what Charlene wanted, for example, $30,000, were figments of his imagination. Information he said he got from his attorney was not accurate either.

Soon after Nick left, he went to the awaiting car Rushing had directed him to go to and this ended his responsibility.

Floyd was briefly relieved that Nick had visited him. He didn't have an inkling that he had only a few minutes of freedom left.

With the taped conversation between Floyd and Nick and the police having listened in from beginning to end, Rushing then began the arresting process. He had prepared for it meticulously hoping the whole thing would go off without a hitch.

For five days, June 17 - 21, Rushing's preparations for the raid on Floyd went on. As commander of the planned assault, Rushing had two teams, each with a sergeant and six detectives, at his disposal on standby. At 4:45 p.m., June 21, Nick Sitto was equipped with the body wire, a recording device for his safety and a device to record his conversation with Floyd. He was reminded about the kind of things he was to discuss with Floyd. Then he was sent off to Floyd's apartment. As Nick was knocking at the door, there were ten armed detectives in plain clothes, with body armor, in unmarked vehicles strategically placed at the perimeter of the La Mirage apartment complexes, with Detective Rushing listening to the recording, in case Nick needed help. Floyd answered the door and ushered Nick some twenty feet down the corridor because Floyd's parents were in the apartment. The two talked for half an hour about the arrangements for the hit, its failure, getting the hitters out of town and the stabbing of Muaid.

Nick returned to the police van and gave them the recorded tape. He was hustled away to a police squad car for his personal safety and to keep Floyd from seeing him when arrested.

Then the police officers got ready to execute a search warrant on Apartment #5213, 6418 Ambrosia Drive. All eighteen detectives and three sergeants were assigned different tasks. Wearing bright yellow raid jackets with the word POLICE in bold black letters printed on front and back, armed with guns and one with a shotgun and an iron tool to knock down the door if need be, these officers were Rushing's back-up as he knocked at the door. "San Diego Police Department with a search warrant demanding entry." The door slowly opened and Floyd stood there wearing a white long-sleeved sweatshirt, a red polo shirt, jeans shorts and tennis shoes. Rushing repeated the entry demand as the police rushed in with drawn guns and secured the apartment. Floyd's father and mother were seated in the living room, their faces pale with fright.

Rushing was proud that his planning had resulted in his achieving the desired goal: disabling Floyd. When he called Charlene after Floyd's arrest and she became jubilant, she had no idea of what Floyd was going through while Rushing interviewed him. But Floyd was in the worst pain of his life. This would be a day forever too hard for him to forget.

San Diego Police Department
June 21, 1995

Rushing began his interview with the usual preliminary questions and noticed an occasional quiver coming from Floyd's back which Floyd said was a spasm. The detainee was visibly nervous but put on an act of indifference

Almost immediately Rushing told Floyd why he was arrested and that there was evidence against him. Floyd said he was only guilty of loving his wife and not having it work. He accused Charlene of making up stories about him through vindictiveness. She was just mad that he would not go to counseling, he said. That was why she made up the spousal abuse story and accused him of being involved in the attempt on her life. His memory was so faulty, or his nerves so on edge he didn't care, but the promise he made about counseling occurred after his arrest for spousal abuse.

Rushing asked Floyd to give his side of the story several times. He stood by his statement that he had nothing to hide. He said he had a case of his own investigating the people in escrow who had been running his business and who had forged checks and done other illegal things like stealing through money orders. He told Rushing that he did not want to go into bankruptcy because it would ruin his credit for life.

Repeatedly he announced he loved his wife, but that he was not going to get anywhere near her. Once, he confessed, he did call her in a weak moment. He just had to find out how she was doing. He complained that his wife would not give him a break, had even called the police just because he did not move out right away.

The subject of a polygraph test came up. Rushing asked him: So if you did take a polygraph what do you think the results would be?

Floyd answered: "That's got me a little bit worried . . . could be a false poly, who knows? "

To all questions having to do with others arrested and the crime of attempted murder, Floyd hastily insisted he had nothing to do with it and if other guys said he did, they were not telling the truth. Rushing told him that others involved had turned in money which Floyd had given them and that made them credible. They could have just as easily run off with the money saying nothing to the police. Their honesty was in their favor. Rushing told Floyd he simply did not believe him. Floyd swallowed hard and tried to revive his former insolent persona. It seemed that each new thing Rushing told him made his attitude of innocence harder to maintain.

"Somebody claims they know me and I don't know them," Floyd repeated. "What is there I would worry about?"

Rushing outlined several times that if Floyd would cooperate it would make his case in court better for him. He told him he would probably be put in the same facility where others involved would be, and for his safety, Floyd would do well to tell Rushing what he knew about all this. Floyd called this extortion. If he went in the same cell with these guys who said they knew him, they might beat the shit out of him or even kill him, his words. He'd prefer not to be with them, of course. He asked about making bail and how long he was going to be held. He was alarmed when Rushing told him he would be arraigned in 72 hours and he did not think he would be allowed out on bail.

Before the officer put the handcuffs back on Floyd to take him downstairs to a cell, he asked him if he wanted to put on his sweatshirt.

"I guess it's a little cold," Floyd admitted. The truth was he was shaking inside from the chill. The deep shit he and Nick had talked about was worse than he thought. He was going to need help to clear himself and he hoped he knew where to find it.

35

Preliminary Justice

After Nick was questioned extensively on June 27, Imad met with Rushing and Bowman. He too recorded testimony regarding his part of the crime of conspiracy, solicitation and attempted murder for which Floyd had been arrested and was presently in jail. Their stories were remarkably alike. Imad and Nick were arrested on June 29.

The District Attorney filed a Felony Complaint against Floyd, James, Marvin and an unknown John Doe. A preliminary hearing was set up. A special hearing for Imad and Nick was held on July 24 and they were released on bail. They would be state's witnesses in a later criminal trial. They were also key witnesses for the prosecution in the preliminary hearing the next day.

San Diego Superior Court
July 25, 1995

Herb Bowman had his investigator, Ron Johnson, meet Charlene and her father when they arrived for the preliminary hearing on July 24. Charlene had left San Diego only a month before. She knew Bowman was a man uniquely qualified to handle this case. She was glad that Ron served as their guide and protector and enlightened them on the proceedings. Having Philip, her Dad, travel with Charlene made her feel secure; she would return alone because he would drive the Caprice back. It had been released from impound.

"You'll be the second one to testify," Ron told them. "First will be Alfuraiji. His part will take all morning. He is in a wheelchair and in bad shape."

Charlene and her father were waiting in the corridor outside the courtroom when they saw the mysterious Alfuraiji. Al Rushing wheeled him toward them from the side hallway. The olive-skinned, silky black-haired man, waiting to be called, was pitifully thin and drawn, appearing uncomfortable with suspended medications and intravenous tubes connected to him in his wide wheelchair.

Court was in session. Al wheeled Muaid in when he was called. Charlene's Dad was allowed to go on in the courtroom and sit in the visitors' gallery. Muaid Alfuraiji's testimony had to do with the stabbing incident which took place late at night on June 12. His wounds were recent, severe and not yet healed. He was still convalescing and would be for some time. Her Dad took notes as to Muaid's testimony because he knew Charlene was dying to know what was happening. She was not allowed in the courtroom until she was called to testify.

Meantime Ron and Charlene talked. He told her his job was great and he really liked running around town interviewing witnesses involved in crimes out of his department, Major Violations. "I do a lot of photo lineups," he said, "and checking out alibis. There are a lot of false alibis people use, but we can almost always disprove them. I guess I'd have to say most people tell the truth. But certainly not all."

"You're an actor, too?" Charlene asked. "Yeh, come to think of it, I have seen you in an episode or two of *Renegade*. You're pretty good."

"Thanks."

"We could say you work in real drama and make-believe drama, couldn't we?"

"Yes, that's true. Real drama, especially crime, is fascinating. Take your case as an example. Floyd certainly made this an intriguing tale."

"You had to be there," Charlene joked, though the remembrance of being shot at and the agony of the events afterward were not amusing.

Soon the doors to the courtroom crashed open. Al brought Muaid out and Charlene's Dad, Philip, followed.

"You guys go have lunch," Ron said. "I'll meet you back here about one o'clock. You'll see the signs; there are good cafeterias in all these court buildings."

"I'm not supposed to talk about Muaid's testimony," Charlene's father said at lunch. "But I can't see what harm it would do. It can't affect your testimony in any way. This young Iraqi was stabbed more than 32 times by three black guys trying to get $70,000 out of him. He just testified that he knew nothing about the money and he tried to tell them, but they hogtied him and literally butchered him. They left him for dead. He is lucky to be alive. He is still in terrible pain. Several times Rushing had to wheel him out to a bathroom behind the courtroom. He was so miserable. Those guys who did this are no more than savages. Alfuraiji can ID all of them."

"What did Floyd look like and what does this have to do with him?" Charlene wondered, knowing little about the complications of this case.

"I think the guys who stabbed him were the same ones who were in the car in front of Lewis Junior High six days before, trying to kill you."

"So, why did they think Muaid had the pay-off money? I don't understand."

"I think they believed his roommate had it."

"Who was that?"

"Someone named Imad. The interpreter said Muaid and Imad were companions, but I am sure he meant roommates."

"So this Muaid didn't testify in English?"

"In Arabic. A few times he burst out in English, but the whole thing was supposed to be in his native language."

When they got back to the courtroom corridor, Ron was waiting for them. "You'll be called next, Charlene."

"I know. Don't remind me. I am not too thrilled about going in there. Floyd will be there and I don't want to see him."

"He looked up at me when I went in," Philip said. "Just ignore him and do your thing. You want him put away, don't you? He looked pale, almost sickly this morning. But he still had that conceited demeanor."

"He can't hurt you now," Ron spoke up. "You're about to hurt him with your testimony. But the real fireworks will come when Sitto takes the stand. Floyd won't know what hit him."

"Who's that?" Charlene asked. "I saw his name in the Complaint." But at that moment the bailiff came out to call her into the courtroom.

Charlene Mitleider, called as a People's witness, having been duly sworn . . .

Bowman: Between the time that you came out here to San Diego and the time you were separated, did he [Floyd] ever talk to you about any financial problems he was having?

Charlene: Shortly after we were married he indicated that his business wasn't doing as well as he thought it would and there was a little money shortage.

Herb continued to question the witness about her husband Floyd's finances and his complaining about money. Floyd's arrest on felony spousal abuse and his threats filled the next moments of interrogation.

Bowman: Did he ever talk to you about getting an insurance policy on your life? Was this policy still in effect when you were legally separated? After you were separated in February, did you stay living at the La Mirage apartment?

To all these questions, an affirmative answer was given. Charlene began to wish they could get to the point. The procedure was unfamiliar to her and she knew she was not going to like it.

Herb got through all questions leading up to her driving routine to the schools and what she was doing on June 6. She described how she parked at Lewis Junior High and how the shooting took place, what her car looked like and what the shooters' car looked like.

Then came a series of questions about the man at the door . She had to look around the courtroom and find Black faces that looked similar to the shooter and the man at the door. She had found the one (James Smith) who she said in the photo lineup most resembled the shooter, but she had to say she was not 100% sure. In her heart she connected the man at the door and the shooter from the gray car, but could not in good conscience swear to it.

Defense attorneys began to bombard her with their questions, Floyd's attorney first.

Bishop: Why is it that you know February 17 is the date that Floyd abused you?

Charlene: I just remember it was three days after Valentine's Day.

Bishop: Did you tell the district attorney's office during that interview of June 23rd of this year that after the shots were fired you ran into the office for help?

Charlene: I believe so.

Bishop: Would it be fair to say that the following statement would be incorrect, quote "At that time security and the principal ran out and asked if I was okay?"

Charlene: Well, as I was running in, they came out to me. That's a correct statement.

The defense attorneys were grasping at straws. They had nothing to go on except what Charlene had told Mr. Bowman in his office before returning home. She didn't even know she was being recorded, but finding small discrepancies did not seem to alter the reality of this crime.

Rutman: If you look at the length of Mr. Smith's hair, could you tell me if the shooter had longer hair or approximately the same?

Charlene: Approximately the same.

Mr. Rutman was the court-appointed attorney for James Smith and his approach was not impressive. He asked Charlene to look at Mr. Smith's ears and nose to compare them with the unknown shooter. He wanted to know about the man who came to the door days before the shooting. He questioned the accuracy of the date and said Charlene had changed it since her statement in the DA's office. Charlene had not. Did Charlene have her porchlight on and was it light enough for her to see the man was wearing a green satiny jacket and which exit did he leave from? He asked about her identification in photo lineups of his client as being similar to the shooter.

Charlene looked at Floyd when Mr. Rutman said, "No more questions, Your Honor." Her Dad was right. Floyd did look sick, but he also looked angry and arrogant. He looked away when he realized their eyes had met. Charlene could tell he wanted to look confident and unconcerned, especially for her. She cared about him but could not allow herself to dwell on that. In her mind the question should be simply put by the judge: Did he try to have you killed? Answer: most definitely yes. Should he be punished for that? Answer: Of course!

What a relief when Mr. Martin, attorney for Marvin Brown, said what was to become Charlene's favorite phrase: No questions, Your Honor.

Ron asked them if they were ready to go back to the hotel. Philip rather wanted to stay and hear more testimony, but Ron said it would be going on for one or two more days. They needed a ride and were leaving the next day anyway.

"Thanks for taking care of us," Charlene told Ron. "My flight leaves in the morning, and Dad will drive the car back as soon as it's released to him."

"I'll take you to the airport. And the car will have some putty and paint filling in the bullet holes before you leave, Phil."

Philip made it back to Missouri with the damaged Caprice. Charlene's parents had it fixed and repainted completely, then brought it to Charlene to continue driving. It was like an old friend, a part of her salvation. Mr. Bowman had said the bullet fragments were only inches away from where Charlene's head probably was. Thank God it was an older model with heavy firewalls which the bullets could not penetrate.

Brach was still working on the case, though Charlene's parents told him they could not pay him any more money. He wanted to stay on the case so badly that he gave them a promissory note for the rest of the money they paid him, saying they would get it back with 10% interest by next February. He could not locate Frankie at first with all his usual tracking devices. The friend seemed to want not to be located.

Among the things uncovered by the private detective was that Floyd's father had once been in federal prison for an offense having to do with an application for a VA loan. The man who had taught his son unethical business practices had done time himself; Charlene remembered that Floyd did not like to admit he was like his father. He did not like the sound of the word prison either.

Charlene had taken steps not to be found in a town away from St. Louis, but it was not a normal life. The anticipation of getting all the bad guys convicted and put away was at the top of her wish list. Next up was a way to rid herself of sleepless nights. If she had a good night's slumber, then she might feel free again.

36

Interrogatories, Lies and Crime Marches On and On

At first Charlene could not adjust to the new pattern of life back home. It was too unsettling. There was no divorce forthcoming and no criminal trial. The trial date for the dissolution of marriage was continued again and again. It seemed that Floyd's arrest had given him the chance to prolong the divorce proceedings; that did not seem fair. Floyd's attorney used his incarceration as an excuse. The discovery was still going on, or at least that is what Charlene heard. Brach said he was running all kinds of computer searches

Brach kept implying to Charlene and her parents that the efforts to nail Floyd had paid off: He had been arrested and bound over for trial. "I told you our investigative procedures would come through," Brach bragged. "At least Floyd is where he belongs." The strangest thing of all was that Chelby wanted Charlene's family to write to the San Diego Police Department and tell them that he was instrumental in the arrest of Floyd and that he deserved a commendation. The same man who would not even return a phone call to Charlene's mother did not deserve anything from them.

Brach claimed that his sleuthing skills would pay off as well. He would take care of everything if Phil and Dorothea would just keep on paying him. He came by asking to borrow more funds from them on a regular basis; his agency needed money for many mishaps and projects. They were beginning to suspect his agency was not entirely on the up and up. The business he ran was not a well-run establishment and had produced few complete reports.

As for the divorce, the same sort of delays occurring in the criminal trial were taking place. A court date in October was the latest set for the criminal trial. The waiting was oppressive.

Brach found out that a new defense attorney had been retained for Floyd by none other than Frankie. In fact Floyd would have at least two other lawyers besides Bishop.

Herb Bowman had been going over evidence seized when Floyd was arrested, preparing for the trial. He called one day wanting to know who Load was. He was quite surprised to find out it was a dog. "Are you sure that's all it stands for? Could it be a person you know?"

"If this has anything to do with Floyd, knowing his penchant for codes and secrecy, it could mean something entirely different, but all I really know is Load is Floyd's dog and his other best buddies."

"This has to do with something we found in Floyd's safe. It may come up in the trial. Do you know John Roland?"

"No, I don't think that is the name of any of Floyd's friends. It could be an alias for his friend Frankie, I suppose. What is it on?"

"It has to do with a ticket to the islands."

"Do you mean Hawaiian or Bahama Islands?"

"I'm not sure, probably the West Indies."

"If I think of something, I'll call you."

"Are you all set to come out for the trial?"

"Yes, but I would like to see a transcript of the preliminary hearing. I felt unprepared at the preliminary because I didn't know you were recording me and that all the defense attorneys knew everything I said."

"I can get you a copy of your statements made at the preliminary hearing, but not the whole thing."

Unbelievably Floyd seemed to be carrying on business as usual. He had sold his store back to Yusuf and Charlene did not understand what happened to the other *sale* to Tarak and why the final sale had not been blocked under the restraining order. She was told the store's liquor license was being held in trust for her. Floyd's sale was being called a *default* sale but the only thing Floyd defaulted on was his rental lease.

Charlene's parents had a phone call from the San Diego business landlord of Hillcrest Liquor to whom Floyd supposedly owed money. He told Dorothea he would sue for it in Small Claims Court and would win; since Floyd and Charlene were married at the time of the indebtedness (and in fact, they were not divorced yet), Charlene would be equally responsible. He threatened there would be other debts, too. Papers were served on Charlene through her parents, not even in the town where she was living. Charlene's father called the DDA for advice. "This subpoena was served on you improperly," the District Attorney said. " Send it back to the issuer. Where it says Address Unknown for Floyd, tell them his address is San Diego County Jail." The court was not informed.

The divorce attorney had told Charlene she could have Floyd's famous Grand Marquis if she wanted to take over the payments. Floyd had made the financing arrangements in St. Louis through a credit union. Charlene asked her mother to call about it.

"Yes," said the credit union representative, "the car has been repossessed and can be purchased. It's out in San Diego at a dealership. You cannot take over the payments unless you are a member of the credit union."

When Dorothea asked about the price and the mileage, the rep said, "we are taking bids on it. The Mitleiders have made a bid but it is ridiculously low. I told them I was sure sorry their son is out there in California in a hospital."

Lies, lies and more lies. For Floyd's parents it was less embarrassing to tell people Floyd was in the hospital than to say the truth: he's in jail awaiting trial; he tried to have his wife killed.

Between Floyd's interrogatories and lies told in all his declarations and all the other ranting done by the people Charlene's parents had paid to help them, it was hard to see if anything true had ever been said.

The divorce was continued and Charlene did not really understand the reason. She was disappointed that Floyd's lies about his finances were not recognized. Early declarations showed his assets outweighed his debts by more than $300,000. Now, only a few months later, following his arrest, he appeared to have nothing.

The TV was on and Charlene heard this answer on Jeopardy: "Ananias," to the question: "Who was the biggest liar in antiquity?" A converted Jew thrown into a bonfire for having lied to St. Peter, they said, from the Bible, Acts 5, 1 - 10. Not so, Charlene judged. The biggest liar is not Ananias, she contended, it is Floyd. Judgment day for Floyd may change Biblical history.

"Do you realize how long this O.J. trial has gone on?" Charlene asked her mother in early October when she called. "I think closing arguments are over now, finally."

"Oh, yes. I heard today that the jury will begin deliberating tomorrow. Then at least there will be something else to watch on TV."

Charlene's parents were to come to her hideout apartment within the next few days. Her Dad was going with her to the trial and her Mom was to stay with the girls.

Charlene had accepted the fact that the trial would not take forever once it got started. That would be soon, according to all her "advisors" and when it ended, most of her fears would be alleviated.

On October 3, the jury reached a verdict on the O.J. trial.

"Can you believe this?" Charlene screamed at her mother emotionally. "Four hours of deliberation after eight months of trial proceedings; how can this verdict be right?"

"You saw what people were saying about it on TV. Geraldo said it was a travesty of justice. A whole lot of people think no one was ever as guilty as O.J. I've even heard people will be out to kill O.J."

"What if Floyd gets off? He is going to get the best of lawyers, I know that. Of course, he has no money according to his court declarations."

"Any attorney he gets will be better than the attorney representing him at the preliminary. The DA doesn't seem to be worried about getting a conviction on Floyd," her mother told her. "When I talked to him last time, he said the only thing missing is that third hired killer."

"And a sane jury."

Six days after the outrageous Simpson verdict of Not Guilty, Charlene's parents arrived. They were barely inside the door when Herb called Charlene again. The trial would be continued until January 1996. They had caught the third shooter and would be having a preliminary for him. He had a connection to Marvin; they had been in a gang together a few years earlier.

All the bad guys would be tried at once.

And Floyd, though incarcerated, had new special interrogatories served on Charlene. As far as she could tell what he really wanted to know was her location. There were questions about her mental health, that of her children and to what degree the marriage to Floyd had been responsible for any health problems.

"He wants to evaluate what he might lose in a civil suit," Brach said. "He might want to make a settlement offer which, if you accept it, would prevent your filing a civil suit against him."

Charlene just wanted to get Floyd's trial behind her, but even more importantly, she wanted to be divorced from him. He had not paid spousal support. He owed her that. He owed her something, Having to respond to the interrogatories, Charlene knew now without a doubt that all Floyd really wanted was to know her whereabouts. He was tracking her down just as he had Pat. The shocker was that even though he was in jail, he had the right to harass her.

Brach tried to report to Charlene as to what was going on in San Diego, but she had very little information.

Her mother contacted the Victims' Advocacy Program in San Diego.

"I don't know why we haven't heard about Charlene's part in this case before," said the director, Julie Bolton. "We have already been assisting Muaid Alfuraiji. He was a victim of a crime in this same case, you know. We'll send your daughter an application for medical assistance."

"Good," Dorothea told her. "She can use the help. So far she has received nothing, no assistance, no compensation nor even any good advice."

"If we had known, we could have put her up in a hotel after the crime. We will offer her someone to accompany her when she comes out for the trial and give her some protection. That's the kind of thing this office does."

"I don't know why the police or the attorney could not have told us this," the worried mother said angrily. "Our daughter was really left out there on her own. She has been the victim of more than one crime."

Except for private protection we arranged for her, there has been nothing, no one, but us. I hope the State of California can at least get her some counseling."

No one had told her she could get help or counseling paid for through the Victim's Advocacy program. Everyone had assumed that her parents had an unlimited amount of money and would pay for it.

Advantage was definitely taken of her concerned parents, senior citizens..They even knew this was true, but would do anything to safeguard the interests of their daughter and granddaughters.

Charlene wasn't sure counseling would benefit her now. Floyd was in jail, but not convicted of anything.

And he was putting out feelers trying to locate her.

"You can't hide from me, you DC. We know your social security number. We'll find you." These imagined words haunted her nights and robbed her of much-needed sleep. Counseling was worth a try.

37

Alone

Charlene saw one psychologist before filing the application for medical assistance through the Victims' Program. She liked Connie very much; because she told Charlene she would get stronger every day by going over what had happened and forgiving herself. She understood.

"It takes time," she assured Charlene, "to stand back and look objectively at these traumatic moments. We tend to internalize unpleasant events. Opening closed doors lets those dark memories out and makes room for new and better things in our lives."

In one of their sessions, Charlene began to think about Floyd's paradigm of fitness activities; he must be missing having a workout room and a running track handy. Cycling was essential to his well-being. It came to her that Floyd, since he admitted the strenuous exercise so many hours a day was pure torture to him, did it for a good reason: it was easier to use up his physical strength, making progress as he did to the goal of a fit body, than to face the truth about his mind. He *knew* there was a problem: that he could not keep promises and commitments, that no matter how much he wanted to be a happily married man, even maybe a family man, his inner being would not let him. The same barrier raised its head each time he thought he had conquered the obstacles and could proceed. "You are going to see a completely different Floyd from now on," he had sworn, "not the old selfish one."

This was a conclusion that made sense to Charlene and helped her with answers to the obscure questions that plagued and mocked her.

Connie guided her to that conclusion. She did that much for her, giving her a glimmer of hope that counseling could have some good results. But Connie's office was so many miles away from her town that she was forced, after the second session, to find someone closer. Dr. Straub*, too, each week she saw him gave her more strength to go on; but riddles were whirling in her mind.

"There is so much I don't understand about what happened."

Charlene knew every word of the drama between Floyd and her, but how "Arabs" were involved, why Muaid was nearly killed, and how her murder was planned were fuzzy areas, giving her a shattered view of parts of her past that were vitally important.

Foreigners were a big part of this, she knew from reading the Felony Complaint sent to her before the preliminary hearing last July.

"Arabs" worked for Floyd at the store, had owned the store before him and were buying it back again. Two men with foreign names had taken money from him to help him find someone to kill her. She knew about foreigners from the Middle East; after all, international students in their home or at their gatherings had taught her a lot about their ways. She had wondered about this before when Floyd had trouble with Issa.

Among the students she had known were men from India, Bangladesh and the Middle East who always seemed alike in many ways. Those who were Muslims were, when newly arrived, reserved, polite and often reverent. One of the international students had introduced her to Omar Khayyam whose verses she read but understood only superficially. It was somehow romantic nonetheless to read his words and one verse remained with her and gathered meaning when her relationship with Floyd had ended and she reflected on foreigners involved.

There was a Door to which I found no Key;
There was a Veil past which I could not see;
Some little Talk awhile of Me and Thee,
There seem'd—and then no more of Thee and Me.
Rubaiyat, Omar Khayyam.

She remembered a student named Rajab who kept quitting his jobs as orderly in hospitals because the "Jew Doctors" were unfair. In so many cases, there was an unspoken hatred of Jews. Charlene was too young to be totally wise about these prejudices, but she had to wonder how tolerant these "Arabs" were.

From the names she had seen and heard about in the commission of this crime, she believed some might still be deceptive and controversial and may have duped Floyd If so this was what Floyd deserved. Like his tendency to brag and to change his mind in the middle of a decision, it was a fatal flaw to be scammed by people others would have distrusted- just because they flattered him. It had to come from something imbedded deep inside his spirit that he cried out for admiration.

She had known students who used their "friendships" with Americans to get whatever they wanted: favors, sex with unsuspecting American girls, money. Only her strong faith and surroundings deeply entrenched in tolerance produced forgiveness in her heart. With incredible naïveté Floyd may have allowed himself to be taken in by the *charm* of some of his associates thinking there would never be anything to forgive. He should have listened to Charlene.

"I can only try to help you understand Floyd," the new doctor explained. "You have told me his manner and his treatment of you. We will get into his personality in some detail."

"I want to know what I did to make him want to kill me."

"We'll explore the possibilities in our sessions. But you must consider that he may have planned for this all along. What you did or said may have had nothing to do with it."

In December a newspaper article was published in the *San Diego Union-Tribune*. Lailani's grandmother sent a copy to Charlene. In it she learned more about who the so-called Arabs were and what roles they played in the crime.

Two employees at Hillcrest Liquor had scammed Floyd out of $15,000 with a promise of more to come for Najah Sitto who was originally approached and would receive a finder's fee. Najah and the other, Imad Aqili, claimed they never really intended to kill anyone. They just saw an opportunity to take money from a man who seemed willing to throw it away. This was as Charlene suspected, money hungry people Floyd did not bother to investigate. Money, not devotion, motivated these employees. Charlene visualized Floyd out of his head at any kind of money loss.

The article went on to say Najah seemed to know Floyd very well. He said Floyd only wanted Charlene for sex. He painted a picture of her as a very easily duped woman. As she read it, it made her feel like a small child being punished for not listening to the teacher. Where did this Najah get his information?

As Charlene and her Dad had already surmised, Muaid was Imad's roommate, said the article. The three hired killers came to collect their $70,000. When Muaid did not, could not, accommodate them, they brutally stabbed him. When Najah and Imad found out what happened to Muaid, they went to the police station. Najah turned over $4,500 of the money they had been paid by Floyd and told the authorities the whole story. These details began to form the picture in Charlene's mind of what had happened up to and even after the attempt was made on her life.

"Charlene," the voice on the phone was saying, "I just finished reading my copy of the article. I think I know who Najah is. I never knew about Imad before, except what Dad heard Muaid say," Mom said excitedly, "but I'd bet you a trip to Disneyland that Najah Sitto is the real name of Nick."

"H'm. Yes. Now that you mention it, that's who it has to be. Nick was always Floyd's Number One Flunky. I never knew his real name. In the article he is quoted as saying he never intended to kill me, or find anyone to kill me. He only wanted the money. Greed again. Everyone wants money. Floyd lied about Nick, trying to make me afraid of him. I don't think he is really that bad, except that he believed too many things Floyd told him." There was a brief pause. "Come to think of it, Floyd may have believed too much of what he heard about Nick. Or else he made it up . . . to scare me."

Al called Charlene a week later and she asked him to verify their suspicions. "Yes, that's Nick all right. How well did you know him?"

"Floyd introduced us long ago. But I never knew his full name. And who is Imad ?"

"Imad also worked at the liquor store, but had only been working there a short time before the crime took place. He knew Tarak. There is a lot you should know about Imad."

"Little by little I am beginning to see the role people played in this thing. But I am surprised by Nick's action in that his coming to the police was of great benefit to me. I was always a little distrustful of him. He had that old charisma, but I still thought of him as something of a crook. I couldn't ever figure him out. Floyd made him seem like such scum. But, I should have remembered, Floyd thought everyone was beneath him."

"I can tell you, Charlene," Al went on, "that Nick told me he always liked you."

"Terrific," Charlene said sarcastically. "In that case he should have ratted on Floyd long before June 6. And if he had not taken the money he would not have had to turn it in to you."

"I assure you, Nick has no great respect for him."

In the same article Nick said Imad was given the famous photo of Floyd and Charlene under the heart. Then it was passed on to the shooters. That photo had played a major role in this conspiracy. Charlene was not forgetting who furnished it.

At their next session Charlene told the doctor about the newspaper article and how it made her feel.

"The more you know about this, the more healing will take place. You have been kept in the dark so far as details about the crime are concerned. You can use this new knowledge to cushion some of your pain."

Quiet Charlene felt so alone in her hiding place. She wanted to go visit her Aunt Bibbie who was now advanced in age and lived only a short distance from her. But she was afraid to venture anywhere; someone else might be looking for her to silence her; she did not want to put her aunt or any other relative or old friend in any kind of danger.

Her contact with her parents and brother was what remained to her of the outside world. Susie had made it clear that she did not want further contact with her after she called her with the news of the shooting. "Will says under no conditions would he ever allow me to testify for you in a civil trial." With that their closeness of many years ended. Charlene tried to understand. After all, Floyd was a threat to anyone close to her. It hurt to lose her friendship and she had been missing those long phone conversations they always had; but what hurt more was Floyd's prophecy. Frankie was a better friend to him than Susie would ever be to Charlene.

Near the end of the year Charlene's parents heard from the private detectives they had been paying that some strange things were happening with Floyd's finances. They did not know what to think, because their research had not always been accurate or correct. But one thing seemed to be true: a check for $15,000 had been used as an initial deposit to open an account for Floyd at First Interstate Bank in April. It was a check from Frankie with a memo notation: Loan/Load. When Charlene saw a copy of it she realized two things. The account was set up to add to the confusion about Floyd's assets. Before Floyd's arrest he had been seen at that bank. The inscription about Load probably signified that she had become a problem and there had to be a way to deal with her—with money. She was sure Mr. Bowman would be interested in this since he had already asked for her help to establish who or what "Load" meant. This code was getting a workout! From the poor innocent dog of Floyd's, living back home with his folks, to the nickname for buddy, it now had a new meaning. Take care of the "dog."

"Dogs never lie about love," she mused, realizing she was not a buddy (therefore she must be a dog!).

Thinking about the amount she also came to the realization that the loan amount was the same total that Floyd had given to the two Iraqis. According to the newspaper article they had been asked to make the arrangements for the killing. Instead they ripped off Floyd for $15,000!

So Charlene was alone in hiding and was living on the money derived from selling her house. She felt nearly penniless, unable to get a grip, finding herself at the bottom of the pit again, struggling to claw her way out. Her only consolation was that Floyd's pit was even deeper. She may have lost money, but he had lost something much more precious: freedom. He was nothing. A man awaiting trial for crimes that might put him away for a very long time.

Her children were faithful in their role as schoolchildren, always excited about homework or something going on at school. They were the lucid part of her.

"Mom," Tracie asked one evening, "what's this word: c-o-n-s-c-i-e-n-c-e?"

"That's conscience."

"It ends with science. Is it some kinda science, like general science we have in the school schedule?"

"No," Jericha answered. "This word doesn't have anything to do with science. But, if you're trying to learn to spell it, one way is to think *con* and *science*. That's how I remembered how to spell it. I don't even know exactly what it means. I think it has something to do with being awake."

"This word means feeling or knowing right from wrong," Charlene explained. "It is good to have a conscience. The word you're thinking of, Jericha, is conscious. It does sorta mean being awake. Unconscious means being asleep, like when you get hit on the head or something like that."

"Mom, does everyone have a conscience?" Jericha wanted to know, struggling to pronounce it distinguishably.

"Unfortunately no. Some people never learn the difference between right and wrong."

"People like Floyd?"

"You got it," she answered.

"It wasn't right not to let my friend Ramona come to our apartment in San Diego, just because she's Black."

"And it wasn't right not to let you go to the dentist when you had a bad toothache," Tracie recalled. "Thanks for helping me with my spelling words. Now tell me what does d-e-s-t-r-u-c-t-i-v-e mean?"

38

Definition of a Sociopath

Dear Floyd,

How do you like jail? Everyone knows you don't really belong there with all those Lou and Spiks. Is the jail luxurious like our apartment was, and are the fitness facilities nice? I remember how much you always liked running the track and yelling at me because I couldn't keep up. And bike rides? These amenities are very important.

And how about clean clothes? I hope the laundry there keeps you fresh-smelling and neatly dressed.

Are the meals prepared by master chefs? I do hope they make them fat free for you.

I bought a new area rug for my apartment yesterday. It is 6' by 8' and is really quite small, but I read in a magazine that most jails have cells 5' × 7' designed for two cellmates. My rug is bigger than your cell. I think of you when I step on it.

I know in the past I cost you a lot of money and my two children ate too much for lunch. Now you are getting free room and board and are saving a bundle. May you enjoy every minute of these accommodations. You deserve them.

Love,

Charlene

The letter had come as a result of the psychologist's treatment. "Write Floyd a letter and tell him what you are feeling," was the assignment Dr. Straub gave to Charlene. She felt some of her frustrations floating away as she wrote.

"That's good," said the doctor. "Your sarcasm affords you some relief from tension. You found several things to say that show his lack of appreciation for you. Being open and direct with him feels good, doesn't it?"

In other sessions they talked about Floyd's sexuality. The doctor said the December article in the *Union-Tribune* could have been right, that he really only married her for sex, considering his other personality traits.

"How could that be? Remember I told you about his history with prostitutes. If just for sex, he didn't need a wife. Prostitutes are available everywhere."

Dr. Straub advised, "You must be prepared to accept the possibility. I'm going to tell you why. You will have to accept this if you honestly conclude it is more than likely true. And you would also have to remember he is the loser. You have much more to offer than that. If he did not really see that, he never deserved you. He did deserve his fate."

He paused waiting for Charlene's comments. As usual he wanted her to talk. She had nothing to say. She was so flustered.

"Men live to ejaculate," the doctor continued. "That he had sex on his mind much of the time is not necessarily a sign that he had no genuine feelings for you. I am sure he did."

There was no resolution in what the doctor said.

Floyd had fooled her big time. He may have planned the murder for insurance money long before they married. Charlene could not make herself believe that. Instead she preferred to think, painful as it was, that early in their marriage when the store was not doing well and he was under the horrific pressure, not being successful-remembering how all-important money was—that he just began to crumble, and she didn't handle things right. All right. They could have split up; but Floyd had to make a profit from it. He had to see her dead, get that big money. He decided to follow his heart's desire for great wealth and get rid of her. That was his *modus operandi* before: anyone presenting a problem had to be eliminated. Only this time, it was not just a matter of getting out of his house. It didn't matter when he planned this. She was always willing to do her part. She told him so how many times, and how many chances did she give him? A million.

She was in the deep black hole again. Discussing the article and its implications put her there.

"When I see the light at the top and I'm trying to get out, as I climb the light gets smaller instead of bigger. I am desperate, frustrated because I can't get out. I just keep on trying, frantically."

"That's the whole thing in a nutshell. You keep trying and you do get out, right?"

"I am never sure I am really out."

"Do you know the term sociopath?" Dr. Straub probed.

"I've heard of it. Isn't it a person who has anti-social behavior?"

"It's much more than that. It is a person who has complete disregard of the rights of others. The sociopathic personality is unable to accept normal restrictions imposed by society. His needs and wishes countermand all. The world sort of revolves around him. He is lacking in compassion. He often goes to extremes to put down other people. He can be cruel and uncaring, though he may bury this trait so deeply you can't see it; on the surface he'll appear pretty normal."

"Floyd to a T."

"One characteristic of the sociopath is aggressive sexual behavior, starting in adolescence. I believe Floyd is a classic example of this personality type. You could not have done anything to change him on a permanent basis."

It didn't matter what the doctor and Charlene talked about. She was absolutely sure of only one thing. She could never trust any man again.

This made her a totally different Charlene, like a No Charlene, a woman with a different soul, a different identity. The new Charlene lost her tolerance, wanting to find a way to repay this man for creating a new kind of hell. Confusion and uncertainty reigned. It was impossible to get past this kind of turmoil. No one could help her.

Courtesy KGTV, Channel
10, SanDiego
Floyd Arnold Mitleider at
his sentencing trial.

Courtesy KGTV,
Channel 10, SanDiego
Lou Brown
accompanies and
comforts Charlene at
the sentencing trial.

Courtesy KGTV,
Channel 10, SanDiego
The other victim,
Muaid Alfuraiji.

Courtesy KGTV,
Channel 10,
San Diego.
Floyd Mitleider,
Marvin K. Brown,
Ivan Darnell Catlin,
James R. Smith, Jr. at
the sentencing trial.

Courtesy KGTV,
Channel 10,
San Diego.
William H. Kennedy,
Presiding Judge
at the trial.

Road signs to detention centers where all the defendants spent time.

New section of Folsom Prison, Represa, California. Among inmates at this correction facility is Floyd Mitleider.

Witness for the Defense whose testimony helped the Prosecution. Taken near the apartment on Georgia Street, the scene of the second crime.

University Avenue, the heart of the Hillcrest Section.

A gray Toyota parked here gave the police something to go on.

Pacific Bell truck with a slogan prophetic to Charlene. Star 69 played a role in her story.

Lewis Junior High parking lot, scene of the first crime.

Four shots rang out hitting the parked car where Charlene sat like a "sitting duck".

The San Diego apartment complex, LaMirage

Rental Office of LaMirage. Redezvous point for conspirators.

Hillcrest Liquor Store. Meetings in the back room and payments for a murder contract took place here.

Joe and Floyd. Owners of Hillcrest Liquor.

Restaurant where Iraqis, plotters and hitman met several times to plan Charlene's murder.

Cliff Brown Automotive. Two men involved in the crime discussed it while they worked here.

39

The Trial

A crime victim prays for quick justice and punishment for the perpetrators of the crime. In addition Charlene needed to validate her diminished existence. Helpless, she doubted the criminal justice system would work. Her family did not stand idly by; they were watchdogs. They wanted to learn How to Believe that good would prevail over evil through the criminal justice system as they observed it in action to the very end.

San Diego, California
Department 28
Superior Court SCD113632

The Case for the Prosecution
Who's Who

Presiding Judge
The Honorable William H. Kennedy

Prosecuting Attorney:

Herbert D. Bowman	Deputy District Attorney
	Major Violator Unit

Defense Attorneys:

Keith H. Rutman	For James Ray Smith, Jr.
Michael W. Owens	For Marvin K. Brown
Donald M. Rosenstock	For Ivan Darnell Catlin
Tom Connolly	For Floyd Arnold Mitleider
Lauri J. Stock	For Floyd Arnold Mitleider
James M. Bishop	For Floyd Arnold Mitleider

Witnesses for the Prosecution known by more than one name:

Najah Albir Sitto	known to Floyd and other non-Arabic-speaking persons as Nick, known to James Smith as Jesse
Imad Kassim Aqili	known to James Smith and non-Arabic-speaking persons as Andy, known to Floyd as Mark
Muaid Hawat Alfuraiji	known to James Smith and other non-Arabic-speaking persons as Michael or Mike

The January 1996 court date having been continued to April 18, the DDA kept in contact with Charlene. The long wait added to her anxiety. She doubted there would ever be a beginning to the trial, let alone an end .

The prosecutor was preparing his case and doing more detailed research some of which still involved the confiscated materials from Floyd's apartment, taken at the time of his arrest. Charlene was called in regard to this evidence. There seemed to be some connection between documents found in Floyd's safe and Floyd's friend Frankie whose name had been placed on Floyd's witness list. Mr. Bowman had called before about Load and a ticket to the islands, but only hinted at what his office thought Floyd might have been planning.

"We think we know a great deal about his friend's part in Floyd's business and the acquisition of the insurance policy. We'll see if any of his friends takes the stand for the defense. We will be ready to cross-examine. Even Floyd may take the stand, incidentally. That might simplify things," the District Attorney concluded.

He sent Charlene the new Felony Complaint which had changed since the preliminary. Ivan Catlin, the third complainant who had been previously listed as "unknown" was the new kid on the block. Ron Johnson had told Charlene that Catlin had been right there under their noses all the time. He had been arrested for a murder and was being held in custody at George Bailey Detention Center.

The charges against Nick and Imad had been changed since the preliminary of the previous year.

A deal had been made; their evil was less than Floyd's, by far.

"I sincerely believe what these two witnesses have stated," Bowman confided. "They corroborate each other's story and have from the beginning, even when they were separated. I know I may have trouble with the jury over this issue. The defense will come down hard on them, too. But they have convinced me."

Reading through the complaint was not pleasant for Charlene. There were counts and allegations including stalking, money given freely and generously by Floyd for his goal of her murder, secret meetings, diabolic discussions and the ultimate deal for $70,000. This was spelled out like campaign plans in a war. Meetings at Hillcrest, Denny's restaurant, some other arranged places and La Mirage were all specified in the written document. Charlene actually remembered seeing Floyd talking to some shadowy figures in front of the rental office at La Mirage. As she read she imagined hearing Floyd ask gruffly: *Who is this, Mark?* And Imad's answer: *This the guy I told you about. He do this job for you. We take care of your wife.* Charlene read every word of the long document with the spooky feeling that she had been there for all these events. She was the subject of the meetings, so she was there.

Mr. Bowman's office arranged her transportation. She arrived with her father in time for her testimony.

Pre-trial motions and jury selection of twelve jurors and three alternates had been done in the early days of May. The *voir dire* concluded, the trial could now begin. Charlene sighed, *Let the games begin.*

Charlene's Day in Court
May 6, 1996

Vivian from the Victim's Advocacy Program accompanied Charlene and sat with her on the bench opposite the big doors leading to the courtroom. Dad went in to listen to opening statements. When he emerged he had notes in his hands.

"I know I'll be called to testify early this afternoon," Charlene told Vivian shakily. "I wish it was all over."

"You'll do fine," Vivian assured her. "Your testimony went very well at the preliminary hearing," Dad said.

At lunch Charlene's nerves became even more ragged. "What did they say in there, Dad?" she asked anxiously. "I wish they would let me in the courtroom."

"They are just setting the groundwork more or less. Bowman, Rutman and Connolly, each expressing his estimation of the outcome of the trial, were the only ones to make opening statements. Owens and Rosenstock opted to give theirs at a later time. To me the most outstanding thing was the playing of a taped conversation between Floyd and Nick. It was part of Bowman's opening and it was very powerful."

Charlene was called to testify. She looked around for familiar faces. She recognized Connolly and Stock by her Dad's description and felt they were somehow diabolic simply because of whom they represented. Defense attorneys were sitting beside their clients making it easy for Charlene to know one from the other. Floyd whispered something to Connolly as she walked toward the bench. She looked straight ahead.

Judge Kennedy was a man of some years who had a slight build and was balding. Under the black robe and his soft façade was a figure whose talent in jurisprudence was immediately perceived. He seemed up to the task ahead of him: digesting the hours and days of argument pro and con dealing with not one defendant, but four, and tricky defense attorneys pitted against a dedicated prosecuting attorney. The chore of the jury was likewise mammoth; a glance at them was all Charlene allowed herself.

Floyd and the other defendants were dressed in white shirts, street clothes-quite different from their attire in the preliminary where they wore dark blue uniform jumpsuits. Floyd's eyes were on Charlene, she could feel them, as she took the stand. When she looked his way, his insolence filled the heavy air surrounding him, as though he was prepared to go on forever incarcerated. She could read his mind: he was satisfied he had gotten away with "burying" his and her money so Charlene could not touch it and that he was about to be acquitted of the crimes charged against him. James and Marvin looked massive beside Floyd, and Catlin was broader in appearance than the other three. Her fast glimpse of them did not distract her.

She swore to tell the truth, stated and spelled her name and concentrated on Herb Bowman's initial questions.

This time Charlene stated she was the ex-wife of Floyd Mitleider. (Dunne had gotten her a bifurcated divorce the month before.) There was a solemn milieu. No one smiled. Charlene was very uptight. It began:

Bowman: When did you first meet Floyd?

Charlene: December 1991.

Bowman: And where was that?

Charlene: It was through a St. Louis dating service.

Herb Bowman clarified all the background questions, about coming to California, when Floyd purchased Hillcrest Liquor, and their marriage. He asked about her children, ages 10 and 13, and when they were enrolled in school. As he asked about Floyd's financial concerns, Charlene's answers inevitably showed the traits of a man bent on making money and lying, a cheap self-centered playboy: no health insurance for wife and stepdaughters, just not enough money in those child support payments, no money available to replace Charlene's car or buy anything for her, really. Were there arguments? Did he decide to sell his business? Did he want to take out a large life insurance policy? Yes, yes, yes. Did he tell you about the arrangements? No.

First Connolly, then all the other defense attorneys, began objecting, especially about the arrangements to sell the store and about the insurance. Judge Kennedy stated the questions and answers about the financial pressures and insurance were applicable only as against Floyd. Conspiracy had not been developed as yet.

Charlene sighed deeply, sat up straighter and looked directly at Herb Bowman, eager for the remaining questions. Suddenly and inexplicably she changed from the fearful, tense, reluctant witness to a confident, powerful one. She realized she had the strength and authority to make the case go the way it should. She would tell the truth, give all the facts, and show by her words that this monstrous man should be convicted and removed from decent society. It was in her hands; she only had to speak.

Mr. Bowman had already told Charlene that Floyd's arrest for spousal abuse could not be brought up in this trial by virtue of some pre-trial motion made by his defense team as they bargained. It had been a part of the preliminary hearing. But when the jury would hear the words "restraining order," what could they believe?

Now questions centered on the insurance policy, beneficiaries and how they continued to fight after the policy went into effect.

Bowman: Was he ever abusive?

Charlene: Yes.

Bowman: What do you mean by that?

Charlene: Yelling at me, yelling obscenities to me, calling me names.

Bowman: What sorts of names?

Charlene: A D.C.

Bowman: What's that mean?

Charlene: A dumb . . .

They would not let her finish. Connolly said they had already addressed the issue and the judge agreed that this trial was not a divorce suit. Questions about filing for divorce and the issuance of restraining orders made it clear, if the jury was as sharp as it seemed, that Floyd had done something bad enough to warrant restraint. So, without even mentioning spousal abuse, Charlene had planted a seed of doubt about Floyd's behavior.

Bowman: Now, in the course of your marriage to Mr. Mitleider, did you get to know an individual by the name of Najah or Nick Sitto?

Charlene: Yes, I did.

Bowman: How did you get to know him?

Charlene: He was one of the workers at the liquor store.

The prosecutor asked about Nick, the hiring of a lawyer on her part and Floyd's, and the disputes over money.

Bowman:'s questions about the divorce proceedings were followed by others about Floyd and his attitude about the IRS. Connolly objected, but the objection was overruled.

Charlene: He told me that he had cheated on his income tax returns for the last few years.

There, she said it. The secret of his physically abusing her was kept, but Floyd's secret regarding the IRS was out. He could not part with his precious money by paying his fair share in the form of taxes. He thought only the masses should pay, his attitude being just like Leona Helmsley's. Floyd's system would never be fully exposed, Charlene thought, but she knew that he had a crooked associate who made out his income taxes on two different forms each year; one showing low income, to be submitted and on it taxes were paid; the other showing high income he needed to qualify for something like an expensive apartment at La Mirage or getting a loan on the purchase of a business. No one knew the truth about his income. It was like his two personalities wrapped in one package, tied with the strings of dishonesty. When Bowman asked Charlene about Floyd's term, or code, for African-American people, everyone objected. Connolly said it was irrelevant and Rutman said it was hearsay as it pertained to Smith. The judge overruled all the objections and Charlene got to reveal this code: Lou. She knew why Rutman objected. Floyd no doubt used that term in any statement he gave and it may have inadvertently implicated Rutman's client. To Rutman, James Smith was a client, but to Floyd, just another Lou, Mark's Lou.

Bowman got to the questions about the children and their schools as of June 1995. Charlene gave their names and the two schools involved: Lewis Junior High and Foster Elementary, the distances from La Mirage and her route in taking them and picking them up. She liked to come to their schools fifteen minutes early in order to get a good parking place, usually the same one every day, she testified.

Bowman: What car were you driving?
Charlene: A 1988 Caprice Classic.

She explained her routine of backing into the place in the row nearest the Lewis building so that her daughter would be able to see her and they could get out easily even though the parking area and driveway were congested.

Bowman: Now, did Floyd know the routine you followed?

Charlene: Yes. And he knew that I was there fifteen minutes early each day, yes.

Bowman: On June 6th, did you follow that routine? . . . Did you go to pick up your kids?

Charlene: Yes, I did.

Bowman: Were you at Lewis Junior High sometime prior to 2:00 o'clock? . . . Did you take your normal spot? . . . What happened next?

Charlene: Well, I was bent over, signing a greeting card. I knew I had a few minutes to kill before dismissal of school. And I saw a gray car in the driveway of the school stop in front of me, and I saw a gun sticking out of the window, the passenger window, pointed at me.

It was hard, almost impossible, to relive that moment. Her voice became unsteady, but unfailingly each frame of that incident happened again. It made her keep her responses truthful as she had sworn to do.

She told of seeing three African-American males in the car, the person on the passenger's side proceeding to fire four shots at her.

Charlene: I had my seat belt buckled on, but I tried to bend down as far as I could to save myself. . .my head wasn't completely under the dashboard, but I bent down pretty far. . . . I could see the barrel of it [the gun] . . . I couldn't see the handle or anything.

Charlene was asked to look around and identify anyone in the courtroom as a perpetrator of the crime against her, but she could only say James Smith looked similar. She described the gray car as a compact type.

Testimony went into details about the call she had received from Floyd on June 1 and the visit from an unknown Black caller before the June 6th incident.

Bowman asked the Court's permission to put up a panoramic photo of the parking lot of Lewis Junior High, marked as Exhibit 3. (Exhibits 1 and 2 were the tape recording and a transcript of it.) She stepped over to the photoboard and pointed with a ruler telling the Court what was there. Her knees were wobbly. She initialed the spot where her car had been parked and where the gray car was when she first saw it.

Exhibit 4 was a photoboard with three views of the Caprice Classic for her to identify. The same procedure was used to introduce a photoboard of two photos of a gray car, Exhibit 5.

Charlene was relieved that a 15-minute recess was announced.

♦♦♦

"Dad, do you think this trial is typical?"

"I wouldn't have any way of knowing. But it can't go as long as, say, the O.J. trial."

"But it might if everyone's testimony rolls as slowly as mine, it could go on for a long time."

After the recess Bowman continued to examine Charlene, this time regarding Exhibit 6, the application for and the life insurance policy for $750,000.00. He verified her signature and the fact that it had been in effect since November 1994.

Charlene was tired of questions and the defense people staring at her. It was not fair that she had to endure being in court instead of at home with her children, and that she had to be drilled and recall the most harrowing moments of her life in front of all these people all because a crime was committed against her. It was more vicitimization. Then came the cross-examination.

Rutman: You testified, I believe, that you arrived at the school at 1:30, is that correct?

And thus began Rutman's line of questioning. How far from La Mirage to Lewis Junior High could not possibly be important, especially since on the day of the shooting she did not go directly; how far away the dark gray vehicle was from her parked car followed and was a further waste of time, as far as she was concerned. He found some small discrepancies between his questions and her answers today and her answers at the preliminary hearing. She knew by Rutman's questions that the man in the green satin jacket who came to her La Mirage apartment must have been James Smith, because Rutman was so quick to ask if she could identify him. Rutman continued to try to impeach Charlene, afraid she might incriminate his client by her observations. His examination of her was an exercise in hollowness.

Owens: Referring to the black male that was at your door at 9:00 p.m., you stated on direct that you got a good look at him; is that correct? Was Mr. Brown that individual?

She could not say for sure that Brown was or was not one of the three individuals who were in the gray car. Owens wanted her to say it was definitely not Brown, but she couldn't. Floyd's "Dream Team" asked her questions next. Stock asked the questions but occasionally consulted with Connolly. Stock had a style Charlene abhorred immediately. She was unfeminine and unattractive with an "I'll get you, my pretty" attitude. Charlene could not help but wish for her a fate similar to her own: that of being stalked, abused and shot at, ordered by a sick man who professed love.

None of Stock's questions was earth-shattering. Charlene could not see how the number of seconds the gray car stopped in front of Lewis Junior High was significant or that the fact the insurance policy was mutual coverage lessened Floyd's intent.

Charlene hoped the jury was watching Ms. Stock as carefully as she. Stock referred to her notes and paced around a lot as she questioned Charlene about her conversations with Nick at Hillcrest; she implied by her questions that Charlene knew him quite well when just the opposite was true. She only knew what Floyd had told her and no doubt he was trying to make her believe Nick was another Frankie who would do Floyd's bidding. Nick was Floyd's "yes man" but not his friend, Charlene knew that now. Thus the idea was to make Nick's story about Floyd's crime seem like a made-up tale. Floyd's attorneys tried to make Charlene's testimony back up that theory. Charlene knew she would have to answer questions in that regard very carefully and of course, truthfully.

Stock: You've heard Mr. Sitto make derogatory remarks regarding women, haven't you?

Objection by Bowman: relevance. — Court: Sustained.

Her continued interrogation was based on very little but nosiness; how long had Charlene lived in St. Louis; had she really wanted to come to San Diego; had she had reservations about moving to San Diego; did Floyd and she have arguments during their two-and-a-half year relationshp prior to marriage; had he once broken up with her because of arguments before their marriage. But the big question she asked Charlene would never have answered.

Stock: And you are currently residing back in St. Louis, is that correct?

Objection by Bowman: relevance.

Court: Yes, sustained.

They thought they could force Charlene to reveal her place of residence by asking about it in court. As hard as Floyd was trying to get this information, Charlene felt sure she had succeeded in keeping herself under cover.

Stock's questions sounded more like what Charlene had expected to hear in a divorce procedure, but no one objected. She thought this unfair, since Connolly had objected when she wanted to tell the court about Floyd's verbal abuse. And as the defense attorney's questions continued it was clear Floyd had prompted her.

Stock: And you hired a private investigator to look into his business dealings prior to the time—look into the dealings that he had been involved in before the two of you got married; is that right?

Charlene: No, I did not hire an investigator.

Stock: Your attorney did that, is that correct?

Charlene: No, my attorney did not.

At this point, Stock flipped through her notes frantically, having not heard from the witness the anticipated answer.

Stock: Did you hire a private investigator to assist you in your divorce proceedings?

Charlene: I've never hired anybody.

Stock: Your attorney's never hired a private investigator on your behalf?

Charlene: My attorney didn't hire anybody. I myself did not hire anybody.

Stock: Did anybody hire a private investigator to look into any issues regarding your divorce?

Charlene: Yes, but it was not by me.

Stock: Okay. Who hired the private investigator?

Charlene: My parents did.

It had been great fun watching her sweat it out. Charlene was surprised that the hiring of a private investigator was known to Floyd. She thought Brach had been discreet. His defense attorneys were trying to make a big deal of this.

Stock: Did this private investigator ever accompany you to court during the divorce proceedings?

Charlene: Not this particular investigator, no.

Stock: Did any private investigator that was investigating your divorce come to the divorce proceedings with you?

Charlene: Yes, after the shooting, for my safety.

Stock was confused and frustrated but went on with incorrect information Floyd had supplied. She implied Floyd had made a lump sum settlement offer of $50,000! Charlene found that hilarious. She had never heard from her attorney of any settlement offer and rather believed that no such offer had been made. This was all part of Floyd's lies.

Remaining questions about Charlene's being frightened by the hang-up phone call and the man coming to her La Mirage apartment were as meaningless as most of Ms. Stock's inquiry. The hang-up call from Floyd was another violation. She was proud of herself for having learned the past this way: "The sun and the moon tell the future. Star 69 tells the past," says a Pacific Bell slogan, so personally appropriate to her. The man at the door was a Lou. Charlene had a question which would never be answered: who was the *someone* in the corner of the porch.

Stock and Connolly had a discussion off the record and decided to ask a few more questions. It was unproductive as Ms. Stock proceeded, trying to put blame on Charlene—for not liking La Mirage, for not appreciating her generous, caring husband, for not providing enough financial support for the two stepchildren. Charlene hoped the attempt to make her look like a gold digger failed as miserably as her attempt to make Floyd look like a typical husband.

Donald Rosenstock was her next questioner. It was his hope to establish there were only two shooters in the gray car, excluding his client of course.

Rosenstock: And you indicated that there might have been a third person?

Charlene: No. I indicated that there was a third person.

Rosenstock: And the age of the person that you do recall was someone who appeared to be in his teens; isn't that true?

Charlene: No. I said possibly a late teen or early 20's.

Rosenstock went over the same material; the age of the men in the gray car, skin color, was the man at her door his client, Catlin; could she identify him as anyone involved in this case.

Charlene truly wished she had observed more carefully when the gray car pulled up in front of her. This whole trial could probably be expedited by her saying: Yes, these are the three perpetrators, X Y and Z. And it was Z whom I saw through my peephole. But she could not be sure and she said so. Her inner being cried out: They are not the real demons here; it is Floyd. He caused it all.

Bowman had a few more questions on redirect.

Bowman: Were you looking through a keyhole when you made those observations?

Charlene: I was looking through my peephole.

Bowman: Your parents hired a private investigator, is that right?

Charlene: Yes, they did.

Bowman: Was there some point after the shooting where there was a divorce proceeding and a private investigator was there?

Charlene: Yes, there was a time prior to Floyd's arrest that my parents felt that it was better for me to be accompanied by a private investigator to a - it was actually a spousal support hearing.

Bowman: And at that hearing, was Floyd present?

Charlene: Yes, he was.

Bowman: And was this private investigator in view of Floyd?

Charlene: He was in view of everybody there.

Bowman wanted to know what she meant by being frightened after the separation. She told the court Floyd had a temper and had threatened her in the past. Mr. Connolly jumped up in his objection, asked and answered, not relevant, but the Court overruled.

Bowman: Did he verbally express anger at you in the past?

Charlene: Yes, he did.

Bowman went into the finances, the money Charlene had contributed to the marriage. She had wanted to contribute to the marriage, she testified. Secretly she was acknowledging to herself that she was a terrible fool; after all she had given, she had nothing and her parents were straining their finances to help her. It should not be this way.

The judge excused Charlene from the witness stand. Because of arguments from the defense attorneys, she was not allowed to stay in the courtroom even though Bowman did not think it likely she would be recalled. Defense attorneys probably thought she could clear up too many of the mysteries they wanted to be left as such.

So again Charlene was to be kept in the dark about the remainder of the testimony. She felt as though she was what the trial was all about, in a way. But as such, she could not be clued into it. It was not fair.

"Thanks for being here with me," Charlene told Vivian. "I have to go home tomorrow. I want to go, but I also want to stay."

"I know what you mean. Good luck on the outcome of the trial," she said, "and with getting on with your life."

That evening Dad got out his notes from the morning session and told Charlene what she missed.

"Bowman has the burden of proof, so his opening statement was lengthy. It was also riveting. He described Floyd as a greedy, cowardly type who married you and then used you as a pawn. He played a cassette tape that was recorded June 21, the same day Floyd was arrested. It was a conversation between Floyd and Nick."

"When Rushing called and told me of Floyd's arrest, he said they had the evidence they needed. Must have been this tape."

"Nick must have worn a wire. He pretends to be a friend who knows all about Floyd's scheme and wants to help him out. Floyd says in a spiteful low-key voice, 'I told those fuckers how to do it, but they fucked up. They missed.' He talks about money paid, the insurance policy and his willingness to try again later. He and Nick use the f-word constantly and shit frequently, like two uneducated mafiosos. You could tell by his voice how afraid he is and how worried he is about the three Black guys. He wants to get them out of town fast. He calls you a fucking bitch throughout the conversation. He also thinks you have the upper hand. He says, 'They got me by the balls,' and that because the attempt has been made and failed, he is in big trouble which he called 'deep shit.' This tape is explosive."

"I want to hear that tape," Charlene said sternly. "I'm going to ask Herb to give me a copy of it."

"He figured to profit from your death in addition to saving himself the price of a divorce settlement. He mentioned that his phone was tapped and that Nick should speak Arabic when he talked to Mark, that's Imad. You know. He sounded desperate."

It was hard to listen to the details, but at least Charlene now understood better Nick's part in the murder plot and what appeared to be a sincere endeavor to help the authorities prove their case against a man he did not really like. Her suspicions about Hillcrest Middle Eastern employees not liking Floyd were right. When Rushing referred to CWs, cooperating witnesses, he meant Nick and Imad. They had testified at the preliminary hearing and would be the most important witnesses in this trial. They were the ones who could nail Floyd. Their testimony was what Ron referred to as the "fireworks" that would do Floyd in.

Charlene was glad Al Rushing had told her of Nick's attitude toward her. Now she was sure Nick would not do things for Floyd. It was all in Floyd's mind. People were deceiving and fleecing Floyd, even more than she suspected before. Would he ever see that his employees and their associates had been the ones after his money and not Charlene?

"Bowman concluded his opening by saying there will be no doubt in the minds of the jurors that Mr. Mitleider solicited and conspired to have his wife killed out of pure greed and selfishness. He is as guilty of attempted murder as the three who did the actual deed," Charlene's Dad read from his notes quoting Bowman.

"A normal person would have been embarrassed to hear himself say the things Floyd said on the tape," Charlene remarked. "He has to have been shocked at least. I am sure he was rehearsing his line, 'I'm fuckin' innocent.' He had to keep his mouth closed, just sit there and listen, but he was erupting inside."

"I could not see any change in his expression. He did share a short conversation with Connolly from time to time," her Dad noted.

He described Rutman's opening, starting with *"Oh, what a tangled web we weave when first we practice to deceive"* which he quoted so cleverly.

"He promised a different picture of what happened in this conspiracy murder-for-hire trial and gave a list of witnesses who would prove his client, James Smith, was innocent of the charges filed against him. James was otherwise occupied when the crimes took place, said Rutman, and he had solid proof.

"Then Connolly spoke. He claimed his client, Floyd Mitleider, was a cheap not so smart SOB, but he was not guilty of the charges. His intent was never to kill his wife, but only to scare her. He wanted her 'out' but never conspired to have her murdered."

"That's not what Floyd says on the tape, is it?"

"Certainly not. Stock made a statement, too, saying Floyd cared so much for you that he took out a $100,000 insurance policy on himself naming you as beneficiary. I saw a report from Brach that showed Floyd had a $100,000 insurance policy on his first wife. The beneficiaries were later changed to his parents."

"Floyd's imperfect memory was used here again in an effort to make him look like a good husband. He must have ranked me higher with a $750,000 policy. But Stock should have checked up on what Floyd told her. Instead she presented his lies as facts."

"Finally the judge told Connolly and Stock that only one could speak for Floyd."

Charlene leaned back in the easy chair that the motel room offered, closed her eyes and tried to picture the smug defense attorneys as they stood before the court.

"I don't like the way it sounds," she whimpered.

"It would complicate things if these three Black guys all had alibis, or if the jury can be convinced that Floyd is not really guilty of these crimes."

"Attorneys do a lot of blabbering at opening and closing statements," Phil said, quickly moving to alleviate his daughter's fears. "These statements are not even put into the court transcript. They are not evidence. It is just talk, in some instances quite absurd."

"Like Connolly's statement that Floyd only intended to scare me coming after the playing of the tape where Floyd talked about murdering me. Scaring me did not require real bullets; they could have succeeded with blanks."

Her Dad would stay on in San Diego and attend the trial for a few more days. Charlene was sent home. She wanted to hear all of what Nick, Imad and Muaid would testify. She had to know what all those defense witnesses had to say. It was more than curiosity. Within her was a profound fear, fear that the defense would somehow prevail and all these defendants would be set free. Guilty men often go free. Good defense attorneys get them off.

After her Dad's stay to hear the testimony of the Iraqis, Charlene's mother, Dorothea, was to come out for the rest of the trial. Her parents promised to keep her posted on the courtroom drama of the trial. She had to know it all. She deserved to be informed, they thought. What all of them wanted to hear most of all was the outcome, the all-important verdicts.

But from this the beginning to the very end of the trial there would be more than tangled webs or practices to deceive referred to by defense attorney Rutman. Charlene was sure of that.

40

The Trial Goes On

There is a colony of more than 50,000 Iraqis in the San Diego, California, area-some are Muslims and others Chaldean Christians who claim descent from the ancient inhabitants of Babylon and Assyria (Iraq today). The involvement and court testimony of three of them is a major element in this story. These Iraqis see American law and order in action.

May 7 through May 16, 1996

Najah Sitto was called by Mr. Bowman to testify regarding his knowledge and actions having to do with Floyd Arnold Mitleider.

His descriptions followed his taped interview with Al Rushing and Herb Bowman of the 27th of June of the previous year.

His testimony illustrated Floyd's confidence in Nick. Nick's aggressive personality reinforced that trust in him. It was on the night of March 22 at the store that he told Nick, "I've had a helluva time with my wife. I'm pissed! She filed for divorce and I'm afraid she'll report me to the IRS." Nick listened to Floyd's complaints: Charlene's ex-husband did not always pay child support; she "was trying to get half" of what Floyd had. He bragged to Nick more than once about the $750,000 insurance policy that he had on Charlene. But Nick was caught off guard when Floyd gave him the big *coup de grace* later that month. Nick recalled and testified to all the things that happened from that time on.

March 30, La Mirage, Floyd asking him to find someone to kill his wife.

April 5, Hillcrest Liquor, Floyd giving Priest $2,500 to kill his wife.

April 9, La Mirage, Floyd again asking Nick to find someone to kill his wife.

April 17, Hillcrest Liquor, Nick asking Andy if he is interested in killing Floyd's wife.

April 19, Hillcrest Liquor, Andy telling Nick he will kill Charlene.

April 22, La Mirage, Floyd offering Andy $100,000 to kill his wife.

April 22, Denny's Mission Valley, Nick and Andy deciding to scam Floyd.

May 9, Hillcrest Liquor, Floyd lowering price to $75,000 for the hit and giving Nick $5,000.

May 14, Denny's Mission Valley, Andy telling Floyd James will help with the hit.

May 15, Andy's apartment, Andy soliciting James' help for $2,000.

May 17, La Mirage, Floyd showing Nick wife's route to take daughters to school.

May 18, Andy's apartment, Nick and Andy explaining the hit to James.

May 19, La Mirage, Floyd promising Andy and James $70,000 for the hit.

May 22, La Mirage, Andy stalking Charlene.

May 23, La Mirage, Andy stalking Charlene again.

May 24, La Mirage, Andy and James stalking Charlene.

May 25, La Mirage, Andy and James stalking Charlene again.

May 31, Hillcrest Liquor, Floyd giving Nick and Andy $10,000.

June 1, Denny's Mission Valley, Floyd telling Nick and Andy his wife is not dead.

June 2, Andy's apartment, Andy telling James he will not do the hit.

June 6, the attempted hit on Charlene taking place; James' telling Andy "the job is done" and admitting that at 2:00 he, along with two friends, had shot her four times, saying they had seen her fall on the steering wheel.

June 12, Andy's apartment, Muaid being harassed and stabbed multiple times.

Nick was examined on all these dates followed by cross-examinations of each defense attorney. Any discrepancy, no matter how minute, between his current testimony and his preliminary testimony was challenged.

Nick insisted that Floyd only trusted him and that the two of them attended Padres and Chargers games at Jack Murphy Stadium, worked out in the weight room at La Mirage and often went out to eat. This was the reason for Nick's having been consulted and informed by Floyd and his getting involved. He admitted that to him Floyd was a jerk that he really did not like at all.

There were objections by all defense attorneys at much of Nick's testimony, but often they were overruled. They even tried to bully him.

Rutman tried to pin him down by asking what deals he had made with the prosecution and how he was going to get out of punishment for his part in this. Nick said that he would take his punishment, that he had done something wrong and deserved something for it. But Rutman threatened possible deportation for lying in court to which Nick replied: "Deportation from where? I am American citizen!"

Rosenstock got Nick to admit that he hated Jews in his cross-examination, but it was stricken from the record.

Connolly's cross was the longest and nastiest. He called Nick a flim-flam artist. Then he played a little game, trying to get Nick to admit that Floyd only wanted Charlene out and that Nick was not telling the truth. Nick really did not understand the word *out*. Bowman objected frequently as Connolly tried to impeach his witnesses.

Imad's testimony which began late that day was still going on the next day. Bowman asked his questions in much the same order he had asked Nick. With few exceptions his testimony was a repeat of the same facts and details as Nick's.

The defense tried even harder to impeach Imad, because he seemed even more inclined to participate in the murder plot than Nick.

Connolly used his same technique about his client, Floyd, only wanting Charlene *out*, but the interpreter could not even translate the expression. Philip heard one San Diego detective say that Connolly's reputation was bad, that he was a sleazy slimeball. Whether this was true or not, he did some odd things in court. Once the judge admonished Connolly's style and conduct. He had been doing "asides" which Judge Kennedy warned him about. Connolly, seeming very overconfident, persisted in saying things like, "That's what I thought" after one of his prodding questions was answered.

After the cross-examinations, redirects and recrosses of Imad, late in the day the testimony of Muaid began.

May 13-14, 1996

"He looked greatly improved over his appearance at the Preliminary when he was still in a wheelchair," Philip reported to Charlene.

When he was finally allowed to step down from the witness stand, Imad was recalled..

May 15-16, 1996

On Wednesday the 15th the infamous Nick/Floyd tape of June 21 was played for the second time in open court.

Floyd's parents were there. They listened attentively with a look of wonderment and doubt on their faces, shaking their heads and acting as though lightning had hit their bodies. They would have to concede that it was truly their son admitting those monstruous things, calling Charlene names and expressing his disappointment that his plan failed and Charlene was not dead.

Police reports and photos were presented for the remainder of the case for the prosecution. Al Rushing gave details as to James' arrest of June 15 at James' apartment and Marvin's at the Brown home on June 17. Testimony also came from Dr. Dandan who had treated Muaid and from Barry Eldridge of the San Diego Police. Ron Johnson testified as to the identifications through lineups. Now the defense had to find fault with the police investigation any way they could.

41

Gentlemen's Agreement

"Two more minutes, Mitleider!" yelled the guard. "Get ready to say your good-byes!"

"I've only got two minutes left?" Floyd gasped. He had called everyone he could. He had to find out if his money was safe and what were the plans to get him out of this stinkin' place. "They just can't leave me here. Shit, I have helped every one of them more times than I can count."

This would be his last call, he thought as he heard the sound of the number he dialed grinding out and ringing. "You have reached the number of . . ." began the message which broke off abruptly since no one was there to accept the charges. "Sorry, there is no answer," the nasal voice of the operator announced.

"Fuck!" Floyd spat out as he slammed the receiver. Now he'd not have a chance to call until the next week, and by that time the trial would probably be over. His face turned red with anger. He pounded his fist on the yellow cement wall.

He thought of the past week, how Charlene's parents had been in the courtroom, taking notes and listening to every word spoken. A lot of good that was going to do them! Still, his parents had not been there since the day the DA played the God-damned tape that that God-damned Nick rigged up. Although he most wanted to see one of his good Load friends, he would even have been happy to see his mother and father. Didn't anyone care? He shoulda skipped town; he had a ticket sent to him. Too bad it was for nine days after his arrest.

"Time's up, Mitleider," yelled the guard. "Back to your cell."

Floyd stood by silently while the armed guard came to him and clamped on the cuffs. The unsmiling guard led him through the rust-streaked walls of the hallway, their steps echoing in the empty space of the bare passageway. The guard unlocked the cell block and gave Floyd a shove.

It was damp and cold and Floyd felt the chill pass through his body causing him to shiver. Inside his cell his talkative cellmate began to chatter just where he had left off when Floyd had exited the cell. "Shut up, you ass." Floyd shouted, stuffing make-believe stoppers in his ears. He sat down on his cot and closed his eyes. He visualized his parents. Yeh, they had tried to help him plea bargain, but the fuckin' DA said it was too late. Why didn't they try to help him sooner?

Hell, this is pure torture, like exercising too much and having your muscles tighten up into painful knots. Not only couldn't he talk to any of his buddies or folks, the court was not going to let him take the stand and defend himself. He could give that jury an earful about that friggin' Nick and what a golddigger Charlene was. But no, his attorneys said No. It was too risky.

He shook with grief and exasperation. There was no future for him, no existence.

42

The Law, The Police and The Iraqis

Rushing's testimony in the trial was lengthy. His experience in police work made the difference between what might have been a miscarriage of justice and what was turning out to be a solid case for the prosecution. As he testified he remembered the details of this unusual case of Iraqis over their heads in trouble. Almost immediately he felt a connection to them, from the moment he visited patched-up heavily sedated Muaid at Mercy Hospital. He was told that Muaid distrusted Blacks, and since two African-Americans had cruelly carved him like a pumpkin, no one could blame him for his attitude. After reassuring this pitiful victim that he was a good police officer attempting to help him in any way he could, in spite of the fact he was Black, he took the reins of the case upon him. Muaid reacted favorably and even though in pain, in and out of consciousness, from the first moment contributed factual information that only a good observer could have provided.

Rushing's next encounter with Iraqis came when the Nick-Imad duo came to him with an incomplete story. They left out their role in this bizarre crime. They told truthfully what they knew about Muaid's terrible experience. Rushing interviewed them, Nick acting as interpreter for Imad. Rushing acted quickly after they supplied the information about James Smith, the only Black friend Imad and Muaid had.

After leaving the police station, Nick and Imad checked into a Motel 6 in San Ysidro not far from the Mexican border. They talked into the wee hours of the night, finally deciding to return to the police.

"James and his friends are probably looking for us right now and we should get protection. The whole story about Floyd's murder-for-hire plan, James' thinking we got paid and the attack on Muaid must be told," Nick proposed to Imad.

Late the next morning the pair was back. This time Detectives Rushing and Marino separated the two Iraqis and interviewed them separately. "We must tell you the truth before more people get hurt."

Nick related the strange tale from A to Z. He said that he still had the $5,500 he got from Floyd and that he would bring it to Rushing because he wanted nothing to do with the money.

Marino interviewed Imad. When the two detectives compared notes, they realized the two Iraqis told nearly identical stories.

When Rushing and Marino accompanied Nick and Imad to Imad's Georgia Street apartment, two important developments took place. Imad discovered several valuable personal possessions had been stolen. Rushing looked through a photo album belonging to Imad and discovered a photograph of Imad, James and Linda taken at Club E. The police used this in the identification and eventual arrest of James. James was arrested after being identified by Imad. The police took photos of James and used them in a photographic lineup which, in their usual procedure, contained filler photos pulled out of their file cabinet. Muaid positively identified #3 (James Smith) as "the one who let the stabbers into our apartment," but surprisingly he also identified photo #5 as the shorter of the other two Black men. The police ignored this identification because it was a filler photo.

Rushing testified proceeding to James' residence at 4450½ Georgia Street and seeing a gray Toyota Tercel in the parking lot in front of the building. The Iraqis told him the car belonged to James' live-in girlfriend Linda Brown. James had a yellow Oldsmobile but always drove Linda's car, the Iraqis reported.

Other events followed in rapid course. Nick brought in $4,500 of the pay-off money, saying the people keeping it for him had spent $1,000 of it. Marvin Brown was discovered through a computer search and the knowledge that Linda's brother had recently been released from prison. Another photo lineup and Muaid identified Marvin as the taller of the two stabbers.

Rushing was most gratified by the fact that he was able to make the connection between Muaid's stabbing and the previous crime of attempted murder of Charlene Mitleider. He pondered over the police reports, the dates, places and people involved spending the entire night of June 16 until he had the pieces of the puzzle in place.

I know Floyd Mitleider is the mastermind of this twisted series of criminal events, Rushing internalized. *All we need is solid evidence.*

The plan for getting this was Rushing's idea: have CW Nick talk to Floyd wearing a wire. Nick would do it, he was sure. The success of that operation had been shown in court, the tape having been played for the jury not once but twice, with printed transcripts distributed for them to follow along.

Marvin's arrest took place with the help of Mark Valdez, Marvin's parole officer. He denied participating in the robbery at Muaid's and offered an alibi for his whereabouts at the time it occurred, but it failed to clear him. The girlfriend he planned to use as an alibi witness, Tanisha Cockrell, could not substantiate his claim.

The careful planning of the raid on Floyd's apartment paid off. Nick's participation in the recorded conversation with Floyd produced invaluable evidence against Mitleider. Rushing was happy to be able to call the young woman who was the first victim of Floyd's vicious crime, Charlene Mitleider, his wife. Then Floyd was transported to Police Headquarters where Floyd made his statement: "I love my wife, but I just can't live with her. I would never do anything to harm her." When he heard this, Rushing thought to himself: okay, you can't live with her, but does this mean she can't live? It was easy to size up this Floyd Mitleider but Rushing followed procedures to ensure that Floyd was regarded as innocent until pronounced guilty by a jury.

The DA's staff studied the tape, scrutinized all the police reports and conferred with Rushing. The criminal case was written up and given to Deputy District Attorney Herb Bowman. Both Rushing and DA investigator Ron Johnson worked diligently to find corroborating information and help the District Attorney's Office make their case strong.

On June 27 Nick and Imad were called to the DA's office and interviewed extensively by Bowman and Rushing. Both were arrested on June 29 for conspiracy to commit a crime, solicitation to commit murder and grand theft of personal property. They were almost grateful for the arrest. They already knew that American justice would be totally unlike the quick and violent justice of their homeland. Along with the prior arrests of James and Marvin, all but one suspect (Ivan Catlin) were in custody. Locating this individual, it was thought, was going to require the best police work they had to offer. Muaid had seen him during his ordeal and gave police a good description of him, identified his filler photo in a lineup and even drew a crude picture of the stabber, a man who, it turned out, looked strikingly like Catlin. Ron, in conducting a computer search on Marvin Brown, found out Ivan Catlin and another Black male were convicted of robberies in 1989; they did time together. Ron continued his probe.

When Bowman determined that Nick and Imad were telling the truth, the original date for a preliminary hearing set for July 18 was postponed. He arranged a preliminary hearing for the two Iraqis on July 24 in which they pleaded Guilty to lesser charges and were released from jail on a $5,000 bond. They knew that their sentence could be three years of jail time when the criminal trial for the other suspects was over. They testified on July 25 and 26. Rushing remembered wheeling Muaid in and out, seeing Charlene and her father there and presuming the case would go forward to trial later. Meantime Ron was on the case for finding the third Black man involved

What a find, Rushing mused. Homicide Detective Lamour called him on October 3 about a photo of Ivan Catlin from his September 20, 1995, arrest for homicide. A photo of Nov. 4, 1994, when Ivan had been a suspect in a different murder case, had been used as filler photo #5 and positively identified by Muaid. It turned out to be the same Ivan Catlin. The police had missed an important clue on June 15. "I also discovered that Ivan was a long-time acquaintance of Marvin," Ron reported, "including gang participation." On October

9 Rushing went to George Bailey Detention Facility and arrested Ivan for robbing and assaulting Muaid. This is what Ron meant when he said the third shooter was "right under their noses." Ivan had accommodated them by getting himself put in jail again, making it simple to arrest him on the new charges. He did appear to be a man who was having trouble staying out of trouble. His arrest rounded out the list of participants in the June 6 and June 12 crimes.

Rushing knew he would be cross-examined at length by the defense attorneys.

One of the examinations by Mr. Connolly was especially strange. He claimed that Nick never mentioned a life insurance policy, that somehow Rushing added something that was not there. The judge allowed a *voir dire* examination of Rushing.

A reexamination of Nick's taped interview of June 14 proved Al's memory was not faulty: Nick really did talk about the $750,000 insurance policy Floyd had arranged in connection with the planned murder of Charlene. Connolly stubbornly argued that the prosecution's transcript of that tape was an enhanced version and did not jibe with his certified transcript of it. The judge had to clarify that the defense's so-called official transcript was no more certified than was the prosecution's and he himself listened to the tape. He seemed exasperated with Connolly who exclaimed: "What I worry about . . . is our reputation. I have been relying . . . I relied on a certified copy, not something I've created."

It was Rushing's excellent memory for details that served to thwart the defense attorney who objected again saying "Floyd Mitleider can't leave the impression with this jury that his lawyer is not playing fair." The judge said he understood but that Connolly's objection was without merit and was overruled.

The rest of the police testimony ended the case for the prosecution. On May 20 the defense was to begin presenting the other side of the picture.

43

The Case for the Defense

Department 28
Superior Court
Monday & Tuesday
May 20-21, 1996

"This trial has been going on so long now. School will be out soon. The kids can't wait," Charlene complained.

"Well, there are just so many delays, like yesterday and today. No court. The defense is going to put on their case starting tomorrow morning. That will take time. . .Surely next week will end it. That's what both Bowman and Rushing have told me. However, there will probably be no verdict until the week after, first week in June."

"I wish the whole thing, final divorce and all, would soon be over. I am convinced that Floyd has made sure no one will find his money. Besides he must be using a lot for his defense."

"I believe we can find out a lot of things through the detectives. Brach tells me it is rather mysterious what happened to a rather large amount of money Floyd had left over after paying off his bank obligations for the store. He is looking into it," Charlene's mother explained.

"Wherever his money may be, it is not bringing him the satisfaction and joy he thought it would," Charlene recalled.

"We won't stop asking questions until we get the real answers," her Mom assured Charlene, "no matter how long it takes."

♦♦♦

Wednesday, May 22, 1996
In defense of James Ray Smith, Jr.

Rutman set out to provide the solid alibis he had promised by calling his first witness, Michael Rabb. He was living at 4525 Georgia Street on June 12, 1995, when the crime was committed. He testified to hearing the unusual sounds from across the street at the 4512 Georgia building in the hours before midnight. He said he saw two men emerge from that building at nearly midnight: one olive-skinned and the other white, and no one else.

Bowman cross-examined the witness and brought out several discrepancies in his testimony from what he had told investigators earlier.

Rutman moved on to Thelma Gibson, manager of a Motel 6 in Chula Vista, who presented a receipt indicating James Smith had checked in on June 6, 1995. She said it was a Monday. The receipt was incomplete, lacking the make and model of the car Smith was driving and the number of persons occupying the room.

Donita Walker was put on the stand next. She identified herself as Linda Brown Smith's[2] hairdresser. She described a series of phone calls and attempted calls around the June 12 crime date. She testified that Smith was going to paint her house but when she tried to call him on the evening of June 12, he was asleep. All the calls were recorded in her appointment book On cross-examination it was revealed that the times and comments regarding Smith were written in a different handwriting and ink color. Ron Johnson had investigated this earlier and Ms. Walker admitted that Linda had added those dates some time in July, reconstructing them from memory. The hairdresser verified that James often drove the gray Toyota belonging to Linda.

Linda was the next witness. She stated that James and she had met on June 6, 1993, according to her, two and a half years ago. (Actually it would have been nearly three years ago.) This had remained a very special day to them. She testified that she knew Imad as Andy and also Nick. Rutman questioned her about Alvin Boudreau and Richard Jenkins with whom James had played cards. She said

[2]Linda and James were married in August 1995 while he was in jail awaiting trial.

that was on Sunday, June 5, and it was the next day that James, her young niece Denise and she went to the Motel 6 in Chula Vista and spent the night.

Cross-examination by Bowman proved her wrong on the dates. She was indignant when Bowman asked if it were true that she had asked Jenkins to provide an alibi for June 6 and he refused. Her car was inoperable during the time in question and was not repaired until June 8. They had borrowed a car from Andy. But Bowman reminded her that she had told an investigator that they drove her Toyota when they went to play cards. He asked her why she had not come forward immediately with the two alibis when James was arrested for crimes occurring on those exact dates. Why, when people were following and frightening her before and after James' arrest she did not call the police, Bowman asked, to which she replied that Bowman was confusing her.

Two police officers who were called to the scene of the Muaid crime testified. Officer Lessa was questioned about the appearance of the apartment when he arrived. Owens wanted to know if he noticed a white powdery substance on a table there. He said Officer Jones who came after him collected evidence. Jones affirmed that there was such an off-white powder on the table, but during Bowman's cross minimized its presence and importance, saying that it was not anything that made him think of a controlled substance. He stated it was some type of dye.

The next witness called was Miguel Garcia. In his capacity as manager of the apartment building where Muaid was victimized, he had been questioned by the police the night of the crime. Garcia stated he was sound asleep when he heard the noises coming from #6 which also awakened other tenants and the lady from #1 who called 911. He stated he never told police that a whole lot of people went to that apartment; he barely knew the man who was injured or his roommate, actually the tenant, who worked at the auto shop down the street.

Rutman prodded him to recall what he had told police, i.e. that the apartment had many people coming in and out. Garcia insisted that all he told anyone who asked was what happened that night.

Owens questioned Garcia along the same lines and was having him look at a police report to refresh his recollection. The judge interrupted, saying they would go on from there tomorrow at 1:30 Outside the presence of the jury the judge asked Owens where he was going with his question; Owens wanted to establish the same thing, that the path in and out of Imad-Muaid's apartment was well-traveled. The judge reminded him that Rutman already asked the question three times and he was not allowing it to be asked again.

"When you tell me what has been going on, I try to pretend I am in the courtroom taking it all in like the jurors. I could not keep an open mind as I hope they are. June 6 was not a Monday. I will never forget that day. It was a Tuesday when the attempted murder took place."

"The witnesses confused days and dates. People like Linda should have been more careful when they first talked to investigators. She probably did not understand the full significance of her statements so soon after the crimes. Later she had time to cook up alibis with James, despite her denials.[3] "

"James was probably committing the crime against Muaid during the hours Donita described," Charlene surmised.

"I want to tell you that Mr. Bowman has been very friendly to me. After Rabb's testimony, Bowman saw me sitting alone in the corridor and told me the two men Rabb saw probably had nothing to do with the case. After Linda's testimony he asked me 'How am I doing?'"

"It sounds like he is doing a good job," Charlene remarked.

"Even Rosenstock approached me. During the afternoon break he asked me who I was and what was my purpose in attending the trial. I never told him anything except that I was interested in the trial."

"He's a little nosy, isn't he?" Charlene noted. "And what was the big thing about Garcia's testimony? Why did the defense want him to say there were a lot of people in and out of Muaid's apartment? What difference would that make?"

"I'm not sure," her mother answered. "Who knows what tricks the defense has up their sleeve?"

---

[3]Linda testified that James and she had not discussed the testimony for court this day; James, however, admitted to having phone conversations with her. Bowman, in his cross-examination of James, stated that from June 23 to July 26 there were 130 to 140 logged phone calls between James and Linda; James verified this.

Thursday, May 23, 1996

Miguel Garcia's testimony continued, with Bowman asking him if any people other than tenants came outside like he did when the noise alerted them. He said No, only people known to him. No one came out of #6; the voice inside was begging for help saying, "I've been shot," and some words in a language Garcia did not understand. The victim implored him to break in. Garcia did and was about to cut his binds when the police arrived. Rutman redirected wanting to know if Garcia was alone when he went around the building and talked to Muaid through an open window. Yes. The other defense attorneys quit.

James Smith took the stand in his own defense, stating he had been employed at Cliff Brown Automotive since mid-April as an apprentice mechanic. He had been offered the job when he went there once to have his yellow 1970 Rally Cutlass repaired. Terry Mustafa hired him part-time. He worked as a self-employed house painter also. He established that he knew Imad Aqili as Andy and Muaid Alfuraiji as Mike and Najah Sitto as Jesse , later learning he was called Nick.

Smith stated he had socialized with Andy and had been to his apartment three times. He described times when they went to Club E together. He said Andy asked him to take some drugs to Chicago, and he had seen Andy in possession of cocaine. Drug use in Andy's apartment was brought up and an attempt was made to make drugs a major factor in the crimes Smith was describing. He detailed having been introduced by Andy to an individual at the Café Sevilla whom James did not want to have anything to do with. He was a Black man with short hair, about the height and weight of James, with two scars on his face and a tattoo on his right forearm. The tattoo turned out to be a symbol of a gang, whose initials "G.D." for Gangster Disciple were inscribed on it. James stated this individual was offended by the Calvin Klein shirt James was wearing, saying CK stood for "Crip Killer." James claimed Mike was involved with the tattooed man as well. He expressed concern about this tattooed man to Andy, and Andy told him not to worry, that he had a gun. James stated he did see this Black guy again before June 6th, in front of Andy's apartment. He was sitting in a gray 2-door Honda Accord with Andy. James said he walked by but didn't speak to them, not wanting a confrontation.

James also stated that he has a photo in his home of Marvin Brown, his brother-in-law, and that Andy had asked him who this man with long hair was. He added that he had seen Andy in possession of a gun at his house, the one described by Muaid, a 4-chambered revolver.

James stated that in his association with Andy he had at times borrowed money from him.

Smith: I wanted to surprise my wife for Mother's Day. I rented a limousine to take her out to dinner.

Rutman: How much did the limousine cost?

Smith: It was 200.

Rutman: So you were short some money, then?

Smith: Yes.

The testimony went to the occasion of Smith's going with Alvin Boudreau to Richard Jenkins' house. Smith repeated Linda's story about going to Motel 6 in Andy's car; he described going to a restaurant and then to Auto Zone to get parts for Linda's car en route; he went over the signing of the Motel 6 receipt, and said he lied about the number of people because it's cheaper.

He claimed he didn't go to Lewis Junior High on June 6 or know Charlene or Floyd Mitleider, never went to Floyd's apartment, nor did he ever search Aqili's apartment, or go there with two other guys. He said he made plans to go to a drive-in movie in South Bay on the 12th; was at Linda's mother's house (8 to 10 miles away) at 7:00 the evening of the 12th, was going to paint Donna's house the next day. He walked down to Andy's but only Mike was home, he stayed only five minutes. He testified that he did not hear from Aqili on the 12th but the next day, Andy came to James with Jesse. They were agitated and wanted James to come over to the apartment. Smith said he did go with them, saw the condition of the apartment and was told Mike got hurt, was in the hospital and might die. Andy and Jesse spoke in Arabic most of the time, leaving James out. They wanted James to go to Denny's with them, but stopped at a gas station at

Texas and Mission. Andy got a page from the police. Andy told Smith that he (Smith) was the only person who could talk to the police. Smith refused because he had tickets.

Rutman: Did you tell him (Aqili) that you would assist him in talking to the police?

Smith: No . . . He got mad. . . . He said that if I didn't help him he was going to kill me. He told me that he was involved in some Arabic Mafia group called Hamas.[4]

James further testified that Andy said he would kill James, Linda and the baby (Linda's niece Nisie) and that he had done a drive-by with the guy James had met at Café Sevilla. On the 14th James heard from Andy again. He kept paging James, said he was going to send police to James' house. There were three cars parked outside, of which James gave descriptions; James thought they were police, told Andy he couldn't talk because police were there.

A recess was called and James was to refresh his memory by looking at the police transcript to see what he said to Aqili. Finally he remembered that he couldn't talk because there was a tap on his phone. Then James testified that since Andy kept calling and threatening, he told him he had found someone in Spring Valley who might be able to transport drugs. This was just to get Aqili off his back.

James testified that he had not spoken to Andy since that day when police were tapping his phone. He admitted to owning the .25-caliber gun which he bought three weeks before his arrest; that he did not return to Aqili's apartment on the 12th and allow Brown and Catlin in; that he does own cowboy boots, but his are brownish tan and dark brown, worn often in the presence of Mike; and that he does not have Andy's phone number, but has his pager number; Andy has his.

Owens cross-examined James Smith wanting to know how long James knew Brown. James said only months before he was arrested. He said Marvin had been in Northern California in prison and had gone to live with his mother on Detroit Street. Owens had anticipated only the last part of this statement.

The judge instructed the jury to disregard James' statement about Brown's having been in prison because it was inadmissible.

[4]James' tale had many instances of lack of finesse. Hamas is an extremist Palestinian group which promotes violent strikes against Israel. To say an Iraqi in the U.S. is a part of this group is an absurdity.

Bowman's cross-examination of James showed his testimony was not totally believable and was memorized, calculated to cover bases and put the blame on Aqili and Alfuraiji. Asking questions about what Smith was wearing, Bowman caught Smith offguard. He forgot his own testimony about the Calvin Klein shirt the mysterious gangster person had insulted. This was not cleared up until Rutman did a re-direct. Rutman had to coach him. Smith's explanation of how he acquired the gun showed lapses in his memory.

"James changed the year date when he first met Linda, but the emphasis is on June 6," Charlene noted

"I know, and his story was so long and drawn-out. I could hardly keep up. But I believe we have the answer to why the defense wanted Garcia to say the Aqili-Alfuraiji apartment was heavily trafficked: they wanted to tie in drugs. Remember when the defense attorneys asked about a white powdery substance? They picked up on the photos taken.

Some white powder was found on the table.Actually the police said it was not drugs. But it might stir up something with the jury if they could say lots of people were in and out of the apartment."

"Mr. Bowman asked 'What do you think?' at one of the breaks during James Smith's long testimony. I told him I was taking abundant notes in case we ever needed material for a fairy tale. He smiled."

"I wonder how the other defendants are going to be. If they convince the jury they are innocent, what might happen to the whole case?" Charlene offered.

"Be patient and reasonable," her mother advised. "These men are all desperate. They will say or do anything to get off, and their attorneys will help them. That's their job."

"I can't help it," Charlene screeched. "I heard so many lies from Floyd, and some people seemed to believe him. Jurors might believe some of these concocted alibis are true!"

Friday, May 24, 1996 Owens waived the opening statement and Brown rested. Rosenstock would not relinquish his right. He made a long opening statement which often sounded like a closing argument.

In defense of Ivan Catlin

Rosenstock began his defense by having a barber, Quiñones, testify about Catlin's Quo Vadis haircut. Catlin's brother was also called. They verified the long-standing existence of Ivan Catlin's pigtail. Rosenstock told the court the identification of his client was inaccurate since the pigtail was not mentioned.

Lorri Hooper from Los Angeles testified she was a friend of Sabrina and Ivan Catlin and that her daughter was Ivan's godchild. This daughter was graduating from Dana Middle School in San Pedro, a few miles from Los Angeles, last June and Ivan wanted to celebrate with them. Lorri and her daughter Nieshia drove to San Diego to pick Ivan up on June 10. They spent their time June 11 and 12 at home but on the 13th they all went to the graduation ceremony. The following day, June 14th, they returned to San Diego. They were together at all times.

Bowman began his cross-examination by asking Ms. Hooper who asked her to testify; answer: Sabrina; when; answer: in October; and when did she first discuss it with Mr. Rosenstock; answer: about a month ago. Catlin was living in San Ysidro at the time Lorri Hooper picked him up. The graduation ceremony attended in June was the subject of Bowman's next questions.

Bowman: Now, at this graduation, did you take any photographs?

Hooper: Our camera broke.

Bowman: Did anyone else take any photographs of your daughter on this occasion?

Hooper: No, the pictures we took, when we got them back, they were messed up.

Bowman: So, you took some pictures, but the camera broke?. . .Well, was Mr. Catlin with you during the ceremonies?

Hooper: Yes.

Bowman: Where was he sitting?

Hooper: We were all sitting in the seats.

Bowman: What day of the week was this?

Hooper: It was a Tuesday.

Bowman: What day?

Hooper: The 13th.

Bowman: Well, certainly they gave out a program or something for this graduation, correct?

Hooper: Yes.

Bowman: Do you have that program with you?

Hooper: No.

Bowman: Was your daughter's name written in the program?

Hooper: Yes.

Bowman: Do you recall what page it was written on?

Hooper: No.

Bowman: Would seeing a copy of that program refresh your recollection?

Hooper: Yeah, if I saw her name.

Bowman had the program marked as People's Exhibit No. 42: Richard Henry Dana Middle School graduation program.

Bowman: Looking at page 4, first column, about 12 names down, do you see your daughter's name?

Hooper: Yes.

Bowman: Would you mind turning to the front of that program and telling us the date written on the front?

Hooper: June 29th.

Bowman: 1995, correct?

Hooper: Correct.

Bowman: Who told you to come and testify?

Hooper: Excuse me?

Bowman: Who told you to come and testify in this case?

Hooper: Sabrina. She asked me would I come.

Bowman: And you lied about the date, didn't you?

Hooper: No.

Bowman: The program says June 29th, correct?

Hooper: Correct.

Bowman: That's the program for your daughter's graduation date, correct?

Hooper: Correct.

Bowman: You just testified repeatedly that it was June 12th, correct?

Hooper: Nope.
Bowman: You didn't testify to that?
Hooper: I didn't say the 12th.
Court: She said the 13th.
Bowman: You testified it was the 13th, right?
Hooper: Right.
Bowman: So you lied, correct?
Hooper: Correct.

This witness was excused and went into the corridor where all witnesses waited. Bowman asked the judge to have the bailiff tell her not to talk to other defense witnesses out there. The judge complied.

Rosenstock called Ernest Elahi next. He was Sabrina Catlin's grandfather. He testified to having transported Sabrina to work and the school-aged children to the bus stop while Ivan remained at home with the baby. Sabrina would call home from work to check on the baby. Elahi continued to provide taxi service in June and until some time in July. The dates gave Catlin an alibi for the June 6 crime.

Sabrina testified to the child care provided by her husband and the transportation her grandfather had given. She specifically remembered having gone to work on June 6. Sabrina said she was led to believe that the graduation was on June 13th. Bowman's cross-examination went into more detail about Sabrina's employment which she claimed was for two different temporary agencies. In early June she had been assigned to Insurance Express, through the So-Cal agency.

"This was the last witness and there will be no more court sessions until Tuesday, May 28."

"That's right," Charlene gasped. "Memorial Day week-end. Too bad you can't come home."

"This close to the end I wouldn't think of it. There has been a lot of speculation about how much longer the trial will last. One of the people I talked to told me the judge is pressing the various defense attorneys about how many more witnesses they would be calling. Mr. Connolly said the possibility of Floyd Mitleider taking the stand on his own behalf depended entirely on how the rest of the defense, especially Smith's, went. He said that Mr. Mitleider's testimony with an expert having to do with a totally different part of the case could happen."

"What kind of an expert? This is strange."

"Really. I also heard there was some bickering between Rutman and Owens. It has to do with some prejudicial questions Brown and Catlin's attorneys did not want Rutman to ask. Smith having an alibi put the other two in more jeopardy because they had been identified by Muaid. If Smith was being framed, and the wrongful identification Owens (and Rosenstock) planned to use in their defense did not work, they might have to prove their clients were being framed too. I don't think Owens liked Smith's story at all," Charlene's mother explained.

"I believe having four defendants being tried all at once has its problems," Charlene added.

"Yes, but if it is only causing trouble for these defense attorneys, we don't care. I heard that ultimately Connolly stated in one of the closed sessions that Mitleider would object vehemently to being placed on the witness stand. There is a pattern of changeability here."

"Connolly is getting advice from the chief of changeability," Charlene laughed. "But, Mom, what did you think of Catlin's alibi? I wondered how Mr. Bowman could refrain from yelling 'You liar!' at that witness from Los Angeles."

"That was perjured testimony nipped in the bud."

Tuesday, May 28, 9:08 a.m.

Scott Fraser, an expert on eyewitness identification, took the stand for the defense. He stated his qualifications and explained scientific research in laboratory studies and experiments.

Rosenstock's questions leaned toward the possibility of inaccurate identifications in this case because of discrepancies in heights and failure to note the distinctive cue of his client's pigtail. Mr. Rutman asked questions about identification of a previously-known subject. Mr. Owens tried to set up hypothetical questions having to do with height but was objected to each time. The birthmark on Marvin Brown's face was brought up and Mr. Fraser said that it would be a distinctive cue.

Bowman asked about the pay Fraser receives for this type of testimony. Then he asked if a distance of 15 feet to nearly touching is ideal for identification, to which Fraser replied Yes. Live lineups are more reliable than photo lineups since participants walk, turn and speak.

Outside the jury Bowman next announced a rebuttal witness regarding Sabrina Catlin's testimony. Both Ivan and Sabrina Catlin were being interviewed back on June 28 by a public defender and on June 29 a parole officer talked to them both.

There was a meeting of the attorneys regarding putting Floyd on the stand. Rutman wanted him to testify under *use immunity* on behalf of his client, James Smith, that he never met or knew Smith. Mr. Bowman objected, saying use immunity could only be granted by the prosecution. Connolly stated he did not want to subject his client to what would be a thorough cross-examination. Rutman's motion was denied.

A stipulation was made by Rutman that he instructed his client not to discuss with police or the district attorney any of the details of the motel or Donna Walker after he took the case. Bowman stipulated that on June 6 the first 911 telephone call made was at 1:38 p.m. regarding shots fired at Lewis Junior High.

Rushing was recalled to the stand. He had made a test run from Lewis Junior High to the Georgia Street area where Smith lived to the exit on E street where the Chula Vista Motel 6 is located. In the middle of the day, it took approximately 10 - 20 minutes to travel to Georgia Street and 15 - 25 minutes to travel Highway I-5 to the border.

Bowman announced another stipulation. On June 13th the first 911 call made regarding screams heard coming from the Aqili-Alfuraiji apartment came at 12:25 a.m. A person identifying herself as Pauline called at 12:31; a person identifying herself as Debra Brave called at

12:35; a person identifying himself as Ernest Green called at 12:36 and a person identifying himself as Michael Rabb called at 12:39 regarding the noises.

Diana Barnes, a rebuttal witness, was then called. She testified that she was managing a temporary employment service, So-Cal, when Sabrina Catlin was employed by the agency. Sabrina worked her first day on June 7 (not June 6) at Arrowhead Insurance (not Insurance Express) and completed service with the agency on June 23.

"Bowman sure got a lot of proof that the Catlins lied, didn't he?"

"Sounds like it. The prosecution got the goods on them. Even Rosenstock can't deny that. Now all he has to hang on to is that much mentioned tail of his client," Dorothea remarked.

"But I am still not feeling confident about how all this will turn out. We don't know what the jurors are thinking and we can't forget how easily and quickly the jury acquitted O.J.," Charlene reminded her mother.

"We'll know before long. Don't even think about acquittals. These guys just cannot go free, especially Floyd."

"You'll be coming home soon now. We are all anxious to see you. The girls are more excited about that than the last day of school. It has been great getting reports from you daily, but your phone bill will be out of sight!"

"Don't worry about that either. It's only money."

44

Case Closed

The case was coming to a close without testimony from all the potential witnesses on the list. The suspense was over. Connolly did not want Floyd to be subjected to cross-examination. And for whatever reason the defense never called Frankie either.

May 29 - May 30, 1996

The Prosecution had two chances to close this case. His lengthy summary of allegations and overt actions, corroborated facts and testimony, physical evidence and convincing proof were designed to leave no doubt in the minds of the jurors of the guilt of all four defendants. Then the Defense had the floor and tried to undo the DDA's statements. The second and last closing or rebuttal ended the case. Charlene, having suffered through the year between the crime and the trial, was confused, troubled by the fact that some of the defending attorneys' arguments sounded too believable. She did not know the two best witnesses for the prosecution well enough to decide, as the DDA had, that their stories were true and that Floyd had done this awful thing to her with the aid of other greedy culprits.

At night she could not fall asleep without the picture in her mind of a Black man with a gun, leaning out of the passenger side of a gray car, slowly, carefully, deliberately aiming the gun at her. Everything was vivid in her picture, except the face of the gun-wielding man. At first glance it was James, no question about it. Then in a second the face changed and the hair of the shooter was long, braided and tied back. She accustomed herself to the fact that Marvin was the holder of the gun until alas, his face changed once more. It was the full broader face of Ivan Catlin so similar to James in many ways.

She began to wish she had not seen their faces in the courtroom so they could not invade her dreams. Soon all the faces were cloudy and had no features at all. She sat up in bed venting a silent scream of complete despair. At that moment she knew she would never be sure who the real shooter was; none of the accused men would ever talk. One word from any of them would have led to clarifying everything, but they remained mute. The mystery hung heavily over Charlene, stifling her, making it difficult for her to breathe freely.

Bowman reminded the jury that the theme of this case was greed, from start to finish, beginning with Floyd Mitleider's desire to collect on a $750,000 insurance policy. He went to another greedy man, Smith, who was willing to snuff out the life of a woman he did not even know. . .for money. And about a week later, Smith and his accomplices were willing to butcher a man who was innocent of everything, even knowledge of these events, for the promise of money.

In his forceful remarks Bowman explained that the jury need find only one overt act in each of the three main crimes in evidence and if anybody in the conspiracy does an overt act, everybody else is liable for it.

Floyd's procedure of asking Sitto for help, the $2,500 he paid Priest (a crime committed right here) and his acts of solicitation and forming of the conspiracy were recounted. All of this having been testified to by Sitto and corroborated by Aqili is also in evidence on the tape-recorded conversation between Mitleider and Sitto. There was a second time that Mitleider solicited Sitto to find someone to kill his wife. But Sitto's plan, along with Aqili, was to take Floyd's money. Meetings at La Mirage and later at the liquor store culminated in the agreement that Floyd would pay $100,000 for the job. Giving Aqili a photo of his wife and details of how he wanted the murder to look, and the giving of a down payment of $5,000 were all overt acts. James got in on it now, at Aqili's invitation and to satisfy Mitleider's desire to have someone "tough" to do the job. Stalking Charlene, more money paid by Floyd and a crucial meeting between

Mitleider, Aqili and Smith in which the price of $70,000 was fixed followed. Floyd gave $10,000 to Sitto to hold for the hitmen who were going to kill Charlene.

Since Aqili's intent was to steal, the conspiracy was now between Mitleider and Smith. Sitto called in the wa-bo signal knowing the money scam had gone as far as it could. Floyd called Charlene about June 1 and found it was a false wabo-wabo; meantime Smith solicited Brown, his girlfriend's brother, telling Aqili, "Hey, I'm gonna do this. I've recruited somebody." Then Smith solicited Catlin. June 6 marked the attempt event as the three assailants drove in a gray compact car to Lewis Junior High and shot at Charlene, narrowly missing her. Her life was saved because a bullet could not get through the fire wall of her car. A bullet fragment found there barely missed her head where she had ducked down.

Once these events had taken place, Smith drove from Lewis Junior High to where Aqili was working at Cliff Brown, reporting, "I've done it with two other people. We've done it. We want our money." Due to the Defense's case we know what Smith did: he drove south to Chula Vista in the direction of Catlin's house in San Ysidro and the border, to hide out at a Motel 6. Smith's actions were within the time frame tested by Al Rushing.

All the testimonial evidence is strong, but the most fantastic piece is the tape-recorded conversation with Mitleider and Sitto. Mitleider wanted his wife dead in a very bad way, lamenting the failure of the "fuckers" to kill her. "They know about the insurance policy," Mitleider told Sitto. There can be no question Mitleider committed solicitation of Priest, Aqili and Smith, was involved in a conspiracy to commit murder with Smith who ultimately involved Brown and Catlin.

As to the stabbing of Alfuraiji, involvement of the three men is circumstantial evidence which should be used to find them guilty of the attempted murder of Charlene.

The courtroom stage was filled again with the same players and as Floyd would have said, "The heat is on." Now, however, the pressure was on the defense attorneys.

Rutman remarked in his closing that the evidence has not proved his client guilty and that in case of reasonable doubt he is entitled to a verdict of not guilty

He said they were disputing the allegations by Najah Sitto, Imad Aqili and Muaid Alfuraiji. These witnesses made mistakes in their testimonies and if it is all right for them, it is all right for Linda and James Smith to make mistakes also. The scam on Floyd and the statement by Aqili and Sitto that they did not want to hurt anybody, they just wanted Floyd's money was illogical, as the payment later on of $10,000 was also, because he had just lost money hiring Priest

Among all the illogical aspects of the accusations, Rutman said the code "wa-bo wa-bo" was just a figment of Sitto's imagination. There were many contradictions in the testimony of both Sitto and Aqili. He said that Linda and James did not have answers for everything, but Aqili and Sitto thought they did.

Mr. Bowman reduced the charges of attempted murder and conspiracy against Sitto and Aqili to obtain their cooperation and they testified with the expectation of leniency.

In his eagerness to impress Mr. Rutman often confused the names Aqili and Alfuraiji and admitted he did so. But he implored the jury to look to the credibility of the witnesses. He denied that Smith had set up an alibi explaining that if that were the case, Smith surely would have saved receipts from the auto parts store.

Rutman's final statement was: "If as you deliberate you cannot find answers to all these questions and you don't know who to believe, that problem is reasonable doubt. You have to acquit James Smith."

Owens' closing argument was an appeal to the jury to take each defendant separately and consider split verdicts. Defendants have the right not to testify and this should not be held against them. Brown's defense could be abbreviated to one phrase: reasonable doubt. Sitto, Aqili and even Alfuraiji were unreliable, lying witnesses. Sitto and Aqili became state's witnesses only after their friend got hurt. He quoted Scott Fraser on the distintive cues being omitted and the erroneous height identification. Misstatemens of the testimony brought objections often, mostly sustained.

Rosenstock, Ivan Catlin's verbose attorney, used the burden of proof borne by the prosecution in his closing. His client had not been proved to have any part in any of the charges and allegations. He said the district attorney was doing all possible to be able to go back to his colleagues and brag about getting convictions. Bowman objected that this was entirely improper and the judge agreed. Aqili and Sitto were characterized as crooks. Scott Fraser's testimony on eyewitness identification was used to disprove Catlin was ever identified by Muaid.

Friday, May 31, 1996

Connolly, assisted by Ms. Stock, stated the jury would have to decide whose story to believe. His client had no connection to Smith and only wanted Charlene followed and scared back to St. Louis. He said Floyd was a businessman and had broken his contract with Sitto and Aqili by asking for his money back. This was Floyd's withdrawal from the conspiracy.

Rebuttal

Bowman used his time before the jury again to clear up confusion. As to Mr. Rutman's statement that unanswered questions equate to reasonable doubt, Bowman explained that this was simply not true. In every single case that's tried there are certain unanswered questions: what Smith did with the gun, what happened to the bloody clothes and what disposition was made of the stolen articles were such questions in this case.

As to Connolly's statements, Mr. Bowman urged the jury to step back and look at the whole picture, not just certain words out of context. It was clear what Mitleider's intent was and absurd to argue that he only wanted his wife followed. This man promised to pay $77,500 and actually did pay $17,500 counting Priest. Mitleider said, "If you don't kill my wife, I want my money back." There was no withdrawal from the conspiracy.

The DDA summed up the arguments by the defense as "either misstatements of testimony or, as in the case of Smith, an effort to

make the jury believe in a create-an-alibi that did not make sense."
Mr.Rutman himself gave up on the gangster/frame-up story in his
closing.

When Bowman moved to the Catlin alibis, he reminded the
jury of Alfuraiji's identification and Catlin's connection with Brown.
The false alibi testimony showed consciousness of guilt.

"The scary part here is they might have gotten away with it
(false alibis) if we hadn't gone out and been able to get that program
and the witness from the insurance company. You would have been
sitting here right now believing that Mr. Catlin had an alibi for those
dates."

At the trial's conclusion the jury's task began. Deliberation would
start on Monday, June 3.

Charlene's mother said, "I wanted to cry, scream, run away as
Bowman went over the details of this horror story again. It is like the
worst scene in a nightmare: to hear how the man I thought loved you
and would take care of you instead planned and spent money to have
you murdered."

"Sorry you had to go through this," Charlene sighed.

"At least it's over," the woman said. "Oh, did I mention that
this last day of the trial I saw a red-headed well-dressed young man
come into the back of the courtroom for the last few minutes before
the judge adjourned? The jury marched out, followed by those of us
in the visitors' gallery, and I had to step in front of this man to get
out. I looked down and saw penny-loafers! I don't know why he was
allowed to stay there. Everyone else had to leave. But I saw him
looking at Floyd and an engaging glance from Floyd to him made me
realize this was Frankie."

45

The Verdict and Penal Codes Violated

June 8, 1996

After all the instructions to the jury and the suggestions given by both the prosecution and defense for the application of them, jurors still had questions.

Juror #8 sent this note to the Court during deliberation: "Can we consider a lesser charge against James Smith in reference to Conspiracy? Can we consider aiding and abedding (sic) or any other minor charges associated with letting Brown and Catlin in that night, not of as a <u>conspiracy</u> to kill Alfuraiji?" The judge answered: "No. Aiding and abetting is not a lesser charge."

June 11, 1996

Juror #7 sent this message to the court just before the verdict was presented by the jury. "Several members of the jury request the identification of the jurors, including the questionnaires used in the jury selection process, not be released and be protected by the court."

The 13-page questionnaire of the prosecution and the 36-page defense questionnaire to which this juror referred covered a whole range of information which almost no one would want made public about themselves, nor would anyone want the family and friends of the convicted felons to know.

On this day the jury had reached its verdict and court was reconvened for the reading of it to the defendants, as follows:

Floyd Arnold Mitleider

Count l.

In the Superior Court of the State of California, in and for the county of San Diego, Department 28, Case No. SCD 113632; the People of the State of California, Plaintiff, versus Floyd Arnold Mitleider, Defendant.

VERDICT: We, the jury in the above entitled cause, find the defendant guilty of the crime of attempted murder, in violation of Penal Code section 664/187(a). (Victim: Charlene Mitleider)... The offense was willful, deliberate and premeditated.

Count 2.

... VERDICT:... find the defendant, Floyd Arnold Mitleider, guilty of the crime of conspiracy to commit a crime, in violation of Penal Code section 182(a)(1). (Victim: Charlene Mitleider). In violation of Penal Code section 187, the jury marked by an "X" for Murder, the type of crime conspired.

Unanimous findings:

Overt Acts No. 1, 2, 3, 4, 5, 6, 7, 8 naming James Ray Smith, Jr., Marvin Keith Brown and Ivan Darnell Catlin as being recruited, traveling to Lewis Junior High School, 5170 Greenbrier, San Diego, and firing four shots into the car in which Charlene Mitleider was sitting in an attempt to kill her.

True.

Count 3.

...VERDICT:... find the defendant, Floyd Arnold Mitleider, guilty of the crime of solicitation of murder, in violation of Penal Code section 653f(b).(Victim: Charlene Mitleider.)

James Ray Smith, Jr.

VERDICTS:

Count 1.

Guilty of attempted murder in violation of Penal Code section 664/187a), the offense willful, deliberate, and premeditated with Penal

Code section 189; armed with a firearm, to wit, a handgun, with the meaning of Penal Code section 12022(a)(1).

Count 2.

Guilty of conspiracy to commit a crime, in violation of Penal Code section 182(a)(1), the jury marked with an X for Murder in violation of Penal Code section 187. Unanimous findings:

Overt Acts No. 1, 2, 3, 4, 5, 6, 7, 8, all the same as for Floyd. True.

Count 3. Guilty of solicitation of murder.

Count 4. Guilty of attempted murder. (Victim: Muaid Alfuraiji).

Count 5. Guilty of conspiracy to commit robbery. (Victim: Muaid Alfuraiji).

Unanimous findings:

Overt Acts No. 1, 2, 3, 4, 5, 6, 7, 8, 9, 10, 11, naming James Ray Smith, Jr. as going to the apartment of Muaid Alfuraiji and Imad Kassim Aqili, 4512 Georgia Street, Apartment 6, San Diego, opening the door and allowing two men to enter, urging Marvin Keith Brown and Ivan Darnell Catlin to do what they came to do, pointing handguns at Muaid Alfuraiji, forcing Alfuraiji to search for money they said roommate Imad Kassim Aqili owed them, binding of hands and feet of Muaid Alfuraiji, putting Muaid Alfuraiji into a bedroom closet, Marvin Keith Brown stabbing him repeatedly and Ivan Darnell Catlin stabbing him repeatedly:

1 through 10

True.

Overt Act No. 11, taking property belonging to Muaid Alfuraiji and Imad Kassim Aqili:

Not true.

Count 6.

Guilty of the crime of torture, in violation of Penal Code section 206, further that the defendant was armed with a firearm, to wit, a handgun. (Victim: Muaid Alfuraiji).

Count 7.

Not guilty of the crime of robbery in violation of Penal Code section 211.

Marvin Keith Brown

VERDICTS:

Count 1, Count 2, Count 4, Count 5, and Count 6 guilty.

Count 3 was not charged against Marvin Keith Brown (solicitation of murder).

Count 7. Not guilty of the crime of robbery.

Count 5 Overt Acts No. 1, 2, 3, 4, 5, 6, 7, 8, 9, 10 (same as to James Ray Smith, Jr.)

True.

Overt Act. No. 11, taking property belonging to Muaid Alfuraiji and Imad Kassim Aqili.

Not true.

Ivan Darnell Catlin

VERDICTS:

Guilty of the same Counts as Marvin Keith Brown, that is, all Counts except Count 3, solicitation of murder (charged only against Floyd Arnold Mitleider and James Ray Smith, Jr.); all Overt Act Nos. true, except No. 11, not true.

Count 7. The crime of robbery, not guilty.

Attorneys for defendant Mitleider asked that the jurors be polled.

Clerk: Were these or are these your verdicts as read?

Individually each juror responded:

All Jurors: Yes.

Court: You may record the verdicts as to Mr. Mitleider. Any counsel on behalf of their respective client wish to have the jury polled? Hearing no response, you may record the verdicts as to the remaining defendants.

Clerk: Yes, your Honor.

Court: [To the jurors] From my perception, this was not just civic duty that you signed up for. It turns out it was long and personal sacrifice. So on behalf of the lawyers, whatever side they're on, and certainly this particular Court and the courts in general, I just have to personally thank you for your time, your attention, your effort and your conclusion. Your necessary contribution as the conscience of this community has just helped make the system work. You're to be congratulated, and that lingering admonition is no longer binding upon you.

Charlene reflected a long time about the verdicts of the jury. Her imagination painted a picture in her mind of the condemned men, especially Floyd, whose face she knew so well. The three hired killers had to be mortified by the word Guilty at the end of each ruling; that the jury discarded the robbery phase of their visit to Muaid gave them no comfort, she was sure. Except for James the shooters had priors, she had been told. In California that meant that the sentences for the present crimes would be doubled or tripled according to the number of priors each had. As for James Smith his sentence would be harsh because he solicited the help of Brown and Catlin, like Floyd had solicited people to kill his wife.

Floyd, sure he would be acquitted, must have revolted inside when he heard he was found guilty. He had been caught and convicted of a crime he had so passionately denied. Lying had always worked before. "I love my wife . . . I would never do anything to harm her," he had believed was sufficient to get him off.

Not only had Floyd been apprehended and embarrassed by his words on the damning tape, he'd been put through an arduous trial. He had exposed his culpability and his dark side as well. This would be totally beyond his comprehension. "I said I was fuckin' innocent, didn't I? Enough!" would be his tacit plea bursting to be said. How he could regard himself as innocent would perplex anyone looking at the case records. It was so Floyd that he would say and expect everyone to believe he was innocent.

Floyd would also be distressed at having spent money on defense attorneys who did not get him off.

Charlene was overcome with torment, knowing Floyd deserved to be found guilty and at the same time wishing he had not done anything of which he could be found guilty. She began to quiver as she thought of the penal codes announced with each verdict. Floyd's code and the penal code he violated in this dynamic encounter were both components of murder; there were two codes for murder.

And before the final word of the judge that day, she was sure Floyd was already planning his appeal. Maybe Frankie would know what to do. He would make it work.

Floyd's most prominent trait, changeability, would appear very soon. He would be bitter and rigidly deny his guilt but in a very short time he would be admitting to himself only: You screwed up, you fool, you fucked up. You traded the unshaken goal to keep your money away from Charlene for a long stint in prison; your Forever Girl is Forever Gone.

46

Escape: Last Chance for Fresh Air

The trial over, Charlene tried the rest of the month of June 1996 to think of other things. The guilty verdicts brought only a partial triumph, enough to be able to relax her vigil somewhat. Why would anyone want to help Floyd in his quest to do away with her now? Even if Frankie was a devoted friend, he would not take the risk of doing anything illegal and getting caught, like Floyd and the three shooters.

The sentencing for the four convicted men was set for early August; plans were underway for Dorothea, her two granddaughters and her daughter to attend the court hearing. Charlene had been invited to speak to the court by the Department of Probation. The purpose for the trip to San Diego would be twofold: to attend the sentencing trial and to enjoy a short vacation.

Conviction was one thing, but sentencing quite another. They could not be sure Floyd would be punished by a long sentence. There would be no closure for Charlene unless Floyd had to stay imprisoned until he was an old man. She knew he would always blame her, the DC for ruining his life.

Charlene wanted her girls to see her stand up to Floyd in the courtroom and say what she thought should be done with him. She wanted them to see justice in action, and the person who had deliberately put them in an unhappy situation now in a deserved unhappier situation himself. They would see what results from breaking the laws of God and man.

They had adjusted to their new crowded place which had become home last summer. The girls had some weeks of this summer to enjoy before the new Fall semester at their respective schools.

Kimber and a new kitty named Butchy took up some of their already cramped space, but they were thrilled to have them make up 2/5 of their family. The girls showered affection on them, calling Butchy their "attack cat" with a "tough gal" name.

Lailani kept in touch with Tracie and Jericha corresponded with one of her school friends who proclaimed Jericha was "cool." Along with Mary, these were their San Diego contacts. They were like cherished passages of the California chapter of their lives. They were apart from the District Attorney's office, the Probation office, the SDPD officers and Charlene's divorce attorney. Their contacts with the "outside world" were very limited. Charlene did not like all the hang-up calls she was getting on her unlisted phone nor other rather strange occurrences. Cars would often pass very slowly in front of her apartment building, sometimes with men leaning out the windows staring her way. There were two new houses for sale in their block. She believed people were looking for them. A large black car passed by one Saturday afternoon while the girls had Kimber and Butchy outside playing in the too tall shimmering grass. It was moving so slowly that its make and license plates were easily noted. A Cadillac, Kansas license number JO 4 6 ? - she couldn't really see the last two numbers. It had very dark translucent windows.

"Don't let your imagination get the better of you!" she warned herself. She had to be her own psychologist. Dr. Straub had not yet been paid by the California Victims' Advocacy Program and he wanted to bill Charlene for their sessions. She had to drop the treatment.

There was an uneasiness, an unconscious fear that maybe she had not heard the last of Floyd Arnold Mitleider.

Tracie was propped up on the couch, nearing the end of her conversation with Lailani one Wednesday afternoon.

"My grandmother wants to speak to your mother," Lailani told her.

"Hi, Charlene. How have you been anyway? We are surely missing you. It is such a shame you had to leave San Diego, and under the circumstances you did."

"We'll be coming back to San Diego next month for the sentencing hearing," Charlene proposed. "We'll see you then."

"I wanted to tell you something interesting that happened," Mrs. Hartford* said with a chuckling enthusiasm. "You know my neighbor Joaquina was down at the Hall of Justice yesterday morning getting some kind of filing forms. On her way back to her parked car on Union Street she spied a beautiful shiny penny on the sidewalk close to the curb. Don't laugh. It wasn't just any ole penny, not an ordinary penny. There was something special about it, all polished, almost glowing, she said. Naturally she picked it up for good luck, brought it home, and showed it to her son when he came in from work. He said, after looking it up in his coin directory book, 'My, oh my. This is a rare coin.' Turns out it may be worth a few hundred dollars. It's called a 'wheatie' or something like that. She said to me, '*Dios mío*, going downtown today was really worth the *pena*. I'm glad I was looking down.'"

"That was good luck all right. You never know when you're gonna have it, or need it, do you? I don't think I've had any for a real long time. Oh, Mrs. Hartford, I have another call. Will you hold a minute?"

The call was from St. Louis. Charlene's mother had just received a FAX from Mr. Dunne's office, a newspaper article in the Crime Watch section of the *San Diego Union-Tribune* about an attempted escape from the city jailhouse beside the courthouse. The inmates had tried to cut a hole in the chain link fence to gain freedom from the jail. It was Floyd and two others. Mom said she would mail the FAX to Charlene right away.

"My God, did you say 'attempted'?" Charlene gasped.

"Yes. They were caught."

"I'm back." She clicked into Lailani's grandmother's line. "We just got a copy of a newspaper article from this morning's San Diego paper about an attempted escape from jail yesterday morning. Hey, this probably happened about the time your neighbor was down there. The courthouse, Hall of Justice and jail are all in close proximity, as I recall."

"It was Floyd?" Mrs. Hartford asked. "Is he still being held downtown?"

"Yes. He is still in jail until the sentencing. They're holding him there until he goes back to court. H'm, h'm, this escape attempt might influence the sentencing. I don't know. But from this article I would say he was a desperate man.

"This was his last chance for freedom. When he gets to prison, it'll be all over. Escapes from prison are almost unheard of. Or at least, that's what I've been told. Depending on to which California prison he is assigned, he may get rough treatment while there, in addition to no chance for escape!"

"I see. You said it's his sentencing trial you're coming out for, isn't it?"

"There wouldn't be any if he had succeeded in escaping."

"I'll look for the article when I get my newspaper in from the street. I'll send you an additional copy when I do."

"Thanks. I'd appreciate that. And we'll be seeing you soon."

Later, the faxed article in hand, Charlene read with intense attention.

CRIMEWATCH.
Tuesday, July 23, 1996

DEPUTIES THWART ESCAPE ATTEMPT BY 3 INMATES. San Diego.—Sheriff's deputies thwarted an attempted rooftop escape from the downtown jail yesterday when they found three inmates trying to cut a hole in a fence. The inmates were spotted about 9 a.m. huddled in a corner of the seventh-floor rooftop recreation area and about to cut a hole in the chain-link fence that encloses the lockup, said Sheriff's spokesman Ron Reina. When apprehended, the inmates were wearing cutoff shorts and tank tops fashioned from jail garb under their issued uniforms. They also had a make-shift rope made of knotted towels and a small blade.

The article concluded with the names of the inmates, one of whom was Floyd Mitleider, recently convicted of attempted murder.

Later Herb Bowman told Charlene it was a saw blade the three men had gotten their hands on. Al said it wasn't a bad plan; it could have worked, except for the informant.

"Do you know if they had any outside help?" Charlene asked Herb.

"Can't say, but if we find any proof that anyone did provide assistance, that person will be prosecuted. We will let you know."

Although she had some haunting suspicions, Charlene really knew only one thing: Floyd had lost his chance for fresh air.

In her dreams that night she saw Floyd quickly shimmying down the towel rope, swinging like Tarzan agilely.

As soon as his feet hit the sidewalk, a waiting cohort grabbed Floyd's waist and started undressing him. The makeshift shorts and tank tops were fringed and unclean, but Floyd dusted them off and ran behind the other man who tripped slightly on the corner of an uneven cement piece, scraping his shoe at the same time.

Sitting straight up in bed, wide awake and in a cold sweat, the realization that this didn't really happen came to Charlene as a peaceful revelation.

But it might happen again, there may be success the second time around. If it failed the second time, there would be a third attempt. Floyd would not stay locked up.

A new nightmare genre had been born. It would be repeated, Charlene knew. Through illusion his control over her still existed. The nightmare would foretell the event.

Dreams, especially bad dreams, had a habit of becoming reality. There was the murdered woman at La Mirage. The event had emerged out of the pall of her mind into a tangible happening, part of which she saw for herself. . . the gurney, the local news. This new dream about Floyd and his aide was not real; Floyd had only attempted escape. He never made the trip down on the makeshift rope to the sidewalk below. Part of this dream may have been true, but she did not know what part.

Her Guardian Angel was still with her, she thought, not allowing Floyd to escape, keeping her safe from his harm.

I am with you always, echoed her Guardian Angel's dulcet voice. Where is Floyd's Guardian Angel? He doesn't believe in them, so how could he have one? They are for the masses. Not for the higher echelon like Floyd. He looks to his own superior strength and makes his good fortune his own way, never giving a weakling an opening. What does an Angel have to do with it?

Floyd's attempt to gain freedom had failed. His cycling days, jogging the track, lying in the sun on a white Hawaiian beach would never come again if he got the sentence he deserved.

The real world turned on and off flickering like a candle. She would ask about the penny tomorrow or whenever she talked to Mrs. Hartford again. She could get Charlene more details from her neighbor. Charlene's paranoia had grown out of Floyd's words; she had to remember that he was often wrong.

Floyd's friends had more sense than to break the law.

That would be asking too much of them.

47

Diogenes is Still Looking

After the long battle in the courtroom drama, Charlene turned to the problem of her final divorce from Floyd.

She needed closure. It was not enough that Floyd had been convicted.

There was information uncovered by private investigation that Floyd had succeeded in removing a large amount of money from one of his bank accounts. Charlene eventually formed the opinion that this was the reason he claimed to take money from his account with which to gamble in Las Vegas. He thought he would be in trouble otherwise. He was nothing but a dishonest man.

"He always wanted me to sympathize with him, saying his store was not making money. I was supposed to feel sorry for him. But he didn't deserve my compassion."

"He never deserved you Period."

"I know. In fact I wonder if there are any really honest people. I feel like Diogenes and I'll keep my lamp on shining everywhere I look."

Charlene still had to wait for the sentencing hearing. Waiting was as hard as searching.

PART THREE

HOW TO SURVIVE

48

A Fair Sentence

A year and two months since the last time they were all together in San Diego, Jericha, Tracie, Dorothea and Charlene were back. When they had left for their destinations in the Midwest, their lives were filled with uncertainties. Now the tableau had changed somewhat. There might be an end in sight.

They stayed at a Best Western across and down the road from the Handlery where they had spent anxious moments before Floyd's arrest. The thin air of August in this part of the country was warm, but not scorching like the heavier air of the Midwest. They were determined to make this sojourn to so lovely a place as wholesome and refreshing as any stay in a pristine site. Floyd had been right about San Diego's high rank among cities in which to live. But he had enjoyed it a fleeting moment only. Charlene and her mother pledged themselves to giving the girls a much needed wonderful experience. In fact they needed one too.

Jericha had her friend Rose come over and swim one day at their motel. They reminisced about the end of the previous school year.

"I kept wondering why you didn't come back to Lewis after that day. No one answered when I tried to call you. The kids told me someone had driven up and shot at your mother's car," Jericha's friend was saying. "I couldn't see what was happening. That was a bad thing. And it was your stepfather? He hired someone to kill her?"

"Yes," Jericha answered as she stepped out of the pool. "But I never thought of him as a father of any kind. I don't want to talk about it, if you don't mind."

"I was sorry you missed the yearbook signing. They gave us the whole afternoon. Some of the kids got rowdy and Mr. Elgin sent them home."

"Par for the course at Lewis," Jericha laughed. "Only the rowdies didn't always get suspended."

Tracie had a sleepover with Lailani. Charlene remembered to ask Lailani's grandmother about her neighbor Joaquina who had the good fortune to pick up a valuable penny off the sidewalk.

"You know Joaquina and her family had sold their house and were just getting ready to move, if I didn't tell you that. In fact she was at the courthouse getting some papers that had to do with the property exchange, I think. I never got to ask her any particulars about that penny. She was sure excited that day, though."

The day of the sentencing, they all woke up extra early. Jericha and Tracie put on their new dresses and stood before the long mirrors beside the closet of the joined rooms.

"Is my slip sticking out?" Tracie asked, absorbed in her grooming.

"Just a tiny bit on one side," Jericha answered.

"Let's see if we can adjust the strap on that side."

"You both look wonderful," Charlene bragged. "We'll get a bite of breakfast downstairs and be on our way."

"Mom, do we have to look at Floyd?" Tracie asked. "Because I don't really want to."

"Me neither," Jericha joined in. "I'm not going to."

◆ ◆ ◆

In the same courtroom where she had testified in May and in which Floyd heard the "Guilty" verdict for his crimes in June, Charlene found herself again where her speech to the court had begun. "I didn't feel like a person at all," was a reverberation which brought her to the task at hand.

"I felt like a big nothing; so through . . . counseling I have found out that what I have to say is important and I am a valuable person, so I'd like to thank you for this opportunity to speak.

"Floyd married me and isolated me 2,000 miles away from my friends and family. I know now that he did that on purpose so I wouldn't have anyone to turn to during the abusive times.

"It started out with belittlements, emotional abuse; and then it turned into physical abuse. It was not just horrible for me, but for my two daughters, also. I could have stood it for just myself.

"He had control of everything, control of the money, what we did, where we went. It was just total control of myself and my daughters; it was his apartment, his car, his money, his say. It was no way to live."

Charlene paused.

"When November came, he came to me with this idea of getting a life insurance policy. It overwhelmed me at the amount, $750,000. I couldn't believe it. I said, 'How can we have this policy when you tell me we can't even afford health insurance for myself and my daughters?' He came up with this story that it was a good deal, a chance of a lifetime. We would get it through his best friend."

Again, Charlene stopped.momentarily. She had to go on.

"My daughters and I tried to cope but it progressively got worse and worse for us." Reliving those bad times, Charlene swallowed hard, then continued.

"On February 17th the abuse led to his arrest. It was his first felony. A week and a half later I filed a restraining order against Mr. Mitleider, and he was supposed to leave our home immediately. He did not leave our home until March 3rd, and then, because I called the police again.

"He didn't care about restraining orders. He just ignored them. I believe he thought he was above orders.

"I didn't see Floyd for months. Nick would come to my apartment when Floyd needed to find out something about court proceedings or taxes. Nick was our go-between. But we had no contact. That's why I was truly shocked when, on June 1st, I had a phone call; and I *69'd it, because I heard heavy breathing and the person wouldn't speak; and lo and behold, who is on the other end of the line but Floyd. I couldn't understand why he's still annoying me and harassing me when we hadn't even seen each other for months. I found out, of course, that he was just checking to see if I was still alive. I know he was terribly disappointed to hear my voice," Charlene hesitated, nearly losing her train of thought.

"The day the attempt was made on my life [it was a] horrible [experience for] me. A mother going to pick her children up from school, sitting in her car, minding her own business, does not expect what happened to me. I was just waiting for the kids to come out when a car stops dead in front of me and [a passenger] starts shooting at me to kill me.

"This man didn't care about innocent children that would have been in the parking lot or children that were dismissed early. He only cared about his needs. He wanted to get that money. He didn't marry me for love; he married me for the love of money. He was greedy and cruel.

"My children and I have been living in hiding for this last entire year. . . [We have] endured a lot of pain. . .

"My parents have had to spend thousands of dollars on a bodyguard during the time when we were waiting for him to be arrested and looking out for me. . . Because he had control of the money, I have had a hard time financially.

"So I would plead with you to give him the maximum sentence, because I don't think anything less would be right. My daughters and I will have to live with this bad experience for the rest of our lives. He should have to give up his comforts and selfish ways for the longest term possible. I have suffered in every way; it is only fair that he should too."

The judge thanked Charlene and got on with the business of the sentence. The discussions had been grueling, even boring to everyone sitting on the back row. Al and Ron had sat through many a sentencing hearing. Al told them they would hear wailing and loud whining if they stayed in the courtroom for the other three's sentencing. Charlene thought it a little sad that no one was wailing for Floyd. Lou Brown was steadfast in his support for Charlene. She looked to the right of her and saw her Mom who looked dejected but managed a smile.

Her two daughters were a little red in the face from the excitement of the moment and the remembering of the past.

Floyd had not blinked an eye but did stare at Charlene during her oration to the court. She thought her speech surprised him; he didn't think she had the stamina for this. She wanted her words to mean something to him: "she spoke out boldly against me; I never thought she would do it," he would say.

Judge Kennedy then continued with his deliberation. At issue was the matter of how much time Floyd should serve for one phase of the crimes of which he was found guilty. "The aggravating factors with regard to Count 3 (solicitation) outweigh the mitigating factors providing for the upper term of 9 years," the Judge noted. He stated the crime involved great violence, great bodily harm, the threat of the same and other acts disclosing a high degree of cruelty, viciousness or callousness. "There is no question that Mrs. Mitleider was particularly vulnerable as a victim in this case and the intended object of this offense. As she has announced, she was completely ignorant of his plans, although he had evinced abusive conduct towards her by way of domestic injuries; and one of the vicious aspects of this thing was that, as she has spoken here today, she was literally a sitting duck, sitting outside a school, of all places, in a parked car when these hired assassins come up and shoot at her. The manner in which the crime was carried out does indicate preplanning and a certain degree of sophistication. The fact that they weren't accomplished at this and missed their intended target doesn't, nevertheless, negate the sophistication intended. The crime involved the attempt to collect on life insurance that he took out of three quarters of a million dollars, pretty heavy motivation for a pretty greedy husband."

"The judge was listening to me after all," Charlene whispered to her mother who was shaking her head affirmatively. "It pays to speak up," she murmured.

"Probation having been denied, it is the judgment and sentence of the court that the defendant, Mr. Mitleider, be committed to the Department of Corrections for the total term of 25 years to Life, plus 9 years."

The judge had already mentioned the attempted escape from jail about which he himself had read in the newspaper. That, he assured Floyd, would be the subject of another case and other punishment.

Charlene had heard of much briefer sentences for men convicted of hiring a killing of their wives; she had also heard of cases in which the convicted man got a life without parole sentence.

She thought about the judge's pronouncement and the extra blink of Floyd's eye when the words reached his ears. He did not smirk or radically change his facial expression. But Charlene knew that it impacted him sharply, it wounded him just as his words and deeds had injured her.

Thirty-four years plus the attempted escape punishment...

Charlene looked down at the baby blue crepe dress she was wearing. There on the left side she was wearing two initial pins her mother and she had combined for Charlene to wear conspicuously: one large D, for her mother's first name and a matching large C, for Charlene. Together they had hoped it might be noticed who was the DC by which name Floyd had called her. The defense attorneys would not let her explain when Bowman asked its meaning.

By now they probably had forgotten, and maybe never did care. But Charlene did believe Floyd noticed in that one blink of his eyes. *Yes, I am here, the DC, but I am not as dumb as you had hoped. You are the one just sentenced to a long prison term.* Charlene felt some insignificant revenge.

It was a fair sentence. Despite pleas and appeals, the sentence would stand and would be served. She had to believe that in order to survive.

49

No Safe Place

The television cameras followed them out of the courtroom and questions were being asked.

"We sincerely hope more can be done for women who are victims of this kind of abuse," Lou Brown told the interviewers. "Our foundation has that in mind. . ."

To their questions Charlene answered that she was grateful to Lou for attending the sentencing with her. She thanked her Guardian Angel, as well. "I know I am a very lucky person," she admitted, "and I hope to find a way to make something of my good fortune, my life. I would like other women to know of my experience, and I would like to warn them," she paused, "to look for the signs, believe in themselves, act on their instincts. It's important."

"I know you're glad this is over," Ron said as they left the courtroom and the television crew prepared to exit the building. "Now you and your pretty little girls can get back to normal."

"It's not that simple," Charlene replied, "but at least we'll try."

"Let us hear from you," said Al, "and if there is anything we can do for you, give us a call."

Outside in the heat of late morning, they all waited for the light to change so they could cross Broadway.

They began walking rapidly, but the walk light had already extinguished by the time they got to the middle ground of the wide street.

"Hello," came a raspy voice from the side of the street they were attempting to reach. There was a small crowd on that side of Broadway, the red bricks of the tall Federal buildings behind them. They looked up to see the slightly graying, bespectacled face of Tom

Connolly. He stared at all four of them, no doubt putting their features in perspective. He was calculating that he had seen this young woman, then her mother in the courtroom. Possibly Floyd had told him that her mother was that person sitting in the gallery day after day, back when the trial was going on.

The light changed and they all began to move. As they passed shoulder to shoulder, an almost indistinguishable greeting was mumbled by Dorothea and Charlene did not say even that. He made her uncomfortable. She remembered how he had insinuated his client Floyd only wanted her "out" and was innocent of attempted murder, and how he had joked about the district attorney's whisking her back to St. Louis. He did pretend to know it all.

"Who was it who told you Connolly had been indicted for some crime? I think it was some kind of molestation?"

"One of the police officers. That's probably why he was not there for Floyd today. He may have been disbarred or something," Dorothea suggested. "He may be out on bail."

"They probably don't make attorneys stay in jail," Charlene said naively.

"Floyd did not have much luck with his attorneys, did he?" Charlene asked, taking Tracie's arm as they crossed the next street, dodging the traffic.

"No, he didn't," her mother replied. "But then he didn't have a good case, either. Who could defend Floyd when he incriminated himself so badly? I will say this in his favor: Floyd learned to say, 'Yes, your Honor,' and 'Yes, sir,' quite well."

It seemed so out of character for a man who had ordered people around, calling waiters Troll, so-called friends Phlegm and his own parents assorted insulting names. he showed respect to no one.

When the short visit to San Diego ended, they flew back to their homes, parting ways in St. Louis where Mom stayed and the other three changed to another plane.

50

Finding a Way

The girls liked their schools. After a year in the system they realized structure and discipline were more conducive to learning than the loose California style. Lessons they had learned in the West were not taught in the schools anyway but in the mist of a strange man's macabre lifestyle.

They were eager to be acceptable, if not superior in the matter of schooling. Around strangers they were extremely subdued but were beginning to be more outgoing with people they knew.

There were problems. Charlene had not been able to get a new social security number and was told she could be tracked down even if she did. Knowing how Floyd had Frankie keep a close watch on his first wife using her social security number, she had not stopped looking over her shoulder, feeling the footsteps of a stalker, imperceptible behind her, wondering who was the Anonymous or Unavailable person shown by her Caller ID without real identity.

"Don't answer unless you know the calling party," Mom had advised when this service was put on her line.

Jericha came home from school one day asking her, "Can we go back to California on vacation next summer? I'd like to take my old yearbook with me and have at least Rose sign it."

"We might have to go back for more divorce hearings by then," Charlene responded. "There is supposed to be a civil trial."

"No," Jericha said, "I mean a real vacation that has nothing to do with Floyd. Grandma said we could go back to Sea World. I wish we could."

"Is that important to you?"

"Yeh. I'm going to forget that day at Lewis. That was pretty awful. And we keep talking about it. Seeing those dolphins swim around that tank freely, having fun, that would be great. They might be happier out in the ocean, but at least the trainers take good care of them," she rambled on.

"But the kids at Lewis thought your mother was a celebrity, remember?" Charlene teased, putting her arm around Jericha's shoulder.

The tension inside her changed slowly to a grin.

"I'm glad you're not a celebrity, if that's what happens to them. Plain ole Mom is good enough for me. Not that you're plain, Mom."

♦♦♦

Charlene went to pick up Tracie and found the black Cadillac with dark-tinted windows parked just ahead of her. Tracie came out the side door of the Middle School. "That same car was here last week," she told Charlene, "and you weren't here yet, Mom. The driver rolled down his window a little bit and asked me my name. Then I saw you'd pulled up at the end of the line of cars and I ran down there."

"Why didn't you tell me about that? I will never be even a second late picking you up again," she swore to Tracie. "And if you see that car after this, remember the rule: 'Don't talk to strangers.' If no other option exists, run back inside the school building. Don't be afraid. Everything will be all right."

Charlene knew there were many explanations for the presence of the black Cadillac. Parents of some other student could have innocently asked Tracie her name, hoping she knew their child. She tried to believe that the explanation was something as simple as that. None of Floyd's connections could be responsible.

Floyd was incarcerated. He would not be eligible for parole until he had spent at least 80% of his sentence in prison. Even then he might be turned down on his first parole hearing. By the time he got out, they would both be pretty old. He should no longer be any kind of threat to her. He might even spend the rest of his life incarcerated. Still he occupied her mind and caused her to feel the deep pain of never having the chance to recapture the love they had known. What had lasted only a brief moment in time had evaporated, as though it had never existed in the first place. It left only an indelible stain.

Those thirty or more years from the time of Floyd's arrest on that fateful day in June 1995 until whatever day he would leave the prison on parole in the 21st century represented futility to the highest degree. For Floyd there was no life. Prison was a special kind of hell. He was a naked soul, eating, drinking, sleeping, watching TV, breathing, but accomplishing absolutely nothing. He was a useless zombie.

As for Charlene, life was a meaningful gift no matter how complex it would play out; her already damaged self-image was lowered by the events of this horror story. With treatment in these long years ahead she had a chance for happiness. She had liberty. She could move about at will, be with her children, go to the movie of her choice, have friends from any walk of life she chose, maybe even a nice boyfriend, and be at limited peace. She had to believe in something. All she needed was time.

"The best way to allay your fears is to jump right in, find an outlet for your energies and do whatever you can to rescue other people. In helping people in recognizing and solving their problems, your own problems seem to go away!" said an angelic voice rattling in her head. "Be glad you are alive!"

Every night the nightmare of Floyd's ever-changing persona tried to emanate again. She opened her eyes trying to keep her promise to see Floyd only in her alert mind. She tried to erase from memory all the bad times, all the suffering and frustration. She glorified all the good times remembering what joy she had known. But like laser scars on her memory the black moments would not be extracted. She climbed out of the unlit hole more nimbly each time. Just as Dr. Straub had said, she always somehow rasped her way out.

One night a resplendent image of a man dressed in a Valentino-like tuxedo was tenderly holding Charlene in a slow dance position. She was radiant in her blue crepe dress, now ballet length, shimmering in the light breeze of the evening. They were lightly dancing on a smooth beach surface while the genial voice sang, *So I sing you to sleep, after the lovin', with a song I just wrote yesterday. . . Thanks for takin' me on a one-way trip to the sun, And thanks for turnin' me into a someone.* The image lulled her into a peaceful slumber and froze in time. It rid her of fear and she felt wildly happy.

Now she felt she could accept that love was gone and she finally knew that Floyd's faults and actions were his alone. She did not influence or cause them. She had turned him into a someone. His ego and his own greed had ruined his life. She refused to let him ruin hers. She would survive. She would sway in his arms as they danced, her dress swirling in the dizzy breeze. She would work hard. She could not allow fears to overtake her life. She had to hang on. She would not spend eternity looking for a mystical safe place. It existed wherever she was with this image in her refreshed mind.

When she got home with Tracie and her two girls sat down at the old oak table to have their snack, she went to the phone directory and looked up a number. "Hello? Is this the Women's Center? I'd like to volunteer to help."

Epilogue

Floyd Arnold Mitlieider

Floyd Arnold Mitleider, K-32161, pled guilty to the charge of attempted escape from jail, Case No. SCD 122623, on October 30, 1996, and received a sentence of four years on December 2, 1996. Restitution fines of $1,800 to be paid to the San Diego Sheriff's Department were levied against Floyd. He began serving his sentence of 38 years to Life in Folsom State Prison on February 11, 1997, in Block Z Section 3. On June 27, 1997, the Department of Corrections amended Floyd's credits for time spent in confinement to zero because of his escape attempt. His MEPD (Minimum Eligible Parole Date) is November 14, 2025. It is reported that when a journalist tried to interview Floyd after the criminal verdict, he at first agreed, then changed his mind exclaiming, "I'm fucking innocent." Appeals were filed on his behalf and on March 21, 2000, he was resentenced to 25 years to Life for Counts 1 and 2, with Count 3 vacated. There was a court error which ended in the dismissal of Count 3 (Solicitation). Ironically the solicitation complaint was supported by abundant evidence presented in court. In addition a piece of paper found in Mitleider's personal effects stored in the Mission Valley Self-Storage facility had written on it: Priest 1 800-915-5019, the telephone number of the first hired assassin he solicited. The printing on the paper is obviously written in Floyd Mitleider's style. The sentence for the attempted escape remained at four years.

James Ray Smith, Jr.

James Ray Smith, Jr., K-15873, at the sentencing hearing in August 1996 thanked Mrs. Mitleider for her honesty and God that no harm has come to her. He is serving 25 years to Life plus Life in Lancaster State Prison.

Ivan Darnell Catlin

Ivan Darnell Catlin, E-44547, was sentenced to 150 years to Life plus 5 years. Said to be dominating his yard at Donovan while in reception there, he is now serving his time in Lancaster State Prison. He had a resentencing hearing in 2000 as well, but his sentence was only reduced to 80 years to Life.

Marvin Keith Brown

Marvin Keith Brown, E-28694, was sentenced to 106 years to Life. He was under medication to quell some mental problem but had not received any medication since June 26, 1996, when the sentencing hearing was taking place in August. He was ill and unable to be present for that hearing and was therefore sentenced a week after the others. He was ultimately placed in the California Medical Facility at Vacaville for evaluation and care. Later he was transferred to Atascadero State Hospital, Unit 11, for mental health treatment and was still there as of February 1998. After treatment he will be sent to another state prison.

Appeals

Appeals had been filed for the four defendants very soon after the trial and sentencing in August 1996. Lorri Hooper's perjured testimony, an out-and-out lie for Catlin, was the subject of a motion for a new trial and appeals from all the defendants. The lengthy appeals filed in the Appellate Court are based on the manner in which the jury was chosen and the ineffectiveness of the defense attorneys., particularly Ivan Catlin's. The documents are so numerous that they had to be stacked on a double level cart on wheels when requested to be viewed. Among documents requested by the Appeals attorneys were 12 volumes of Reporter's Transcripts and 7 volumes of Clerk's Transcripts. Final opinion having been rendered resulting in resentencing for Mitleider and Catlin, the appeals process has now ended.

Restitution Hearings

Restitution hearings were heard on September 13, 1996, and September 24, 1996. The court set restitution for all four inmates at $7,440.87 for Charlene and $99,270.65 for Muaid Alfuraiji. Restitution fines for each man were set at $200. A hearing regarding the sum of $4,500 paid by Floyd to Najah Sitto, which was turned over to police on June 15, 1995, resulted in the placing of that sum in Muaid's counsel's trust fund pending resolution of Charlene's domestic matter and order for judgment. Both Floyd's divorce attorney and defense counsel attended the hearing to protect Floyd's interest. The judge suggested this was an admission of guilt on his part; if he had nothing to do with this money, why was he represented by two attorneys? Bishop (defense attorney) told the judge Floyd Mitleider wanted to attend this hearing and his client was upset that he was not allowed. (He must have been interested in the $4,500 of which he purportedly had no part, being innocent of the whole case. According to his statements to the SDPD, his wife had made up the whole story about being abused and fired upon.) Being married to Floyd had cost Charlene considerable money for which in return she had a miserable short marriage featuring abuse and heartbreak. At a hearing held on March 22, 2000, Charlene was awarded the money described, plus the interest it had accrued in the nearly five years it had been placed in a trust account. It seemed to be an instance of true justice that money originally given by Floyd for the purpose of killing Charlene was instead received by her in the form of restitution.

About Dorothea Fuller Smith

Dorothea Fuller Smith is a retired French and Spanish teacher who has written for the literary review of her college, St. Louis Community College (St. Louis MO). She also wrote a feature article, "Maid of Orleans" which was published in the New Orleans Times-Picayune. Dorothea specializes in short stories about contemporary life and poetry.

She became intensely involved in the events of this non-fiction title, *Two Codes for Murder*, based on a crime which was committed against her daughter in San Diego, California. As the terrified mother of the victim, the author writes with authority and conviction and all the events have touched her personally and deeply.

Dorothea resides with her husband in Missouri where they are enjoying life, their children and their grandchildren. Along with her husband, she plans to take a long trip to see the parts of the world not already visited and forget about the events of the last half of the last decade. Thankful her daughter is still among the living, no thanks to the greedy man she had married, she has no regrets about time and money spent. Neither has she any forgiveness in her heart.

About DiefFesco Publishing

DiefFesco Publishing was established in 1999 by Philip and Dorothea Smith with a mission and intent to publish informative books, both non-fiction and fiction, which directly and indirectly help people.

DiefFesco's books will advise readers in an entertaining way on various subjects, such as dealing with an abusive marriage, growing old and using herbs both in the culinary arts and as medicine.

DiefFesco Publishing is a small, independent publisher located in Missouri. It is a member of the Publisher's Marketing Association (PMA), The St. Louis Publisher's Association (SLPA), and the Small Publishers Association of North American (SPAN).

What people have said about Two Codes for Murder

"What a story. Best of luck to your daughter."- *Anita Miller, Academy Chicago*

"Your story is interesting. . . You have done some fine work here. . ."-*Rod Colvin, Addicus Books*

Two Codes for Murder effectively and quickly hooks the reader's interest with a Prologue set in a courtroom in 1996. Much of the account reads with the intimacy of a journal. . .the reader thus gains insight into the psychology of abuse in a compelling way."-*Richard N. Côté, The Côté Literary Group*

"*Two Codes for Murder* is more than a book on domestic abuse and a woman's growing awareness of the dark side of the man she married. Floyd was so secretive and deceptive that he used codes to try to conceal his underhanded activities as well as his action to try to have Charlene murdered. The true crime tale is also part detective story and part police procedure. It has all the elements of a gripping TV drama."-*Henry Berry, Book Reviewer, The Small Press Book Review*

True Crime at Its Best

The explosion of words in *Two Codes for Murder* details the cunning preparation for a crime with extensive use of deceit and codes. Incomparable as a women's issue, the crime and its solution are authentically told through police reports, courtroom drama and the eyes of the bewildered victim.

A young St. Louis single mother dreams of a lasting marriage and a move to San Diego, anticipating a lifetime of bliss with a man in her life she has decided to believe in. Instead, the marriage turns out to be a nightmarish existence with nothing but heartbreak and terror, and then two heinous crimes.

Fearing for her life and her children's safety she gives up her dream and goes into hiding, at first unable to convince authorities that this man she has called husband for a few months is an incredibly cruel and selfish monster. He is a deviate who loves only money, himself and mysterious buddies who are clones of himself. He mistreats the young children and thinks nothing of abusing his new bride.

Middle Easterners add to the intrigue, confounding the criminal acts and their roles in them. But the duped, stalked woman, guided only by her courage and determination that justice be done, will not be discarded so easily. She is inspired by the story of Nicole Simpson and a defiance she has never known before.

A jewel of effective detective work, the investigations and court proceedings will fascinate crime buffs but all readers will admire and deeply empathize with the victim.

Domestic Violence Resources

National Resource Center on Domestic Violence
800/537-2238 or 800/553-2508 (TTY)
Comprehensive information and resources

Resource Center on Domestic Violence
Child Protection and Custody
800-527-3223
http://www.nationalcouncilfvd.org
Information, materials, and consultation related to child
protection and custody.

Health Resource Center on Domestic Violence
888-792-2873
http://www.fvpf.org/health
Resources, information, referrals and support for those
interested in developing a health care response to domestic
violence.

Family Violence Prevention Fund
http://www.fvpf.org
415- 252-8089
Domestic violence resource dealing with immigrant
communities and the special needs of battered immigrant
women.

Communities Against Violence Network
http://www.cavnet2.org/
An interactive web site that brings together advocates and
experts to share information and resources about
domestic violence, including within the gay and lesbian
community, stalking, sexual assault and rape.

Violence Against Women Online Resources
http://www.vaw.umn.edu/
Up-to-date information on interventions to stop violence
against women.

National Coalition Against Domestic Violence
http://www.ncadv.org/
NCADV is dedicated to the empowerment of battered
women and their children and is committed to the
elimination of personal and societal violence in the
lives of battered women and their children.

Famvi.com
http://www.famvi.com/
Range of information about shelters and abuse from
an online magazine. Includes articles and resources.

Cybergrrl Safety Net
http://www.cybergrrl.com/dv.html
Resources for women in abusive relationships.

Safe Horizon
http://www.dvsheltertour.org/
Essential information for battered women and a
virtual tour of a domestic violence shelter.

Shattered Love, Broken Lives
http://www.s-t.com/projects/DomVio/domviohome.HTML
An on-line chronology of a series of articles produced by
The Standard-Times of New Bedford, MA
following six months of investigating domestic violence.

Domestic Violence Handbook
http://www.domesticviolence.org/
Resources and information about domestic violence.

Domestic Violence Resources
http://www.silcom.com/~paladin/madv/
List of on-line resources, shelters and information about
domestic violence.

National Domestic Violence Hotline
http://www.ndvh.org/
Each month, nearly 11,000 callers - victims of domestic
violence, their families and friends across the U.S.
Receive crisis intervention, referrals, information and
support in many languages.

Crisis Support Network
http://www.domestic-violence.org/
California 24-hour toll-free support for victims of
domestic violence and their friends and families.
Also articles and help for victims.

Domestic Violence:
Safety Tips For You And Your Family

IF YOU ARE IN DANGER, CALL 911
or your local police emergency number

To find out about help in your area, call:
National Domestic Violence Hotline:
1-800-799-SAFE
1-800-787-3224 (TTY)

In an Emergency

If you are at home & you are being threatened or attacked:
Stay away from the kitchen
Stay away from bathrooms, closets or small spaces where
you could be trapped
Get to a room with a door or window to escape
Get to a room with a phone to call for help
Call 911
Think about a neighbor or friend you can run to for help
Get medical help if you are hurt
Take pictures of bruises or injuries
Call a domestic violence program or shelter

Mail Order Form

You can use the following order form to mail your order to us. Sorry, but mail orders are in checks, money orders or cashiers checks only. If you'd like to use a credit card to purchase any of our products, visit our Web site at http://www.TwoCodesForMurder.com or call us at 1-800-224-8389.

Please send your completed order form and payment to:
DiefFesco Publishing
PO Box 140098
St. Louis, MO 63114

Your Name: _____
Phone: _____
E-mail: _____
Address_____
Street: _____
City: _____
State _____   Zip Code: _____
Autographed Message:

Two Codes For Murder: # of Books _____
Cost: $16.95 per book $ _____
Sales Tax*: $ _____
Shipping: $ _____
TOTAL: $ _____

*Sales Tax is 7.325% for orders shipped to Missouri address.
**Shipping charges listed apply only to personal orders shipped within the United States.

Shipping Charges

Standard shipping charge $2.55 per order, Priority $3.75 Add .75 additional for each book up to four books. For orders of five or more, or orders shipped to an international address, call for shipping quote.

(Prices subject to change without notice.)

Mail Order Form

You can use the following order form to mail your order to us. Sorry, but mail orders are in checks, money orders or cashiers checks only. If you'd like to use a credit card to purchase any of our products, visit our Web site at http://www.TwoCodesForMurder.com or call us at 1-800-224-8389.

Please send your completed order form and payment to:
DiefFesco Publishing
PO Box 140098
St. Louis, MO 63114

Your Name: _____

Phone: _____

E-mail: _____

Address_____

Street: _____

City: _____

State _____   Zip Code: _____

Autographed Message:

Two Codes For Murder: # of Books _____

Cost: $16.95 per book $ _____

Sales Tax*: $ _____

Shipping: $ _____

TOTAL: $ _____

*Sales Tax is 7.325% for orders shipped to Missouri address.
**Shipping charges listed apply only to personal orders shipped within the United States.

Shipping Charges

Standard shipping charge $2.55 per order, Priority $3.75 Add .75 additional for each book up to four books. For orders of five or more, or orders shipped to an international address, call for shipping quote.

(Prices subject to change without notice.)

**If you'd like more information
and help regarding domestic violence,
please visit our Web site at:**

www.TwoCodesForMurder.com